THEOPHANY

SUNY series in Ancient Greek Philosophy

Anthony Preus, editor

THEOPHANY

The Neoplatonic Philosophy of
Dionysius the Areopagite

ERIC D. PERL

STATE UNIVERSITY OF NEW YORK PRESS

Published by
STATE UNIVERSITY OF NEW YORK PRESS,
Albany

For information, contact State University of New York Press, Albany, NY
www.sunypress.edu

Production, Laurie Searl
Marketing, Anne M. Valentine

Library of Congress Cataloging-in-Publication Data

Perl, Eric David.
  Theophany : the neoplatonic philosophy of Dionysius the Areopagite / Eric D. Perl.
    p. cm. — (SUNY series in ancient Greek philosophy)
  Includes bibliographical references and index.
  ISBN-13: 978-0-7914-7111-1 (hardcover : alk. paper)
  ISBN-13: 978-0-7914-7112-8 (pbk. : alk. paper)
  1. Pseudo-Dionysius, the Areopagite. I. Title.

BR65.D66P35 2007
186'.4—dc22

                                                                    2006021969

                          10 9 8 7 6 5 4 3 2

CONTENTS

ACKNOWLEDGMENTS

Thanks are due to Dr. Robert Wood of the University of Dallas, who made the writing of this book possible; and to my graduate students at the University of Dallas and the Catholic University of America, in teaching whom I have learned most of what is presented here.

NOTE ON TRANSLATIONS

There is still no adequate English translation of the Dionysian corpus. The best, that of John Parker,[1] is both highly imperfect and largely unavailable; while the most recent and widely available, that of Colm Luibheid,[2] is so far from the Greek as to be almost a paraphrase rather than a translation, and disregards Dionysius' use of traditional philosophical terms. Hence I have provided my own translations of passages cited from Dionysius, making them as literal as possible without egregiously violating English usage.

For Plotinus, I have used the translation by A. H. Armstrong in the Loeb Classical Library,[3] with my own modifications where I have judged these to be necessary for the sake of clarity or precision; and for Proclus' *Elements of Theology*, I have used the translation by E. R. Dodds,[4] also with modifications. All other published translations are cited in individual notes.

ABBREVIATIONS

I. WORKS OF DIONYSIUS

CH   *On the Celestial Hierarchy*
DN   *On Divine Names*
EH   *On the Ecclesiastical Hierarchy*
Ep.   *Epistles*
MT   *On Mystical Theology*

II. OTHER WORKS

El. Th.   Proclus, *The Elements of Theology*

INTRODUCTION

This book is the fruit of more than twelve years' study and teaching of the thought of Dionysius the Areopagite,[1] together with that of Plotinus and Proclus, *as philosophy*: not, primarily, as a late antique cultural phenomenon; nor as an influential episode in the history of Christian theology; nor as "mysticism," if that be taken to mean something other than philosophy; nor as a series of texts with ascertainable relations of influence and citation; but as philosophy, i.e. as a rationally justified, coherent account of the nature of reality. Such a philosophical exposition of any body of thought demands more than an explanation of what the philosopher says and of the sources from which he derives his doctrines. It requires, above all, an account of the argumentation, the sequence of reasoning that supports and leads to his positions. Only by understanding this argumentation can we truly grasp the meaning of the positions themselves.

In the case of Dionysius, such an understanding is particularly difficult to achieve because he notoriously eschews argumentation in favor of proclamatory exposition. (See Ep. VII.1, 1077B–1080A.) But that does not mean that his thought is not open to philosophical interpretation and presentation. It simply means that we must look for its underlying argumentation elsewhere, in the philosophical tradition from which his thought derives. To take a prime example, the central Dionysian doctrine that God is "beyond being" is not merely a phrase or a theme which has a discoverable history in Plato and Neoplatonism, nor is it merely a vague assertion of divine transcendence. Rather, within the Neoplatonic context, it is the conclusion of a definite sequence of philosophical reasoning, and only in terms of that argumentation can its precise meaning be correctly grasped. The same is true of other characteristic Dionysian themes such as procession and reversion, evil as privation, hierarchy, mystical union, and symbolism. The textual "source" of a given idea in Dionysius may be Proclus, or Plotinus, or some other writer, pagan or Christian; but its real philosophical origin is a certain line of reasoning, and this is what I aim to bring to light.

The purpose of this study, therefore, is not to contribute to the extensive *Quellenforschung* that has already been undertaken on Dionysius, but rather to elucidate the meaning and grounds of his vision of reality by looking back through the philosophical tradition to recover the structures and argumentation

1

that underlie it.[2] To expound Dionysius in this way, it is necessary to give not merely references to his textual sources, but extensive explanations of the thought of earlier philosophers, especially Plotinus and Proclus.[3] Hence this book is an exposition not only of Dionysius himself but also of central aspects of Neoplatonic thought in terms of their philosophical foundations.

The understanding of Dionysius in philosophical terms has been obfuscated by a widespread bias against Neoplatonism among Christian theologians, who have produced most of the scholarly work on Dionysius. To Luther's well-known and still living condemnation of Dionysius as *plus platonizans quam christianizans*,[4] Christian defenders of Dionysius too often reply, in effect, *non platonizans sed christianizans*.[5] The study of Dionysius by Christian theologians has thus tended to fall into a pattern of accusation and exculpation: some contend that he is fundamentally Neoplatonic and therefore not truly Christian,[6] while others attempt to vindicate his Christianity by showing that he is not really Neoplatonic.[7] The prevailing assumption on both sides is that Neoplatonism is a Bad Thing and is fundamentally incompatible with authentic Christianity.[8] Both sides tend to share a somewhat simplistic and philosophically unsophisticated conception of Neoplatonism, and, indeed, a somewhat narrow and monolithic view of what counts as authentic Christianity. Such approaches preclude a genuinely philosophical understanding both of non-Christian Neoplatonism and of Dionysius.

In relation to this ongoing controversy, therefore, the subtitle of this book is deliberately and doubly provocative. First, by characterizing Dionysius' thought as *philosophy*, I indicate my intention to approach it as a philosophical scholar approaches that of Plato, Aristotle, Plotinus, or Proclus, asking first and foremost not the theologian's question of whether it conforms to a predetermined notion of what is genuinely Christian, but the philosopher's question of what it means and how it is justified. Second, by characterizing it as *Neoplatonic* philosophy, I intend not to condemn but to celebrate it, regarding Neoplatonism as a profound and well-argued understanding of reality and as the most promising resource to which we may turn in our present intellectual and cultural predicament.[9] Rather than either convicting or acquitting Dionysius of Neoplatonism, conceived as a capital offense for a Christian theologian, I propose to reclaim him as a Neoplatonic philosopher who not merely appropriates certain terminological or thematic elements from Plotinus and Proclus, but takes up their deep philosophical insights into his own thought.

Because the aim of this study is to articulate Dionysius' understanding of reality in its specifically philosophical dimension, I have for the most part left aside his discussions of trinitarian doctrine, christology, and liturgy.[10] In presenting Dionysius purely as a Neoplatonic philosopher, however, I have no intention of impugning his Christianity. For unlike most of the theologians who have studied Dionysius, I see no fundamental opposition between Neoplatonism and Christianity, and hence no need to decide on which side of this supposed disjunction Dionysius belongs. This position depends in part on a subtler and to some degree unusual interpretation of Neoplatonism, which brings it closer to what are often regarded as uniquely Christian doctrines. Many of the points which are often said to represent Dionysius' Christian transformation or rejection of Neoplatonism, such as the immediate creation of all things by God, or God as ecstatic love, can in fact already be found in non-Christian Neoplatonism. The need to justify this reading of Neoplatonism further accounts for my extensive discussions of Plotinus and Proclus.

This study is structured not as a sequential commentary on the Dionysian corpus but as a series of closely interconnected essays, aiming to present his thought in its philosophical aspect as a coherent whole. The essays build on one another, in a sequence which, for chapters 1–6, follows the topics addressed in chapters I, IV, V, and VII of *On Divine Names*. *Divine Names* I presents the principles of divine unnameability and nameability, in terms of God's transcendence of all thought and being and his manifestation in all things. *Divine Names* II and III are parenthetical: chapter II is Dionysius' explanation of why he is not doing trinitarian theology in this treatise, and chapter III is a preliminary exhortation to prayer. Chapters IV, V, VI, and VII discuss the divine names Good, Being, Life, and Wisdom, respectively, in order of their universality. However, the account of Life in chapter VI adds little philosophical content to the preceding chapters. After chapter VII, the *Divine Names* ceases to have an easily discernible philosophical order,[11] although its discussions of various additional divine names contain many points of philosophical interest. In terms of philosophical structure, therefore, the fundamental chapters of the *Divine Names* are I, IV, V, and VII, and my essays are arranged in accordance with this sequence. In each case, however, I draw not only on the associated section of the *Divine Names* but also on the entire Dionysian corpus, treating it as an integrated whole whose parts can and should be read in relation to each other.

Chapters 1 and 2 correspond in subject-matter to *Divine Names* I, discussing, in chapter 1, the radical transcendence and unknowability of God, and, in chapter 2, the immanence and manifestation of God in all things.

Chapter 3 corresponds to *Divine Names* IV.1–17, presenting this doctrine in its dynamic aspect by discussing Dionysius' account of God as Goodness, Beauty, and Love in terms of the cycle of remaining, procession, and reversion.

Chapter 4 corresponds to *Divine Names* IV.18–35, addressing the problem of evil as it arises from such an understanding of reality.

Chapter 5 corresponds to *Divine Names* V.1–3, discussing the hierarchical structuring of being in relation to the doctrine of being as theophany.

Chapter 6 corresponds to *Divine Names* VII, discussing the nature and modes of cognition within such an understanding of being.

Chapter 7, finally, presents Dionysius' philosophy of symbolism as it emerges from this metaphysics and gnoseology, and is linked primarily with *Celestial Hierarchy* I–II.

In a manner that perhaps deliberately parallels his own doctrine of divine names, the author of the Dionysian corpus remains invisible: he lies hidden behind his works and can be known only as he is manifest in them, so that the very name *Dionysius* inevitably refers to the content of the works rather than to the author.[12] The absence of biographical information about the author encourages a reading of the works in purely philosophical terms, simply as a body of thought. At the same time, perhaps in part because of his pseudonymity, Dionysius has tended to be studied not *sine* but *cum ira et studio*, and few expositions of his thought even make a pretense of neutrality.[13] The present study is no exception: my own love for Dionysius will be patent throughout. But this love is accompanied by, or rather is one with, an equally great love for Plato and Plotinus, and above all for divine philosophy itself.

CHAPTER ONE

BEYOND BEING AND INTELLIGIBILITY

In recent decades there has been a surge of interest in "negative theology,"[1] of which Dionysius is a leading exponent, and hence many studies of this feature of Dionysius' thought.[2] Rarely, however, do such studies attempt to present the philosophical argumentation that underlies his teachings. The doctrine that God or the One, the first principle of reality, lies beyond being and beyond thought, for Dionysius and his Neoplatonic forebears, is not an ungrounded starting point or an article of faith but rather the conclusion of a rigorous sequence of philosophical reasoning, and only by following this argumentation can we truly understand the doctrine's meaning. Neoplatonic and Dionysian "negative theology" and "mysticism" is an aspect of rational metaphysics, and must be interpreted and evaluated as such. The aim of the present chapter, therefore, is to expose the philosophical grounds and meaning of Dionysius' negative theology by showing how the argument behind it is developed in the Greek philosophical tradition that Dionysius draws on and continues.

The foundational principle of Neoplatonic thought is the doctrine that to be is to be intelligible. The identification of being, τὸ ὄν, that which is, as that which can be apprehended by νόησις, intellection, is the basis not only for the Platonic and Neoplatonic identification of being as form or idea (εἶδος, ἰδέα), and the associated view that the sensible is less than completely real, but also for the Neoplatonic insistence that the One or Good, the source of reality, is itself "beyond being." To arrive at a philosophical understanding of Dionysius' doctrines of being and of God, therefore, we must begin by examining the meaning and grounds of this principle, and then see how its implications are unfolded in Platonic and Neoplatonic philosophy.

The idea of being as intelligible is implicit in Greek philosophy from the very beginning. The philosophical enterprise, insofar as it is an endeavor to think reality as one whole, always already presupposes that being as such is able to be grasped by thought. This presupposition is first made explicit by

Parmenides: "For you could not know that which is not, for it is impossible, nor express it; for the same thing is for thinking and for being [οὔτε γὰρ ἂν γνοίης τό γε μὴ ἐόν (οὐ γὰρ ἀνυστόν)/οὔτε φράσαις. Τὸ γὰρ αὐτὸ νοεῖν ἔστιν τε καὶ εἶναι]."[3] Parmenides indicates here, first, that thought is always the apprehension of some being. For whatever is thought is necessarily thought as something, i.e. as some being. Τὸ μὴ ἐόν, that which is not, cannot be thought, for to think absolute non-being would be to have no object or content for thought, to be not thinking anything, and hence not to be thinking. We may recall here the Thomistic principle, derived at long re-move from this Parmenidean insight: "Being falls first in the conception of intellect . . . Wherefore being is the proper object of intellect [*Primo autem in conceptione intellectus cadit ens . . . Unde ens est proprium objectum intellectus*]."[4] Whatever is thought is thought most basically and generically as some being, which may then be specified by various determinations. Second, Parmenides in this passage affirms that being extends no further than that which can be apprehended by thought, that there cannot be anything beyond the reach of thought. It would be incoherent even to postulate an unintelligible being, a being that cannot be thought, for to do so would already be to think such a being. Parmenides' fragment thus brings to light the obvious but vital point that to think being, that which is, at all, is already to presuppose its intel-ligibility. To think being is to think it *as thinkable*. Indeed, it follows not merely that being and intelligibility are coextensive, as Parmenides plainly asserts, but that intelligibility is the very meaning of being: by *being* we can only mean "what is there for thought," for since thought cannot extend to anything else, "anything else" is mere empty noise—in short, nothing (τό μὴ ἐόν). If 'being,' "that which is" considered as one whole, has any meaning at all, then it necessarily means "that which is available for thinking," i.e. that which is intelligible. That which is, then, is (wholly and solely) that which can be apprehended by intellection, and intellection is (wholly and solely) the apprehension of that which is.

Plato's understanding of being as form or idea (εἶδος, ἰδέα) is a direct consequence of this identification of being and intelligibility. Although in many ways critical of his awesome father figure Parmenides, Plato wholly adopts the doctrine of τὸ ὄν, that which is, as τὸ νοητόν, that which can be apprehended by intellect, and makes it the center of his metaphysics (e.g. *Phaedrus* 247c7–8; *Timaeus* 27d6–28a3). Consequently, what is real, for Plato, is the "looks" (εἴδη) that sensible things display to the mind, the universal natures or "whatnesses" that characterize them and can be definitively grasped in thought.[5] The forms, and only the forms, are "really real," precisely be-cause they and only they are altogether intelligible. Form is "what is there for thought," and therefore it is τὸ ὄν. Its complete reality consists in its perfect intelligibility. Conversely, sensible instances, on Plato's view, are less than really real in that they are constituted as multiple appearances of the unitary forms, apprehended not by intellection but by sensation and opinion (δόξα), the apprehension of appearance rather than reality (see esp. *Republic* 476a4–7). As appearances or images, sensibles are not mere illusion, or nothing (as Parmenides may have believed), but neither are they being itself, the reality which appears, the universal natures apprehended by intellect. They are rather, as Plato says, "in between" "that which altogether is," i.e. intelligible reality, the forms, and "that which altogether is not," i.e. nothing. The "in between" status of sensibles, *qua* appearances, and the perfect reality of the forms, are together correlated to the mode in which each is cognized. "That which altogether is [τὸ ... παντελῶς ὄν] is altogether knowable, while that which in no way is is in no way knowable" (*Republic* 477a2–3), whereas "if something should appear such as at once to be and not to be, this will lie in between that which purely is and that which wholly is not, and neither knowledge nor ignorance will be about it, but again what appears between ignorance and knowledge," i.e. opinion (*Republic* 478d5–11). Plato's levels of being are correlated to levels of cognitive apprehension, and this is just because being is identified with intelligibility.

Contrary to Parmenides, however, Plato regards being, *qua* intelligible, not as simple but as complex, a multiplicity of interrelated forms. He argues, explicitly in opposition to Parmenides, that "relative non-being," or difference, must be included in the altogether real. Each form *is not* any of the other forms, i.e. is different from them, and thus shares in Difference (*Sophist* 255e4–6, 258d7–e3). Difference, no less than identity, is necessary for and constitutive of being. But this doctrine of being as an internally differentiated multiplicity of forms is itself a consequence of the intelligibility of being. As Plato points out, the forms are intelligible only in relation to each other, by the method of "collection and division," whereby the less universal forms are identified as differentiated specifications of the more universal, and the more universal forms are understood as unities overarching and pervading a multiplicity of less universal ones (*Phaedrus* 265c8–266c1; cf. *Sophist* 253b8–e2). The forms' differences from and relations to one another are necessary conditions for their intelligibility. "For through the interweaving of the forms with each other discourse [λόγος] comes to be for us" (*Sophist* 259e5–6). Thus, it is precisely as intelligible that the altogether real must be a multiplicity of distinct, interwoven forms.

Plato's doctrine of the Good as that which "provides" being is also grounded in the identification of being and intelligibility. In his well-known criticism of Anaxagoras in the *Phaedo*, Socrates says that when he first heard Anaxagoras' claim that "intellect [νοῦς] is the orderer and cause of all things . . . it seemed to me in a certain way good that intellect be the cause of all things; and I thought, if it was so, that the ordering intellect orders all things and establishes each thing in whatever way would be best" (97c1–6). In other words, an explanation of things as conforming to the demands of intellect necessarily accounts for them in terms of goodness. Socrates goes on to say that in failing to give explanations of this kind, Anaxagoras "made no use of intellect" (*Phaedo* 98b8–9). Plato here indicates, then, that goodness is the principle of intellectual understanding and of intelligibility itself. The intellect by nature demands to see goodness in its object in order to understand, to make sense of it. Any thing, event, action, or process can be intellectually understood only in terms of the good which is the ultimate "why" for it. And whatever can be so understood, whatever is intelligible, is so only because and insofar as it is ordered on the basis of goodness.[6] Consequently, those "physicists" who give merely mechanical accounts of nature "think that, truly, the Good and the Right [τὸ ἀγαθὸν καὶ δέον] do not bind and hold anything together" (*Phaedo* 99c). The position presented here, then, is that it is indeed the Good that "binds and holds all things together," precisely because only if this is so can "all things" be understood by the mind at all.

This argumentation underlies Plato's representation of the Good in the *Republic* under the image of the sun. Just as the sun, by providing light, makes it possible for sensible things to be seen and for the eye to see them, so the Good provides that which makes the forms able to be known and the intellect able to know them (*Republic* 508b12–c2). The Good, in other words, is the enabling source of intelligibility and intellection. "When [the soul] is fixed upon that which truth and being [ἀλήθειά τε καὶ τὸ ὄν] illuminates, it thinks [ἐνόησέν] and knows and appears to have intellect [νοῦν]; but when [it is fixed] upon that which is mixed with darkness, upon that which comes into being and passes away, it opines and is dimmed and changes its opinions up and down and seems then not to have intellect [νοῦν οὐκ ἔχοντι]" (*Republic* 508d4–9). The fundamental meaning of "truth" (ἀλή-θεια), as Heidegger never tires of pointing out, is "unconcealedness." The truth of the forms is their unconcealedness, their availability or accessibility to the mind—in short, their intelligibility. And this, Plato says, is provided by the Good. For in the absence of goodness, consciousness, attempting to understand reality, is like the eye in the absence of light: it is at a loss, it flounders, it cannot "see" its objects; it "does not have intellect." Just as there can be neither visibility nor vision without light, so there can be neither intelligibility nor intellection without goodness. Consequently, as Plato goes on to say, "That which provides truth to the things known and gives power [i.e. the ability to know] to the knower is the form [ἰδέαν] of the Good" (*Republic* 508e1–3). In other words, any and all beings, i.e. the forms, are intelligible only in virtue of the "look of goodness" that they have and display.[7]

But Plato here says that the Good provides to the forms not only ἀλήθεια, or intelligibility, but also τὸ ὄν, the status of being beings.[8] Later, he says that "to the things that are known, not only their being known is present by the Good, but also their being and reality is present to them by it" (*Republic* 508e1–3). This claim can be justified only on the basis of the identity between being and intelligibility: precisely because the status of being consists in availability to intellectual apprehension, the Good, in providing the latter, constitutes the forms as beings, as that which is. Since anything can be intellectually grasped only in virtue of its goodness, the Good is the only possible "why" for being *qua* intelligible, which is to say for being *qua* being.

Plato goes on to say, in what is for Neoplatonism perhaps the single most important passage in his works, that "the Good is not reality, but excels beyond reality [ἐπέκεινα τῆς οὐσίας] in seniority [πρεσβείᾳ] and power" (*Republic* 508e1–3). Since the Good provides being and intelligibility to the forms, which taken together constitute οὐσία, reality, the whole of what is, it is itself not merely one of them, a member of that complex whole, but lies "beyond" it. As that by which the forms are intelligible and are beings, the Good is ontologically prior to the forms, and in this sense "older" than being, and makes them to be, in this sense transcending them in power. The precise ontological status of the Good in relation to the forms and to intellect remains ambiguous, since Plato also calls it an "ἰδέα" and an object of intellection; but Plato at least recognizes here that being, as the multiplicity of the forms, cannot be ultimate, that it depends for its existence and intelligibility on a principle that transcends it, and identifies this principle as the Good.[10]

Plotinus adopts and develops Plato's understanding of being. Following Plato, he identifies being as the unified multiplicity of purely intelligible, eternal forms, and he regards sensible things as not true beings but images or appearances of the forms. But Plotinus, far more explicitly than Plato, identifies being not only as the object but as the content of thought and therefore as Thought, or Intellect, itself.[11] For (to summarize and paraphrase his arguments) if being were external to thought, then the actual content of thought, what thought apprehends, would not be reality itself but some image or impression of it. Thought, therefore, on this view, could never reach reality (see e.g. V.5.1.20–27; V.5.2.1–9). Rather, as Plotinus argues in a Platonic adaptation of Aristotle's theory of knowledge, intellection, in that what it apprehends is pure idea, contains its object in itself and hence is what it thinks (see e.g. V.9.5–8). Conversely, being, as form or idea, can be nothing but the content of thought, and is therefore not other than the intellect which thinks it. Intellect and the intelligible meet and are one as intellection. "All together are one, Intellect, intellection, the intelligible [νοῦς, νόησις, τὸ νοητόν]" (V.3.5.43–44), and "we have here, then, one nature, Intellect, all beings, truth" (V.5.3.1–2). Here Parmenides' insight reaches its fulfilment: being and thought are not merely coextensive but identical, because being can be nothing but the content of thought and thought can be nothing but the apprehension of being.

As intelligible and intelligent, Plotinus argues, being or Intellect is necessarily complex, internally differentiated, and indeed is constituted as being and as Intellect by the differentiation of the forms from one another within it. For any being can be intelligible, and hence can be a being, only if it is determinate, a distinct "this:" "A substance [οὐσίαν, reality] must be some one particular thing [τόδε . . . τι], something, that is, defined and limited" (V.5.6.6–7). But since a being can be determinate or defined only by distinction, by being "marked off" from other beings, intelligibility, and therefore being, depends on the differentiation of the beings, or forms, from one another. "The objects of thought . . . must have otherness in relation to each other" (V.1.4.39–40), and "the thinker must apprehend one thing different from another and the object of thought in being thought must contain variety" (V.3.10.40–42; see also V.3.10.30f). Being as a whole, therefore, is intelligible, and so is, only in virtue of the internal differentiation of the forms from one another, and this differentiation is constitutive of being itself. The differentiation of one being from another is what makes all things to be intelligible and so to be.

Each form, or being, then, is constituted as a being by its proper determination. "This is why they [the contents of Intellect] are substances; for they are already defined and each has a kind of shape. Being must not fluctuate, so to speak, in the indefinite, but must be fixed by limit and stability; and stability among intelligible things is definition and shape, and it is by these that it receives existence" (V.1.7.23–27). In the absence of differentiation, distinction, and determination, and hence in the absence of multiplicity, there is no intelligibility and therefore no being. The doctrine that being is constituted by determination or differentiation, and that it is therefore necessarily multiple, is a direct consequence of the principle that to be is to be intelligible.

Plotinus' doctrine that being or Intellect is not the first principle but derives from the One or Good, which itself lies "beyond being," is a further consequence of the same line of thought. Since every being is intelligible, and hence is, only in virtue of the determination whereby it is what it is, every being depends for its existence on that determination. Again, every being must have unity, must be some one being, in order to be; but being as a whole and each being within it involves multiplicity of content, without which it would not be intelligible. Therefore, each being can be only in virtue of the unity by which it is this one being: "It is by the One that all beings are beings, both those which are primarily beings and those which are in any sense said to be among beings. For what could anything be if it was not one?" (VI.9.1.1–3). In short, for any being, to be is to be finite and unitary, and hence to be dependent on the unifying definition by which it is the one being that it is. Having discovered that being as such must be dependent, Plotinus therefore turns to the One as the ground or source on which being depends, that by which all beings are beings. All beings depend on, and in that sense derive or proceed from, the One or Good, as the "definer" (V.1.5.8–9)[12] or "measure of all things" (VI.8.18.3), which makes all things to be in that it provides the unifying determination whereby each being is itself and so is.[13]

This reasoning offers a very clear and precise explanation of what Plotinus means by describing the One as "beyond being." Whatever Plato may have intended by this phrase, Plotinus' interpretation of it is unambiguous. Since to be is to be intelligible and therefore finite, any being whatsoever is dependent on its determination and is thus derivative. Hence, to be is to be derivative. No being, therefore, can be the first principle, and the first principle cannot be any being; for if it were any being it would be finite and hence not first but dependent on its determination. Further, it would be one member within the complex totality of all beings, rather than the source of that totality. This would mean that it would have various attributes, such as being, intelligibility, unity, and so on, in common with the other beings; and for Platonic thought, whenever different things share (or "participate in") a common attribute, that attribute itself, as the one nature by which all the participants are such as they are, is ontologically prior to the participants. If, therefore, the first principle were a member of the totality of beings, it would not be first. The One, therefore, "is not equal to the other units so as to be one of their company; otherwise, there will be something in common between it and those which are included in the count with it, and that something in common will be before the One itself" (V.5.4.14–17). Again, if the One were a member of the totality of beings, i.e. were a being, it would be differentiated from the other beings within that totality (see V.5.13.20–24), and so would be determinate, finite, and dependent. In short, no common term whatsoever, including 'being,' can embrace both the One and its products, for the One would then be included within the totality and differentiated from others within it. Plotinus thus interprets "beyond being" in a purely negative sense, as meaning, only, that the One is not any being. "This phrase 'beyond being' does not mean that it is a particular thing—for it makes no positive statement about it—and it does not say its name, but all it implies is that it is 'not this' " (V.5.6.11–14). And this presupposes the understanding of being as that which is intelligible and, as intelligible, necessarily determinate:

> Since the substance which is generated [from the One] is form . . . the One must be without form. But if it is without form it is not a substance; for a substance must be some one particular thing, something, that is, defined and limited; but it is impossible to apprehend the One as a particular thing: for then it would not be the principle, but only that particular thing which you said it was. But if all things are in that which is generated [from the One], which of the things in it are you going to say that the One is? Since it is none of them, it can only be said to be beyond them. But these things are beings, and being: so it is 'beyond being.' (V.5.6.2–11)

Here Plotinus summarizes with exceptional clarity the reasoning behind, and meaning of, his doctrine that the One is "beyond being."[14]

Plotinus has sometimes been interpreted to mean by "beyond being" merely "infinite being," a phrase which he himself could not use because in his inherited philosophical lexicon 'being' (ὄν) comports finitude.[15] But such a reading misses the point. Not because of an accidental restriction on the usage of the term 'being,' but because of the philosophically grounded principle that to be is to be intelligible, being necessarily entails finitude, so that 'finite being' is a redundancy and 'infinite being' a contradiction in terms. To be is to be something, and to be something is to be finite. We must therefore take Plotinus at his word when he insists that the One is nothing (οὐδέν), not any being, not any thing at all (e.g. VI.9.3.41).[16] "That [i.e., the One] is not anything [οὔ τι], but before each and every thing, and is not a being [οὐδὲ ὄν]; for being has a kind of shape of being, but that has no shape, not even intelligible shape. For since the nature of the One is generative of all things it is none of them [οὐδέν . . . αὐτῶν]" (VI.9.3.38–41; cf. III.8.9.55). If Plotinus, very occasionally, uses expressions which suggest that the One in some sense is, this is simply an inevitable impropriety, in that thought and language necessarily treat whatever they treat as a being. In the light of Plotinus' more careful and frequent philosophical precisions, such passages merely serve to lend support to his position that it is not possible or appropriate to speak or think the One at all.

Thus we come to Plotinus' apophaticism or "negative theology." To think or refer to the One at all, even as "cause," as "it," as "that," is, inevitably, to treat it as a being, for thought and language can deal only with beings. Hence Plotinus says, "Even to say 'cause' is not to predicate something accidental of it, but of us, that we have something from it, while that is in itself; but neither ought one who speaks precisely say 'that' or 'is'" (VI.9.3.49–52). This crucial passage makes clear that when he speaks of the One as the cause of all things, Plotinus is not attributing being and causality to the One, but is merely indicating the secondary, derivative status of being. Initially, therefore, all language about the One, like the phrase "beyond being," must be purely negative in meaning. Even the term "One," Plotinus suggests, "contains only a denial of multiplicity" (V.5.6.26–27). The One, then, is not one in any positive sense, i.e. having the attribute of unity; nor is it simple, i.e. having the attribute of simplicity.[17]

But Plotinus' apophaticism does not consist merely in negative language, for even such language still represents conceptual definition and intellectual apprehension: to say that the One is "not this" is, inescapably, to think it as something else; to say that it is not multiple or complex is to think it as unitary or simple. In the end, Plotinus says, we must negate even such negative definitions, including the name One itself: "But if the One—name and reality expressed—were to be taken positively it would be less clear than if we did not give it a name at all; for perhaps this name [One] was given it in order that the seeker, beginning from this which is completely indicative of simplicity, may finally negate this as well" (V.5.6.31–34).[18] Genuine apophasis, then, consists not in negations but in the silence of the mind, rising above thought altogether: "Now if you want to grasp the 'isolated and alone' you will not think [οὐ νοήσεις]" (V.3.13.32–33). Thus we return once more to the correlation between being and thinking, such that all being is the object of some thinking, and hence does not include the One, and all thinking is the apprehension of some being, and hence does not attain the One.[19]

Dionysius adopts his doctrine of God as "nameless," "unknowable," and "beyond being" from the Neoplatonic tradition established by Plotinus, and his thought can be understood only in that context.[20] His "negative theology" is not fundamentally a theory of theological language but a philosophical position taken over directly from Neoplatonism, although, as in Plotinus, it has implications for language in that words are discursive expressions of intellection and hence cannot apply to God. Dionysius expressly adopts the Parmenidean and Platonic account of being and thought as coterminous, and therefore locates God beyond both together: "For if all knowledges are of beings and have their limit in beings, that which is beyond all being also transcends all knowledge" (DN I.4, 593A). Dionysius' God, like the One of Plotinus, is transcendent, not in a vague, unspecified sense, but in the very precise metaphysical sense that he is not at all included within the whole of reality, of things that are, as any member of it. If he has no "name," this is because he is not anything at all. God is not merely beyond "human thought" or "finite thought," as if there were some "other" sort of thought that could reach him, or as if his incomprehensibility were simply due to a limitation on our part, but is beyond thought as such, because thought is always directed to beings, and hence to that which is finite and derivative.[21] When we hear that God is beyond being, we inevitably imagine some thing, a "superessentiality," lying above or outside of being. But this fails to realize the meaning of "beyond being," because it still thinks of God as something, some being.[22] Rather, we must recognize that for Dionysius, as for Plotinus, God is simply not anything, not "there" at all. If our thought cannot attain to God, this is not because of our weakness but because there is no "there" there, no being, no thing that is God. Understanding Dionysius within the Neoplatonic tradition to which he belongs, we must take him at his word and not seek to mitigate the force of his negations by interpreting his thought in the light of later theories which attempt to allow for "infinite being" and thus break with the fundamental Neoplatonic principle that to be is to be intelligible and therefore to be finite.[23]

Consequently, Dionysius' so-called negative theology, like that of Plotinus, is not merely negative, if by that we mean, as is commonly said, that "we cannot say what God is but only what he is not."[24] For negation, no less than affirmation, is still an intellectual activity and as such necessarily identifies its object in conceptual terms and so treats it as finite. To say "God is not such-and-such" is to regard God as something, some being, distinguished from other beings by the lack of some feature that they possess, and thus to circumscribe God in thought. To deny any attribute of God is

still to treat him as a conceptual object, defined by the possession or privation of various attributes. Hence Dionysius carefully explains, near the beginning of the *Mystical Theology*, that although in ascending to "the cause of
all things" we must, at one stage, deny all attributes of all things to him,
nonetheless we must "not think that the negations are opposed to the
affirmations, but much rather that that which is beyond the privations is
beyond every affirmation and negation" (MT I.2, 1000B). Later, having denied
of God all attributes, whether sensible or intelligible, he concludes, "Nor is
there any affirmation or negation whatever of it . . . since the all-perfect and
single cause of all things is above every affirmation, and the transcendence
of that which is simply freed from all things and beyond the wholes is above
every negation" (MT V, 1048B). In the end, then, we cannot say what God
is not any more than we can say what he is, because God neither is nor is
not anything at all—and this, of course, is still to say too much.

Similarly, Dionysius is not content to say simply that God is ineffable,
unknowable, or incomprehensible. To say "God is ineffable" is to describe
him, to ascribe the attribute of ineffability to him, and thus to contradict
oneself.[25] When we say that God is unknowable or incomprehensible, we
inevitably imagine some being that cannot be known, something as it were
"out there" beyond the reach of thought. This is inevitable because thought
always, necessarily, intends some being. But here again we contradict ourselves, for we are thus thinking that which we are claiming to be beyond the
reach of thought. Hence Dionysius uses terms such as ὑπεράγνωστον (DN
I.4, 592D; MT I.1, 997A) and ὑπεραρρήτως (DN I.4, 592D): God is not
merely unknowable but beyond unknowing, not merely ineffable but beyond
ineffability. And of course, even these are still words, names, conceptual
definitions, and must be transcended.

Ultimately, then, for Dionysius as for Plotinus, negative theology consists not in any words or thoughts whatsoever, however negative or superlative, but in the absolute silence of the mind. We must "honor the hidden of
the divinity, beyond intellect and reality, with unsearchable and sacred rev-
erence of mind, and ineffable things with a sober silence" (DN I.4, 592D).
More precisely, Dionysius says that the union of minds with the "super-
divine light" takes place "in the cessation of every intellectual activity [πάσης
νοερᾶς ἐνεργείας ἀπόπαυσιν]" (DN I.5, 593C) and that "ceasing from our
intellectual activities we throw ourselves into the ray beyond being as far as
possible" (DN I.4, 592CD). Likewise, in the *Mystical Theology*, he explains
that we are united with the altogether unknown "in the inactivity of every
knowledge [πάσης γνώσεως ἀνενεργησίᾳ]" (MT I.3, 1001A), and that
"entering into the darkness above intellect we find not little speech
[βραχυλογίαν] but complete non-speech [ἀλογίαν] and non-intellection
[ἀνοησίαν]" (MT III.1, 1033C). As the repeated references to the cessation
or absence of νόησις indicate, this is not mere mystical hyperbole or an
attempt to articulate some sublime experience, but rather the strictly philo-

sophical consequence of the identification of being and intelligibility: as long as any speaking or thinking is taking place, we are necessarily in the realm of beings, of things that are, and hence are not attaining to God. A "God" who either is or is not anything at all, who could be grasped by thought whether positively or negatively, would not be God but a being, and as such finite and created.[26] "And if anyone, having seen God, understood what he saw, he did not see [God] himself, but something of those things of his which are and are known [τῶν ὄντων καὶ γινωσκομένων]" (Ep. 5, 1065A). Only this Neoplatonic argumentation enables us to grasp the meaning and philosophical justification of Dionysius' extreme "mystical" formulations.

We may be inclined to ask whether such a radical treatment of divine transcendence means that God simply disappears from view altogether, in such a way that, as has been remarked, "the truth of negative theology is atheism." But Dionysius' Neoplatonic negative theology transcends atheism no less than it does theism. To be sure, Dionysius is not a theist, since theism, as ordinarily understood, involves the claim that God exists (whatever qualifications may then be added concerning the "mode" of his existence); and many misunderstandings have arisen from attempts to interpret Dionysius and other Neoplatonists theistically and thus not to take with full seriousness their insistence that the One or God is beyond being and is not anything at all, that no common term whatever can embrace both God and his products. But neither is Dionysius an atheist, for on his principles it is no more correct to say "God is not" than to say "God is" (i.e. is a being). Simply to deny that God exists, to say "God is not" or "There is no God" is still to consider God as some (putative) being, and then to deny that there is such a being, as when we say "There is no tenth planet" or "There are no unicorns." This still treats God as some distinct conceptual object and so fails truly to intend God at all. Neoplatonic and Dionysian negative theology, on the other hand, refuses to consider God as anything at all, whether to affirm or to deny the existence of such a thing. Indeed, both "theism" and "atheism" are distinctively modern phenomena which cannot properly be read into Neoplatonism. In the words of Jean-Luc Marion,

> The distinctive feature of modernity does not at all consist in a negation of God . . . Modernity is characterized in the first place by the annulling of God as a question . . . What then is found set in play in a negation or an affirmation of God? Not God as such, but the compatibility or incompatibility of an idol called 'God' with the totality of a conceptual system where the being in its being marks the age . . . Theism or atheism bear equally on an idol. They remain enemies, but brother enemies in a common and insurpassable idolatry.[27]

Theism and atheism are brethren born of modernity, where God is reduced to "the supreme being" and true transcendence is lost. Since, for Dionysius, it is as inadequate to deny that God is anything as to affirm that he is anything, we must now turn to Dionysius' metaphysics of creation in order to see how God is not merely no thing but "all beings and none of beings" (DN I.6, 596C), "all things in all things and nothing in any" (DN VII.3, 872A), how namelessness coincides with all names and silence with the word.

CHAPTER TWO

BEING AS THEOPHANY

Dionysius frequently says that although God is not any being, he is the cause (αἰτία or αἴτιον) of all things (e.g. DN I.1, 588b; I.3, 589b; I.7, 596C; MT I.2, 1000B; IV, 1040D; V, 1048B), and as such can be named by all the names of all beings. "It is cause of all beings, but itself nothing, as transcending all things in a manner beyond being . . . But since . . . it is cause of all beings, the beneficent providence of the Thearchy is hymned from all the effects" (DN I.5, 593C–D). Taken at face value, this would seem to violate all that has been said about God's transcendence. To describe God positively as "cause" would be to regard him as a being and ascribe to him the attribute of causality, disregarding Plotinus' careful explanation that to call the One "cause" indicates only the dependence of beings and does not predicate anything of the One. But Dionysius is by no means so obtuse. When he calls God "cause" he does not mean this in the modern sense, in which one being is the cause of other beings, and God as the "first cause" is the "supreme being."[1] Indeed, the very expression "cause of all things" indicates, as Dionysius says, that all things are effects, or creatures, and hence that God is not one of all things. Dionysius' understanding of God as "cause," justifying the ascription of all the names of all things to him, depends on a distinctively Neoplatonic sense of causation, and we must therefore once again turn to Neoplatonic philosophy to grasp the meaning of his doctrine.

Since, in Neoplatonism, to be is to be intelligible and hence to be determinate, the determination of any thing, the totality of features by which it is what it is, by which it is itself as distinct from anything else, is the cause of being to that thing.[2] The causation in question, therefore, is not the "horizontal" causation of one thing by another within the same ontological order, as when we say, for example, that parents are the cause of their offspring or an earthquake is the cause of a tidal wave. It is rather the "vertical" causation[3] of a lower ontological level by a higher one, as when we say that the intelligible form Fire (i.e. "fieriness") is the cause of sensible fires in that it makes them to be what they are, to be fires, and so makes them to be. Plotinus expresses this kind of causation when he contrasts the "effortless" productive power of intelligible form to the merely ancillary action of bodies on each other: "[T]he making [of the sensible cosmos by Intellect] is done without noise or fuss, since that which makes is all real being and form" (V.8.7.24–25) and again, "One might certainly call the powers of fire and the other bodies great; but it is by mere inexperience of true power that they are imagined burning and destroying and crushing . . . But these destroy, because they are destroyed, and help to generate because they are generated themselves; but the power in the intelligible world has nothing but its being and its being beautiful" (V.8.9.32–37). The same principle, that formal determination is the cause of being to that which it determines, is evident in Plotinus' account of how all making is in fact contemplation, which, we must remember, is identical with its intelligible object. "Making, for it [Nature, i.e. the lowest level of Soul which makes the sensible cosmos], means being what it is, and its making power is coextensive with what it is. But it is contemplation and object of contemplation, for it is a rational principle [λόγος]. So by being contemplation and object of contemplation and rational principle, it makes in so far as it is these things" (III.8.3.18–21). As Plotinus says later in the same treatise, "all things are a by-product of contemplation" (III.8.8.26) in the sense that they depend for their existence on their formal determination, which, as an intelligible idea, is also an act of thinking.

This is true not only of the production of the sensible cosmos by Nature or Soul, but also of the production of Soul by Intellect and of Intellect by the One. Soul, says Plotinus, is "defined by its parent [τοῦ γεννήσαντος] and, so to speak, given a form" (V.1.7.41–42). Throughout Plotinus' hierarchy of production, the higher level acts as form or determination relative to the lower which receives it and is at all only by receiving it. Most fundamentally, as we have seen, the One is the "cause" of all things as that by which each being is intelligible, is itself, is the one distinct being that it is, and so is. As the universal principle of determination whereby all beings are beings, the One itself has no determination and hence is not anything intelligible, any being:

> Intellect, having come to be, is manifest as all things themselves. But [the Good] is enthroned upon them, not that it may have a base, but that it may base the form of the first forms, itself formless. And in this way Intellect is to soul a light upon it, as the [Good] to Intellect; and when Intellect also defines and limits [ὁρίσῃ] the soul it makes it rational by giving it a trace of what it has. Therefore Intellect is a trace of that [Good]; but since Intellect is form and is in extension and multiplicity, that [Good] is shapeless and formless; for thus it makes form [εἰδοποιεῖ]. (VI.7.17.34–41)

We have already seen that, according to Plotinus, to call the One "cause" means only that being, *qua* determinate, is dependent. At every level, indeed, Plotinian "emanation" or "procession," the production or causation of a lower level of reality by a higher, is nothing but the dependence of what is determined on its determination. The "production" of the lower level is not in any way an event or a process; rather, it is simply a description of the dependence of the lower on the higher. As Plotinus says,

> [T]hose are not right who destroy the image-universe while the intelligible abides, and bring it into being as if its maker ever planned to make it. For they do not want to understand how this kind of making works, that as long as that higher reality gives its light, the rest of things can never fail: they are there as long as it is there; but it always was and will be. We must use these [temporal] words because we are compelled to want to signify our meaning. (V.8.12.21–27)

The "light," of course, means the intelligible determination in virtue of which anything is what it is. Still more concisely, Plotinus says, "Of necessity, then, all things must exist for ever in ordered dependence upon each other: those other than the First have come into being in the sense that they are derived from other, higher principles [γενητὰ δὲ τὰ ἕτερα τῷ παρ' ἄλλων εἶναι]. Things that are said to have come into being did not just come into being . . . but always were and always will be in process of becoming" (II.9.3.11–14). As this makes clear, the lower level "comes to be" not in the sense of having an origin, but only in the sense that it is dependent on its superior.

The causation in question, therefore, is nothing other than Platonic participation: that which is determined, the "effect," participates in its determination, the "cause," i.e. has it as its nature or attribute, and thereby is what it is. Plato frequently refers to the forms as that "by which" their instances are such as they are,[4] and, therefore, describes a form as the cause (αἰτία) which makes its instances such (*Phaedo* 100b1–7). "It seems to me, if anything else is beautiful besides the Beautiful itself, it is beautiful through nothing else than that it participates in that Beautiful; and all things I say likewise . . . Nothing else makes [ποιεῖ] it beautiful than the presence or communion of that Beautiful . . . but that all beautiful things are beautiful by the Beautiful" (*Phaedo* 100d4–8). Only by understanding Platonic participation, then, can we understand the relation because cause and effect in Neoplatonism, and therefore the sense in which, for Dionysius, God is the cause of all things.

A Platonic form is the intelligible nature, present in many things, by which they are such things. As such a nature, it is at once immanent in and transcendent to the instances that participate in it. It is immanent, in that it is present in them as the nature or character by which they are such instances; and it is transcendent, in that, as one and the same nature in many different instances, it is other than and unconditioned by each and all of them.[5] Where, among the beautiful things in the world, is Beauty? Everywhere and nowhere: everywhere, in that wherever there is a beautiful thing, there is Beauty, as the nature which it has by which it is beautiful; nowhere, in that as one universal intelligible nature it is other than the many beautiful things and is not confined to any one of them. The form's transcendence is thus a strict implication of its immanence. The instances depend on the form to be such as they are, while the form, as a unitary intelligible nature capable of appearing in many instances, is independent of them. The instances, so to speak, owe everything to the form, as that by which they are what they are, while the form, as the nature which, by appearing in them, makes them what they are, owes nothing to the instances.

Plato indeed interprets participation as the multiple appearing of the one form in many instances: "Each [form] is itself one, but, as they appear everywhere by communion with actions and bodies and each other, each appears many" (*Republic* 476a5–7). The individuated character of a sensible thing, e.g. the beauty of Helen, is a differentiated appearance of the one form, in this case Beauty itself, and the form itself is in the instance in that it appears here, and, by so appearing, makes the instance what it is, e.g. beautiful. All that we find in sensible things, then, are images, presentations, or appearances of intelligible forms.[6] As appearances, sensible things are not beings additional to the forms and so do not constitute another "world." An appearance of a being—e.g., to use a Platonic analogy, a reflection in a mirror—is not another being: when a man stands before a mirror making a reflection, there is still only one man there.[7] But to say that sensibles are appearances is not to say that they are illusions, or not real at all. An appearance of a real thing is not the real thing itself, nor is it another real thing, but neither is it nothing. When we see a reflection, we are not seeing nothing, or suffering a hallucination; nor are we seeing something other than what is being reflected. In seeing the appearance, we are seeing the real thing, as it appears; and yet we are not seeing the real thing itself (as Plato would say, "itself by itself") at all. An appearance is and is not that which appears. It is in just this sense that since the forms are that which is, sensibles, as appearances of the forms, both are and are not, or are "in between" being and non-being (*Republic* 478d5–11). The different "levels of being" in Plato are in fact different modes in which reality may be given to cognition. Each form, or being, may be apprehended, by intellect, as it is, as one, as the single intelligible nature that it is; or it may be apprehended, by sense, as it appears, as many, as the character of this or that instance, differentiated from its appearances in other instances. The difference between intelligible forms and sensible instances is the difference, not between two kinds of reality, but between reality and appearance.

Plotinus adopts this understanding of participation, the relation be-tween the determined effect or product and its causal or productive determi-nation, as the appearance of the cause in the effect. He often describes the form that is present in a sensible as an "image" of the form in Intellect (e.g., V.9.3.36–37; V.9.5.18). This might seem to indicate a distinction between the immanent character and the transcendent form. But he is careful to explain that this does not mean that the transcendent form is not present in the sensible, and that this "image" is not another form, but is only the differentiated presence or appearance of the transcendent form itself. This is indeed the theme of the whole of *Ennead* VI.4–5, "On the Presence of Being, One and the Same, Everywhere as a Whole." Here he explains that the "image" perceived in the sensible is in fact the immediate presence of the transcendent form: "[T]he things in matter are images, and the Forms hold the rank of archetypes . . . But now we must speak more precisely and not assume that the Form is spatially separate and then the Idea is reflected in matter as if in water, but that matter, from every side grasping (and again not grasping) the Idea, receives from the Form, over the whole of itself, by its drawing near to it all that it can receive, with nothing between" (VI.5.8.13–21). It is one and the same form, the "archetype," that is wholly present in all its instances. But for Plotinus, as for Plato, it appears as many to sense perception, and these differentiated appearances of the form are what Plotinus calls "images": "[I]t is not correct to divide that same up into the many, but rather to bring back the divided many to the one, and that one has not come to these many, but these because they are scattered have given us the appear-ance [δόξαν] that also that has been taken apart" (VI.4.7.4–8). The form is present in the sensible in that it appears here in a differentiated mode: "[I]t is not then divided up into parts, but seems [δοκεῖ] to be so divided to the recipient" (VI.4.14.13–14). And this apparent division, or differentiation, is due to sensation's limited mode of apprehension: "For it is sense-perception, to which we are paying attention when we disbelieve what is now being said, which says that is here and there, but reason says that the 'here and there' has not come about by its being extended but the whole of what is extended has participated in it, while it is not itself spaced out" (VI.4.13.2–6). In other words, sensation apprehends a form as it appears, as the character of this or that particular instance ("here and there"). But what appears and is appre-hended differently in different things is one and the same intelligible form, which is neither confined to one instance nor divided up among many.

Plotinus sums this up by saying of the form that "it is all present, but it is not all seen in everything, because of the incapacity of what underlies it. But it is present, numerically identical everywhere" (VI.5.11.30–32). Thus, for Plotinus as for Plato, intelligible being is at once transcendent to and immanent in the sensible: "There is nothing, therefore, surprising in its being in all things in this way, because it is also in none of them in such a

way as to belong to them" (VI.4.3.17–19). The entire discussion makes it
very clear that the "image," the form seen in the sensible particular, is not
something other than the transcendent, archetypal form in Intellect, but is
sensation's lesser, differentiated apprehension of that very form itself. The
higher level is the "cause" of the lower, then, in the sense that the latter is
the differentiated appearance or presentation of the former to a lesser mode
of cognition. The higher "makes" the lower as a reality, by appearing, makes
the appearances of itself.[8]

      This is, in turn, the sense in which all beings are caused by the One.
Just as all fires are fires by having, or participating in, the intelligible form
Fire, so, since anything can be only by being one, all beings are beings by
having, or participating in, the One. "But that which comes after the origin
[i.e. Intellect or Being, coming after the One] is, somehow, under the pressure of the One,[9] all things by its participation in the One [πάντα μετέχον
τοῦ ἕν]" (V.3.15.25–26; cf. V.5.4.1–4). Here again we can see just why the
One is beyond being: just as the form Fire, as that which is common to all fires,
whereby they are fires, is not itself one of the fires, so the One, as that which
is common to all beings, whereby they are beings, is not itself one of the
beings. And just as any form is at once transcendent to and immanent in its
instances, so the One is at once transcendent to and immanent in all beings:
transcendent, in that it is not identified with or confined to any one of them;
immanent, in that it is present to all as that by which they are beings:

> [The One] is there and not there; it is not there because it is not
> in the grasp of anything, but because it is free from everything it is
> not prevented from being anywhere. For if, on the other hand, it
> was prevented, it would be limited by some thing else, and . . . God
> would go just so far, and would not be independent but a slave to
> the beings which come after him. The things, therefore, which are
> in something are there where they are; but everything which is not
> somewhere has nowhere where it is not. For if it is not here, it is
> clear that another place contains it, and it is here in something else,
> so that the 'not somewhere' is false. If therefore the 'not somewhere'
> is true and the 'somewhere' is false . . . it will not be absent from
> anything. But if it is not absent from anything and is not anywhere,
> it is everywhere independent. (V.5.9.13–24)

If the One were merely "other" or "separate," it would be another being, and
so would be limited in relation to others. Precisely as transcendent, infinite,
beyond being, it must be not separate but present to all beings. And precisely
as present to all beings, it is not any one of them, and so is transcendent.

      Proclus' doctrine of causation as participation may seem to be different
from that of Plato and Plotinus, because he distinguishes between the "participated" terms (μετεχόμενα), i.e. the individuated properties, each of which

belongs to a particular instance, and the "unparticipated" term (ἀμέθεκτον), the universal that is numerically one for all the instances and hence does not belong to any of them:

> All that is unparticipated produces from itself the participated . . . For on the one hand the unparticipated, having the relative status of a monad (as being its own and not another's, and as transcending the participants), generates terms capable of being participated. For . . . it will give something of itself, whereof the receiver becomes a participant, whilst the given subsists as a participated term.
>
> Every participated term, on the other hand, becoming a property of that by which it is participated, is secondary to that which is equally present to all and has filled them all from itself. That which is in one is not in the others; while that which is present to all alike, that it may illuminate all, is not in any one, but is prior to them all. (*El. Th.*, prop. 23)

Thus, for instance, there is a difference between the unitary universal form Fire (the "unparticipated") and the fieriness of a particular fire (the "participated"), which is numerically distinct from that of other fires. Participation, conceived by Plato and Plotinus as a two-term relation between the participant and the participated, now becomes a three-term relation among the participant, the participated, and the unparticipated. Taken at face value, this would separate transcendence from immanence, for the transcendent cause, the unparticipated, is not present in the instance as its property, and what is present in each instance as its property, the participated, is not the unitary transcendent cause. At the highest level, this distinction takes the form of Proclus' distinction between the One itself and the "henads" or gods, the many different unities in which beings participate (see e.g. *El. Th.*, prop. 116).

Closer examination, however, reveals that Proclus' meaning is not fundamentally different from that of Plato and Plotinus. For the "participated term" is in fact nothing but the differentiated presence of the "unparticipated" cause in the effect. It is distinct only in the sense in which, for Plotinus, the "image" in the sensible is distinct from the "archetype." In this very proposition, Proclus says that the unparticipated term "will give something *of itself*" in which the recipient participates, and this "something of itself" is none other than the participated term. Thus the unparticipated term is "present [παρόντος] to all and has filled them all from itself." Indeed, it is precisely in order that the cause may be "present to all alike" that Proclus distinguishes it from the participated terms, each of which belongs uniquely to one of the effects. The purpose of the distinction, then, is not to keep the unparticipated term aloof from the participants but to guarantee its unconditioned presence to them all. Shortly afterward Proclus says, "Thus the engenderer [i.e. the unparticipated cause] is established beyond alteration or diminution, multiplying itself [ἑαυτὸ πολλαπλασιάζον] in virtue of its generative potency, and furnishing from itself secondary substances" (*El. Th.*, prop. 27). These "secondary substances," the participated terms, then, are the multiple, differentiated presences of the universal cause in the participating effects.

Proclus corrects the seeming separation between transcendence and immanence in a passage that closely parallels Plotinus' accounts of the simultaneous transcendence and immanence of the forms to sensibles and of the One to being:

> Every cause which is separate from its effects exists at once everywhere and nowhere . . . [W]e mean by 'cause' that which fills all things naturally capable of participating it, which is the source of all secondary existences and by the fecund outpouring of its irradiations is present to them all. But by its mode of being, which has no admixture of the spatial, and by its transcendent purity it is nowhere: for if it is separate from its effects it is enthroned above all alike and resides in no being inferior to itself. If it were merely everywhere, . . . it would not exist separately prior to them all. Were it nowhere without being everywhere . . . it would not be omnipresent in that sense in which causes are capable of immanence in their effects, namely by unstinted self-bestowal. In order that as cause it may be present in all that can participate it while as a separate and independent principle it is prior to all the vessels which it fills, it must be at once everywhere and nowhere.[10] (*El. Th.*, prop. 98)

The cause is "separate" in the sense that it is not conditioned by its effects, not in the sense that it is not present to or immanent in them. The unparticipated term, then, is simply a universal determination *considered as* one and the same, and hence transcendent to its instances; while the participated terms are the same determination *considered as* differently present in each instance.[11] Thus we return to the notion of appearance, of the different modes in which the same content may be given to cognition.

From all of this it follows that the causation we are considering is not the making of an additional thing, the production of one being by another being. The effects are not more things, additional to the cause. Rather, since all that is found in the effects is the differentiated presence of the cause, the effects are contained in the cause. Whatever content we find in an appearance must be present in the reality which is appearing. As Plotinus says, "The last and lowest things, therefore, are in the last of those before them, and these are in those prior to them, and one thing is in another up to the First, which is the Principle. But the Principle, since it has nothing before it, has not anything else to be in; but since it has nothing else to be in, and the other things are in those which come before them, it encompasses [περιείληφε] all the other things" (V.5.9.6–10). The One, then, contains in itself, or better, is the undifferentiated containment of, all beings. Conversely, all that is found in the effects, and hence the effects themselves, are nothing but differentiated appearances of the cause.

The cause, therefore, is the enfolding or *complicatio* of the effects, and the effects are the unfolding or *explicatio* of the cause,[12] its presentation or appearance in differentiated multiplicity. Thus Plotinus remarks, "[S]ince in things which are generated it is not possible to go upwards but only to go downwards and move further towards multiplicity, the principle of each group of things is simpler than they are themselves . . . There must therefore be a concentration [συστῆναι] into a real one outside all multiplicity and any simplicity whatsoever, if it is to be really simple" (V.3.16.6–16). As this "concentration," the One is not any one thing, but all things without distinction: not all things as a multiplicity, for that is not the One but being or Intellect,[13] but all things "at once," without the differentiation which constitutes them as themselves, as intelligible, and hence as all things, as being. "But how is that One the principle of all things? Is it because as principle it keeps them in being, making each one of them exist? Yes, and because it brought them into existence. But how did it do so? By possessing them beforehand. But it has been said that in this way it will be a multiplicity. But it had them in such a way as not to be distinct: they are distinguished on the second level, in the rational form [λόγος]"[14] (V.3.15.27–33). As we have seen, distinction, and hence multiplicity, are necessary conditions for intelligibility and therefore for being. Precisely as all things without distinction, the One is not any thing, i.e. beyond being. "The One: all things and not even one; for it is the principle of all things, not all things, but all things transcendently [ἐκείνως]; for in a way they do occur there; or rather they are not there yet, but will be" (V.2.1.1–3). The phrase "not yet, but will be" clearly indicates the absence of the differentiation by which all things are all things. To use a Plotinian image (see V.1.11.11–13), we may think of all things as the many different points on the circumference of a circle. If we imagine all the points moving toward the center, each along its own radius, the circle will become progressively smaller. When all the points meet at the center, the circle will "blink out" altogether. That is the One: not any thing, but the undifferentiated containment of all things.

Conversely, then, all things are nothing but the "unfolding" of the One, its presentation in differentiated multiplicity. What constitutes beings as not the One but as all things, as being, is their differentiation from one another. They are beings in that they are distinct from each other and therefore determinate and intelligible. What distinguishes each being from the others is also what distinguishes each being from the One. Each being is not the One, precisely in that it is differentiated from other beings, is determinate, is intelligible, or, in short, in that it is a being. All things are other than the One, but the One is not other than all things, for the One,

Plotinus says, "has no otherness" (VI.9.8.34). All the otherness is on the side of being, for the otherness of being from the One consists not in the One's being defined over against being, but in the otherness, within being, of one being from another.[15]

As differentiated, finite presentations, all beings are appearances of the One. In that they are intelligible, they are the One as it is given to and apprehended by Intellect, which is to say not as the One, the undifferentiated containment of all things, but as differentiated, i.e. as being. Since to be is to be intelligible, to be is to be given to thought, to be manifest, to be appearance. The differentiation of beings from one another, in virtue of which they are intelligible and are beings, constitutes them, therefore, as appearances of the One. Thus Plotinus explains that being is established as the multiplicity of forms, and hence as being, in, by, and as Intellect's differentiated apprehension of the One: "Therefore this multiple Intellect, when it wishes to think that which is beyond [thinks] that itself which is one, but in wishing to attain to it in its simplicity comes out continually apprehending something else made many in itself" (V.3.11.1–4). The content of Intellect, which is the whole of being, is the One as it is given, as it appears to and in Intellect, which is necessarily as many. Thus Plotinus says that "being is a trace of the One" (V.5.5.14; cf. VI.7.17.39), or, equivalently, that Intellect is an "expression" (λόγος) or "image" of the One (V.1.6.45; V.1.7.1).[16] Just as a Platonic form is one and makes its instances to be such instances by appearing many, so that the contents of the instances are differentiated appearances of the form, so the One "makes" all things by appearing multiply, so that the entire content of being is the differentiated appearance of the One in Intellect.

When Neoplatonic vertical causation, or "procession," is understood as the dependence of the determined on its determination and hence as the differentiated appearance of the unitary determination, it becomes clear that the production of the effect is not an activity on the part of the cause, distinct from the cause itself. It produces the effect—which, we must remember, means only that the effect depends on it for its identity and hence its existence—simply in that it is determination. The determination as such is the productive activity for that which it determines. The cause does not first exist as itself and then also appear or unfold itself and in that sense produce its effects. Rather, the cause is nothing but that which is appearing, nothing but the unity, the enfolding, of the effects. As Plotinus says of Nature, "Making, for it, means being what it is, and its making power is coextensive with what it is" (III.8.3.18–20). Similarly he says of the forms, "But this, the [intelligible] All, is universal power [δύναμις πᾶσα]" (V.8.9.25), i.e. the productive power by which the sensible cosmos has any existence at all. Each level is best understood not as the producer but as the production of its consequent, the constitutive power by which the latter is.

At the highest level, this means that the One is not something, some being, which both is, or is itself, and also appears and in that sense causes all things, but is rather the causing, the production, or the making of all things. Thus just after describing the One as "all beings and not even one," i.e. all things without distinction, Plotinus says, "This, we may say, is the first act of generation: the One, perfect because it seeks nothing, has nothing, and needs nothing, overflows, as it were, and its superabundance makes an other" (V.2.1.8–10). This can only mean, not that the One is a being which "overflows," which would contradict Plotinus' entire metaphysics, but that the One is Overflow itself, the differentiating or appearing by which all beings are. Plotinus frequently expresses this by referring to the One as not any thing but "the power of all things" (III.8.10.1; V.1.7.10; V.3.15.33; V.4.1.36; V.4.2.39; VI.7.32.31), i.e. nothing but the production of beings, the enabling condition by which they are beings. One of his best images for this point is his comparison of the One not to an object which gives off light but to the ambient light itself whereby things are visible:

> For even the light of the sun which it has in itself would perhaps escape our sense of sight if a more solid mass did not lie under it. But if someone said that the sun was all light, one might take this as contributing to the explanation of what we are trying to say; for the sun will then be light which is in no form belonging to other visible things . . . This, then, is what the seeing of Intellect is like; this also sees by another light the things illuminated by that first nature, and sees the light in them; when it turns its attention to the nature of the things illuminated, it sees the light less; but if it abandons the things its sees and looks at the medium by which it sees them, it looks at light and the source of light. But . . . Intellect must not see this light as external. (V.5.7.13–23)

Just as light is not any of the illuminated things but is present to them all as the condition by which they are visible, so the One is not any of the intelligible things, or beings, but is present to all of them, as the condition by which they are intelligible and hence are beings. And just as light is involved in every act of seeing as the condition of visibility but is not itself an object of sight as the illuminated things are, so the One is involved in every thought as the condition of intelligibility but is not itself the object of any thought. This image also captures the doctrine of being as the appearance of the One: light cannot be seen by itself, as pure light, but only as it is defined or rendered "concrete" in a distinct illuminated thing, so that all that is seen in any visible thing is a differentiated, determinate appearance of light itself.

Proclus, likewise, insists that there can be no distinction between a cause and its causing.

> Every productive cause produces the next and all subsequent prin-
> ciples while itself remaining steadfast. For if it imitates the One, and
> if the One brings its consequents into existence without movement,
> then every productive cause has a like law of production. Now the
> One does create without movement. For if it create through move-
> ment, either the movement is within it, and being moved it will
> change from being one and so lose its unity; or if the movement be
> subsequent to it, this movement will itself be derived from the One,
> and either we shall have infinite regress or the One will produce
> without movement. (*El. Th.*, prop. 26)

The One, therefore, is production itself, since otherwise its producing would
be a "movement," and so is any cause in relation to its consequent. "But
every producer remains as it is, and its consequent proceeds from it without
change in its steadfastness . . . Full and complete, then, it brings to existence
the secondary principles without movement and without loss, by itself being
what it is" (*El. Th.*, prop. 27). If the cause produces by being what it is, then
its producing is not other than itself and hence the cause is (nothing but)
the producing of its effect. Proclus expresses this most clearly when he remarks that the One's production of all things is not, properly speaking, an
activity at all:

> If, then, these entities [i.e., Soul and Intellect] produce by their
> existence alone, far more so does that One which is above them
> produce all things by the very fact of being one, not requiring any
> other activity to accompany its being one . . . [S]o then it created all
> things without employing activity. But if in using these very words
> *created* and *produced*, we use terms proper to activity . . . we apply
> these terms to the One from the realm of beings, signifying through
> terms denoting activity the activity-less manifestation [ἔκφανσιν]
> of all things from it.[17]

Here the doctrine of production as manifestation, rather than the making of
additional things, becomes explicit. For Proclus no less than for Plotinus, all
reality, no matter how many levels and triadic subdivisions may be found within
it, is nothing but the unfolding, the differentiated presentation, of the One.

We are now in a position to see what Dionysius means when he describes God as not any thing but the cause of all things and hence subject
to no name and to all names. The operative principle is the Neoplatonic law
that "the things that belong to the effects pre-exist in the causes [προένεστι
τὰ τῶν αἰτιατῶν τοῖς αἰτίοις]" (DN II.8, 645D). Since determination is the
cause of being to that which it determines, God is the cause of all things in
that he is present to all things as the constitutive determinations by which
each is itself and so is. God is the "illumination of the illumined and principle

of perfection of the perfected and principle of deification of the deified and simplicity of the simplified and unity of the unified ... and, to speak simply, the life of living things and being of beings [τῶν ζώντων ζωὴ καὶ τῶν ὄντων οὐσία]" (DN I.3, 589C). He is present to all beings as being, the universal character common to all beings such that they are beings: God "neither was nor will be nor came to be nor comes to be nor will come to be; rather, he is not. But he is being to beings [αὐτός ἐστι τὸ εἶναι τοῖς οὖσι]" (DN V.4, 817D). Likewise he is present to all living things as life, the universal determination by which they are living things as distinct from non-living things. But the determining, constitutive divine presence is not limited to such exalted attributes as being and life, but includes all the features of each thing, which constitute it as that distinct thing, as itself, and hence as a being. "In the cause of all things the paradigms of all beings pre-exist ... Paradigms ... are the being-making determinations [οὐσιοποιοὺς ... λόγους], pre-existing unitarily [ἑνιαίως] in God, of beings, which theology calls pre-determinations [προορισμοὺς], and good wills, determinative and creative [ἀφοριστικὰ καὶ ποιητικά] of beings, according to which the beyond-being both predetermined and produced all beings" (DN V.8, 824C). Here these "paradigms" or λόγοι contained without distinction in God, are explicitly identified as the defining or determining principles which make beings to be. God is thus present in each being as its determining or defining λόγος, by which it is itself and so is. All the features of all things, therefore, are God-in-them, making them to be by making them what they are, so that God is not only being in beings and life in living things but "all things in all things [τὰ πάντα ἐν πᾶσι]" (DN I.7, 596C).[18]

This constitutive presence of God in all things is what Dionysius variously calls the "powers," "participations," "processions," "providences," "manifestations," or "distributions"[19] of God. All these expressions refer to God's causal presence in things as their intelligible determinations. "If we have named the hiddenness beyond being God, or life, or being, or light, or word [λόγον], we are thinking [νοοῦμεν] nothing other than the powers brought forth from it to us, which are deifying, or being-making [οὐσιοποιοὺς], or life-producing, or wisdom-giving" (DN II.7, 645A). As Dionysius here indicates, this is the justification for the naming of God. Since whatever feature we find in any being is God-in-it, God is truly "named" with all names of all things. Hence he is not only "nameless" but "many-named" (DN I.6, 596A), bearing all the names of all things.

Dionysius' God, then, like Plato's forms in relation to their instances or Plotinus' One in relation to all things, is at once transcendent and immanent. He is transcendent, as we have seen, in that he is not a being at all, not included within reality as any member of it. And he is immanent in that he is immediately present in all things as all their constitutive determinations. As Dionysius says, "the being of all things is the divinity beyond being [τὸ γὰρ εἶναι πάντων ἐστὶν ἡ ὑπὲρ τὸ εἶναι θεότης]" (CH I.4, 177D).

This seemingly paradoxical formulation is perfectly straightforward in the light of Neoplatonic metaphysics: God is the being that all beings have, by which they are beings, and as such is beyond being in that he is not himself one of them, one of the things that have being. Dionysius expresses this simultaneous transcendence and immanence in his account of God as light, reminiscent of Plotinus' image of the One as ambient light rather than an illuminated being: "The goodness of the Godhead which is beyond all things extends from the highest and most venerable substances to the last, and is still above all, the higher not outstripping its excellence nor the lower going beyond its containment, but it both enlightens all that are able, and crafts [δημιουργεῖ][20] and enlivens and holds together and perfects, and is the measure of beings" (DN IV.4, 697C).[21] As light, God does not stand at the peak of the hierarchy of beings but transcends and permeates the whole, transcending it in that he is not any member of it, permeating it in that he is present throughout as the illumination, or determination, by which all things are.

Dionysius articulates this transcendence and immanence, adapting Procline terminology, by saying that the divine processions are "unparticipatedly participated [ἀμεθέκτως μετεχόμενα]" (DN II.5, 644A). This may seem to make his doctrine different from that of Proclus, in that for Dionysius it is the unparticipated God himself in whom all things participate, whereas Proclus distinguishes the immanent, participated terms from the transcendent, unparticipated term.[22] But this difference is only apparent, for as we have seen, Proclus' participated terms are nothing but the differentiated presence of the unitary unparticipated term in the participants. Dionysius' "processions" are participated in that they are the differentiated presence of God in all things, but they are participated "unparticipatedly" in that, since the same God is differently present in different things, he is not confined to, or in that sense "possessed by," any of them. Despite differences of expression, the structure of participation, implying at once transcendence and immanence, remains the same in Plato, Plotinus, Proclus, and Dionysius: one and the same term is present in many different things, and as what is the same in all of them (immanent), it is other than and unconditioned by all of them (transcendent).

But if all the determinations of all things are the presence of God in them, then God is not merely "in all things," as if he were in something other than himself. Rather, God is the whole content of reality, "all things in all things." God "is all things as cause of all things, and holding together and pre-possessing [συνέχων καὶ προέξων] in himself all principles, all limits [συμπεράσματα] of all beings" (DN V.8, 824A–B). The various features, characters, or natures, the determinations (συμπεράσματα) found in a thing, constitute the entire intelligible content of that thing, all that there is in it for the mind to encounter. And since to be is to be intelligible, they constitute the whole of the thing itself. A being can be nothing but the totality of its intelligible determinations, down to the least details by which it is this particular thing and no other. The divine processions are "in" all things, then, not as contained in something other than themselves, but as constituting their entire content. God is the "cause" of all things, and so subject to all names, therefore, in that the entire intelligible content of all things, and hence the whole of reality, is nothing but the differentiated presence of God.

Conversely, therefore, God is not some being other than all things (the very formula is an absurdity) but is rather the entire content of reality, i.e. all things, without differentiation, without the distinctions from one another by which they are all things. Here again we find the Neoplatonic doctrine of *complicatio* and *explicatio*, enfolding and unfolding: the cause (here, God) is the undifferentiated containment of the effects, and the effects (here, all things) are the presentation of the cause in differentiated multiplicity. Thus Dionysius says that the "ray beyond being . . . can neither be thought nor spoken nor contemplated in any way at all because it is transcendent to all things and beyond unknowing, and pre-contained in itself [ἐν ἑαυτῇ προειληφυῖαν] at once [ἅμα], in a manner beyond being [ὑπερουσίως], all the limits of all substantial knowledges and powers" (DN I.4, 592D–593A).[23] "All the limits of all substantial knowledges and powers" means all the intelligible contents of reality, the "termini" or objects of knowledge, and Dionysius here expressly conjoins their containment in God "at once," i.e. without distinction, with their containment in him "in a manner beyond being" (and also, of course, beyond thought and beyond unknowing). Still more plainly, he says that the "cause of all things . . . pre-contained in itself all beings, simply and indeterminately [πάντα δὲ ἁπλῶς καὶ ἀπεριορίστως ἐν ἑαυτῇ τὰ ὄντα προείληφε]" (DN I.7. 596C–597A). Consequently, Dionysius says not merely that God is "in" all things, but that he is "all beings and none of beings [πάντα τὰ ὄντα καὶ οὐδὲν τῶν ὄντων]" (DN I.6, 596C), or better, "all things in all things and nothing in any [ἐν πᾶσι πάντα ἐστὶ καὶ ἐν οὐδενὶ οὐδέν]" (DN VII.3, 872A). Dionysius here follows the thought of Plotinus, who, as we have seen, says not only that the One is present in all things, but that it is "all things and not even one" (V.2.1.1). Dionysius' God is all things in all things in that whatever intelligible content is found in any thing, and so the thing itself, is God-in-it, in the distinct way that is constitutive of that being; and he is nothing in any, in that he is not any one thing, distinguished from others within the whole of reality and constituted by that distinction. Like the One of Plotinus, he is beyond being just in that he is all things without distinction.

If God is the *complicatio* of all things, all things without distinction, then, for Dionysius as for Plotinus, the differentiation of beings from one another is what makes being as a whole, the totality of the things that are, distinct from God. It is this differentiation that constitutes all things as all things, as being, as that which is, rather than God. But if being is being, or is, in virtue of differentiation, then God himself is this very differentiation. Thus Dionysius says that God is named "the Different, since God becomes providentially present to all things and all things in all things for the preservation of all" (DN IX.5, 912D). He goes on to say, "Let us consider the divine difference . . . as his unitary multiplication [τὸν ἑνιαῖον αὐτοῦ πολυπλασιασμὸν] and the uniform processions of his multiple-generation [πολυγονίας] to all things" (DN IX.5, 913B).[24] This account of God as the productive differentiation by which beings are distinct, are themselves, and so are beings, recalls Plotinus' description of the One's production, which is not distinct from the One itself, as "overflow," and his statement that the One is not merely simple but "beyond any simplicity whatsoever" (V.3.16.15). Still more clearly, it echoes Proclus' account of production as the cause's "multiplying itself," where there is no distinction between the cause and its productive self-multiplication, so that the cause is the very differentiation whereby it is differently present in, and so constitutes, its effects. For all three philosophers, the One or God is not a "simple monad," devoid of difference and multiplicity but possessing simplicity and unity. As the very differentiation whereby beings are beings, he is neither simple nor differentiated but "beyond" both, and constitutes at once the unity of being and the differences within it: "From this [God as the Good] are all the substantial existences of beings, the unions, the distinctions, the identities, the differences, the likenesses, the unlikenesses, the communions of opposite things, the unminglings of united things" (DN IV.7, 704B). The center of the circle, the undifferentiated containment of all things, is not "first" a simple monad which "then" in addition to being itself also produces or undergoes differentiation. Rather, the containment is itself the unfolding, the overflow, multiplication, or differentiation, by which beings are distinct and so are beings.

For Dionysius, then, as for Plotinus and Proclus, the whole of reality, all that is, is theophany, the manifestation or appearance of God.[25] For the entire content of any being is God present in it in a distinct, finite way, and, in virtue of this distinction and finitude, knowable in that being as its intelligible content. It is just as distinct, or finite, that God is present in the being, or that the being is a presentation of God. For to be "present" means to be given or available to thought, i.e. to be intelligible. And as intelligible, as given to thought, God is apparent, or manifest, in and as the being. To be present, to be manifest, to be finite, to be distinct, to be intelligible, are ultimately all the same, and all are elaborations of the only possible meaning of "to be." The understanding of being as theophany is thus a strict consequence, developed in the Neoplatonic tradition, of the original principle that to be is to be intelligible.

To say that reality is the appearance of God, however, may be misleading, if it is taken to mean that God is, so to speak, "there," behind or inside all the appearances, an object prior to and apart from them. If God is not any being, then what is reality the appearance *of*? Such a question again attempts

to reduce God to a "what," a being, an object of thought, violating all that
has been said about divine transcendence and about all being as appearance.
When we speak of reality as the appearance of God, we must remember that
since all reality is theophany, God, as "that which appears," is not another
being, another member of reality. The doctrine of being as theophany means
not that God is and is himself, and also appears, but rather that God is
nothing but what is differently present, or appears, in and as all things. To pass
from appearance to what is appearing, from being to God, is not to pass from
one thing to another thing. Rather, since God is not another thing but the
enfolding of all things, to go from beings to God is to gather the whole
diverse content of reality together, and in so doing, since being necessarily
involves multiplicity and distinction, to pass beyond being.

It may be felt that such doctrines make Dionysius into a mere "monist"
or "pantheist." God, he insists, is not something other than the world but is
"all things in all things." Again, if being is nothing but theophany, does this
not imply that the world is not real at all, but only appearance? Such objec-
tions, however, represent a failure to understand the Neoplatonic metaphysics of manifestation and intelligibility. Dionysius' metaphysics is not a form
of "pantheism," if by this we mean the doctrine that all things are God. On
the contrary: every being, precisely in that it is a being, i.e. something distinct, finite, and intelligible, *ipso facto* is not God. Indeed, since to be is to
be intelligible and therefore to be finite, to be *means* to be not God. This,
again, is precisely why God is beyond being. Every being, then, absolutely is
not God. Nor are all things, taken as a totality, God, for "all things" is plural,
a multiplicity of distinct intelligible beings.[26] The God of Dionysius is "all
beings and none of beings," "all things in all things and nothing in any," and
in these formulas the "all" can never be separated from the "none." As all
things *without distinction*, God is neither any one thing nor all things in their
plurality. All things, *qua* all things, the whole of reality, are absolutely other
than God.

But if Dionysius is not a monist or pantheist, neither is he a dualist,
regarding God as another being over against the world. All things are not
God, but God is not therefore something else besides all things. Such a notion,
as the very words indicate, is manifest nonsense. If God were another being
besides his products, he would be included as a member of a more inclusive
totality, subordinated to a more embracing universal term, and distinct from
the other members and therefore finite.[27] If God were merely other than the
world, he would be another thing and so not truly transcendent, but contained
in the world. All things are other than God, but God is not other than all
things.[28] Since all things are not God, Dionysius is not a monist; but since God
is not something else besides all things, neither is he a dualist.

Dionysius, like his fellow Neoplatonists, is able to negotiate a way
between monism and dualism by means of the Platonic concept of appearance, taken up into the doctrine of being as theophany. The relation between

an appearance and that of which it is an appearance is not a relation between two beings: the appearance is not another being, additional to that which is appearing. But in that the appearance, *qua* appearance, is not that which is appearing itself, neither is this a monistic reduction of the appearance to what is appearing. As Plato says, with reference to the status of sensibles as appearances of the forms, they are not being itself, the forms, but neither are they non-being, or nothing. The appearances both are and are not the reality; they are "in between" being and non-being. So, for Dionysius, beings are not additional things other than God, in such a way that God and the world would constitute two things. But neither are they nothing, or illusion, as in a monist philosophy. Wherever we look, we are not seeing God, in that every being, every object of thought, is not God; and wherever we look, we are seeing God, as he appears, for every being, every object of thought, is nothing but a presentation or appearance of God.

To say that the world is the manifestation or appearance of God, then, is not to say that it is not real.[29] Rather, Dionysius' Neoplatonic point is that reality itself is appearance: to be real means to be intelligible, to be given to thought, and thus to be appearance.[30] To go beyond appearance, in this sense of what is given to thought, is to go beyond being. As Dionysius' Neoplatonic metaphysics is neither theism nor atheism, so also it is neither monism nor dualism, but can only be called, for want of a better term, "theophanism."[31] The relation between appearance and that which appears is irreducible to either unity or duality and cannot be expressed in any terms other than those of appearance, manifestation, image, expression. Only through this Platonic concept is it possible to understand Dionysius' metaphysics or to make sense of the relation between the world and God without reducing the world to God (monism) or God to a being (dualism).

CHAPTER THREE

GOODNESS, BEAUTY, AND LOVE

The dependence of the determined on its determination, and thus the dependence of all beings on God, is understood in Neoplatonism not merely as a static relation, but as a dynamic, though non-temporal, "motion" or "process."[1] This is the cycle of remaining, procession, and reversion (μονή, πρόοδος, ἐπιστροφή), which is already present in Plotinus' thought but receives systematic articulation in Proclus: "Every effect remains in its cause, proceeds from it, and reverts upon it" (El. Th., prop. 35). For Plotinus and Proclus, the One is not only the containment of all things and the source (ἀρχή) from which they come, but also the end (τέλος) toward which they go. Dionysius adopts this doctrine in its Procline form, and it underlies his entire account of God as the Good, the Beautiful, and Love in chapter IV of On Divine Names. To understand this cycle in philosophical terms, we must explain why, in Neoplatonism, the One is also called the Good, for it is this name that best expresses God as at once the ἀρχή and the τέλος of all things.

We saw in chapter 1 how Plato argues that goodness is the principle of intelligibility, for anything can be intellectually understood only in virtue of its goodness. To be intelligible, then, is to be good, and the intelligible determination or form in each thing, by which that thing is what it is, is that thing's way of being good. Consequently, Plato says that the Good provides "truth and being," i.e. intelligibility and hence the status of being beings, to the forms, and so is itself "beyond being." Every form, therefore, is a specification, a distinct mode, of goodness.

Aristotle, too, argues that the formal cause of a thing is one with its final cause, as that which determines its shape, structure, and function, and so accounts for the thing's being what it is (Physics II.7, 198a26, 198b3; II.8, 199a33). For Aristotle as for Plato, finality, or goodness, is the principle of unity and intelligibility: the end to which a thing is directed endows the thing with unity, with identity, with intelligibility, making it to be the one

distinct "what" that it is.[2] Hence, for Aristotle, the final cause of any thing
is the fundamental ground of its being what it is. The form or "whatness" in
a thing, therefore, is its distinct way of being good.[3] Thus it is as a final cause,
an object of desire, that Aristotle's God, who is pure form and hence purely
good (see *Metaphysics* XII.7, 1072b29), is the principle of actualization for
the cosmos as a whole (*Metaphysics* XII.7, 1072a26, 1072b3).[4]

Following these Platonic and Aristotelian principles, Plotinus argues
that the form, the constitutive determination of any thing, is that thing's
way of being good. "But shall we then define the good according to each
thing's excellence? But in this way we shall refer to form and reason-principle
[εἶδος καὶ λόγον], certainly a correct manner of proceeding" (VI.7.19.9–
12). Each level in Plotinus' hierarchy of reality, as productive determination,
as the principle of order, of unity, of identity to the next level down, is what
is good for its consequent: "Is it then so that the good for the last and lowest
among beings is what lies before it, and there is a continuous ascent which
gives that above a thing to be good for what is below . . . ? . . . For form is the
good for matter . . . and soul for body . . . and virtue for soul. And now, still
higher, there is intellect, and above this what we call the first nature"
(VI.7.25.18–28). In general, Plotinus says that "everywhere what comes as a
good is form" (VI.7.28.2). At every level, then, goodness is intelligibility,
increasing in intensity as we ascend from body to soul to Intellect (see
VI.7.25.25ff; VI.7.28.20ff.). The goodness in a thing is its distinct way of
being intelligible, and so its distinct way of being a being. Thus, as Plotinus
says, being as such is "boniform" [ἀγαθοειδὲς]" (VI.7.16.5), and "each form
is good and boniform" (VI.7.18.25–26). Since goodness is the principle of
intelligibility, and to be is to be intelligible, goodness is the universal and
constitutive character of all being.

From this point, it is not hard to see why goodness and unity are
interchangeable, why the Good is the same as the One. The goodness in any
thing is the determining identity which makes that thing the one being that
it is. "For all things, the principle is the end [τέλος ἅπασιν ἡ ἀρχή]"
(III.8.7.17).[5] The τέλος, the end, the good of the whole, is what coordinates
or unifies all its multiple content so that it is one being rather than an
indefinite multiplicity, and hence is its principle. Conversely, the unity of
any thing, that very integration of all its contents into one whole, is what
renders the thing good, successful at being what it is. Unity and goodness in
a being are the same, as the principle of identity whereby the thing is intelligible, is one thing, and so is a being. "The form . . . approaches and com-
poses that which is to come into being from many parts into a single ordered
whole; it brings it into a completed unity and makes it one by agreement of
its parts" (I.6.2.18–21). The Good, then, is the same as the One, as the
universal formative principle by which all beings are beings. As Plotinus
explains, the Good is "not . . . good for itself, but for the others" (VI.7.41.29–
30), not a good thing but that by which beings are good, manifest in each
being as its goodness, its unity, its intelligibility.

Proclus summarizes this reasoning most clearly:

> Every good is unitive of what participates in it, and every unification
> is good, and the Good is the same as the One.
>
> For if it belongs to the Good to conserve all beings . . . and if
> what conserves and holds together the being of each thing is unity
> (since by unity each is maintained in being, but by dispersion dis-
> placed from existence), then the Good renders one and holds to-
> gether by unification whatever things it is present to.
>
> And if it belongs to unity to bring and keep beings together,
> by its presence it makes each thing complete. And so being unified
> is good for all things.
>
> But again, if unification is in itself good, and the good unifies,
> then the simply Good and the simply One are the same, making
> beings one and so making them good . . .
>
> Goodness, then, is unification, and unification goodness; the
> Good is one, and the One primally good. (*El. Th.*, prop. 13)

To be intelligible, to be one, to be good, and hence to be, are all the same.
All the varied content of reality, therefore, consists of the many different
modulations of goodness, of unity; all the different ways in which beings are,
are so many different ways of being one and good. Thus we return to the
conclusion that all being is the "unfolding" of the Good, and the Good is the
"enfolding" of all being.

The One or Good, therefore, is the principle of intelligibility, and as
such the ἀρχή or source of all things, by being their τέλος or end. Thus
Plotinus says, "And the One is on both sides of them; for it is that from
which they come and to which they go; for all things originate [ἄρχεται]
from the One and strive towards the One. For in this way they also strive
towards the Good; for nothing whatever among beings could have come to
exist or endure in existence if its striving were not directed towards the One"
(VI.2.11.25–29). This does not mean merely that the same principle has two
distinct roles, as if the name *One* indicated it as source and the name *Good*
indicated it as end. The point, rather, is that the One is the source, endow-
ing beings with intelligibility and thus making them to be, precisely *as* the
Good, the end toward which they strive. Conversely, all things strive toward
the Good precisely *as* their source, that on which they depend in order to
be. "For all things reach out to that [i.e. the One] and long for it by necessity
of nature, as if divining . . . that they cannot exist without it" (V.5.12.8–9).
Thus both One and Good indicate the first principle as the ground of intelligibility and hence of being, at once and identically source and end, ἀρχή
qua τέλος and τέλος *qua* ἀρχή.

The understanding of causal determination as at once ἀρχή and τέλος
for the determined effect underlies the Procline cycle of remaining, procession, and reversion. "Remaining" has already been explained: it refers to the

enfolding or undifferentiated containment of the effects in, or rather as, the cause. Remaining is the identity of the effect with the cause, in the sense that the content of the effect is nothing but the differentiated presentation of the cause. Procession, in turn, is the unfolding or differentiation whereby the effects are different from each other and therefore from the cause, and so exist at all as distinct, determinate beings, as effects. "If . . . [the effect] should remain only, without procession, it will be indistinguishable from its cause, and will not be an other which has arisen while the cause remains. For if it is other, it is distinct and separate . . . In so far, then, as it has an element of identity with the producer, the product remains in it; in so far as it differs it proceeds from it" (*El. Th.*, prop. 30). For this reason, although Proclus usually says that the effect proceeds from the cause, he can also say that the cause proceeds to the effect, and both formulations have the same meaning (e.g. *El. Th.*, props. 21, 25).[6] To say that the effect proceeds from the cause means that it depends on it and in that sense "comes from" it, and this dependence consists in the effect's being nothing but a differentiated presentation or manifestation of the cause: an appearance "proceeds from" that which appears. Likewise, that which appears goes forth in appearing multiply and so constitutes its appearances, and in that sense the cause "proceeds to" the effects.

Reversion, in turn, signifies the relation of the effect to the cause as its end, or goodness. Since the causal determination of any thing is its way of being good, it is the end toward which the effect tends, and this tendency of any thing toward its cause as the good for it is its reversion. "[A]ll things desire the Good, and each attains it through its proximate cause: therefore each has appetition of its own cause also" (*El. Th.*, prop. 31). Thus reversion, like procession, can be indifferently ascribed to the cause or to the effect (e.g. *El. Th.*, prop. 144): the effect reverts to the cause, i.e. tends toward it, as its end; and the cause reverts the effect to itself, i.e. moves or "attracts" the effect to itself, as its end. Both formulations describe the ontological "motion" of the effect toward the cause, its acquisition or possession of the determination whereby it is good, is itself, and so is.

Reversion, therefore, is neither temporally nor even ontologically subsequent to procession, as though the effect "first" proceeds from its cause, or comes to be, and "then" becomes good by reverting to its cause. Since the end that endows a thing with intelligibility is the causal determination by which it is, the effect can be at all only in and by acquiring or reverting to its cause. Reversion, no less than procession, is constitutive of the effect, in that the very existence of anything consists not only in its proceeding from but also in its reverting to its cause. As Proclus says, "through that by which there is being to each thing, through this there is also being good" (*El. Th.*, prop. 31), because the thing's being what it is, and so being, consists in its being good. Since there is no real distinction between its being and its being good, there is no order of priority and posteriority between procession and reversion, but both at once and equally are the establishment of the effect as a being. Hence Proclus can argue from reversion to procession as well as from procession to reversion: "For if [a thing] reverts by nature, it has existential appetition of that upon which it reverts. And if so, its being also is wholly dependent on the principle upon which it reverts existentially . . . And if so, its procession is from that upon which it reverts" (*El. Th.*, prop. 34).[7] This makes it clear that the effect's dependence on its determination is its reversion to it no less than its procession from it.

Since, then, to be, for anything, is to revert to its cause, the proper mode of being for each kind of thing is its mode of reversion.

> Every being reverts either existentially only, or vitally, or also cognitively. For either it has from its cause existence [τὸ εἶναι] only, or life [τὸ ζῆν] together with existence, or it has received from thence a cognitive faculty [γνωστικὴν . . . δύναμιν] also. In so far, then, as it only is, it makes an existential reversion; in so far as it also lives, a vital one also; in so far as it has knowledge likewise, a cognitive one. For as it proceeds, so it reverts . . . Appetition is in some things, then, according to existence [αὐτὸ τὸ εἶναι] only, which is a fitness for the participation in their causes; in others, according to life [τὴν ζωήν], which is a movement towards the higher; in others, according to knowledge [τὴν γνῶσιν], which is a consciousness of the goodness of their causes. (*El. Th.*, prop. 39)

This is, in effect, a Neoplatonic elaboration of the Aristotelian principle, "To be, for a living thing, is to live" (*On the Soul* II.4, 415b12). Each thing is reverting to its cause simply in being the kind of thing that it is, in exercising the activities proper to it as such a thing. The "merely existential" reversion of an inanimate being, such as a stone, consists simply in its existing *as* a stone, its being hard, heavy, brittle, and so on. These features are its activities, the characteristic modes of behavior (resisting pressure, tending downward, shattering when struck, etc.) that constitute it as a stone rather than some other sort of thing. Hence they are its way of being what it is, of possessing its constitutive determinations, i.e. of reverting. Likewise, a plant's "vital" reversion is its living, its exercising the vital functions of growth, nutrition, reproduction, and so on, which are its proper way of being, as a living thing. And if "to be, for a living thing, is to live," then to be, for a cognitive thing, is to exercise cognition, which is the mode of being, and hence of reversion, for such things. In general, to be a thing of a certain kind, which means to be in a certain way, is to perform the activities proper to such things, and this is the thing's reversion, its possessing of its proper determinations. Reversion is thus the very being of all things, in the mode proper to and constitutive of each. As Plotinus says, nothing could be at all if it did not tend toward the Good.[8]

The Neoplatonic understanding of the being of a thing as its reversion to its cause means that the "coming to be" of the effect, its being "made" or produced by the cause, is not merely passive. Its being is indeed received in it, which is simply to say that it depends on its causal determination. But this dependence is an *active* receptivity on the part of the effect. Reversion represents existing as the activity of a being, of that which is: any being can be only by actively receiving its identifying determination, which is to say by performing the act-of-existing in its proper way, by enacting or "living out" its constitutive nature. Hence, the effect, or being, has a positive, active role in its own production, its being made to be. "Being caused" is an activity of the effect. Thus in Plotinus, as we have seen, Intellect constitutes itself as the multiplicity of intelligible forms, i.e. as the whole of being, in its reversion to the One, its looking to the One and taking the One into itself.[9] "That which is produced reverts to [the One] and is filled, and becomes Intellect by looking towards it. And its rest towards that makes it being, and its gaze upon it, Intellect. Since it rests towards it so that it may see, it becomes at once Intellect and being" (V.2.1.10–13; cf. VI.7.15.11–23; VI.7.16.13–20). The same is true analogously at every level: the product comes to be, or is, in and by reverting, taking its prior into itself. So also, Proclus speaks of effects as being "generated by reversion [κατ᾽ ἐπιστροφὴν ὑφισταμένων]" (*El. Th.*, prop. 37).[10] Reversion, in fact, is nothing other than participation, the participation of the determined effect in its causal determination, considered as an activity of the participant.

There is, then, no real distinction between procession and reversion, for both represent nothing but the dependence of the effect on the cause, considered as a dynamic relation productive of the effect.[11] Participation, the differentiated presentation of the causal determination in the effect, is at once a giving, a "going forth" of the cause to the effect and of the effect from the cause (procession), and a receiving, a "turning back" of the effect to the cause (reversion). The entire cycle of remaining, procession, and reversion, the *exitus-reditus* pattern that characterizes Neoplatonism, is simply the dependence of the determined on its determination, considered dynamically as the effect's coming from and going toward that in which it participates and on which it depends in order to be. As Proclus says, "Thus all things proceed in a circuit, from their causes to their causes" (*El. Th.*, prop. 33).

This cycle, as articulated by Proclus, underlies Dionysius' account of God as the Good or Goodness,[12] Beauty, and Love in chapter IV of *On Divine Names*. "It is the Good . . . from which all things originate [ὑπέστη][13] and are, as brought forth from an all-perfect cause; and in which all things are held together, as preserved and held fast in an all-powerful foundation; and to which all things are reverted as each to its own proper limit; and which all things desire" (DN IV.4, 700AB).[14] Or more summarily, "Every being is from the Beautiful and Good and in the Beautiful and Good and is reverted to the Beautiful and Good" (DN IV.10, 705D). We have already seen how, for Dionysius, all things are contained in and proceed from God, in that all the determinations, and hence the whole content, of all things are the constitutive presence of God in them. Having laid out the Neoplatonic doctrine of the One as the Good, we are now in a position to understand these determinations of beings as their goodness, by possessing which they are. Thus Dionysius explains at length that all beings, from angelic intelligences down to inanimate things, have their proper perfections or activities from and through the Good (DN IV.2, 696B–D), and then summarizes this by saying that the Good "gives form to the formless [τὸ ἀνείδεον εἰδοποιεῖ]" (DN IV.3, 697A), which is to say that it makes things be by making them intelligible. The formal determination of each being, then, is its goodness, and so is the presence in it of God, the Good, Goodness itself, by which it is good and so is.

The reversion of effects to their cause, in turn, forms the basis for Dionysius' account of the ontological love or desire of all things for God. Like Plotinus and Proclus, Dionysius explains that the very existence of all things depends on, or rather consists in, their desire for, or reversion to, God, the Good. As Proclus says that "through that by which there is being to each thing, through this there is also being good,"[15] so Dionysius says of the angels, for example, that "by desiring [Goodness] they have both being and being good [τῆς ἀγαθότητος . . . ἐφιέμεναι καὶ τὸ εἶναι καὶ τὸ εὖ εἶναι ἔχουσι]" (DN IV.1, 696A). It is only in desiring Goodness, by appropriating or actively receiving it, that they are at all, and clearly this is true not only of the angels but of all things. Thus Dionysius says later, "By all things, then, the Beautiful and Good is desired and loved and cherished[16] . . . and all things, by desiring the Beautiful and Good, do and wish all things that they do and wish" (DN IV.10, 708A). The most fundamental activity of any being is to be, and any "other" activities (e.g. living and thinking) are not additional to this but are modes or specifications of the activity of being.[17] No being, then, can be without desiring or reverting to God, i.e. receiving him as its constitutive determination, its goodness. All things come to be, they *are*, only in at once and identically proceeding from and reverting to, and in that sense loving, God.

The very being of each thing, then, is its possessing, receiving, reverting to God according to its proper mode. Thus, after saying that the Good is that "to which all things are reverted . . . and which all things desire,"[18] Dionysius continues, "the intellectual and rational cognitively [γνωστικῶς], the sensitive sensitively, those without a share in sensation by the natural motion of vital [ζωτικῆς] desire, and those which are not living and are merely beings merely by their fitness for existential participation" (DN IV.4, 700B; cf. DN I.5, 593D). This paraphrases Proclus' account of the modes of reversion, with the insertion of a sensitive mode, proper to irrational animals, between the cognitive mode belonging to angels and human beings ("the intellectual and rational," respectively) and the vital mode belonging to plants.[19] The proper activity which constitutes each thing as what it is, which is that thing's distinctive mode of being, is its way of reverting to God. A stone in merely existing as a stone, exercising the characteristic activities of being hard, heavy, and brittle; a plant in living, an animal in living sensitively, a human being in living rationally—in short, each thing simply in being what it is, i.e. in being in its proper way, is desiring or tending toward God, the Good, in its proper way, actively receiving him as its determination. Thus to revert to God is to proceed from him and to proceed from him is to revert to him.

As in Plotinus and Proclus, then, a being's reversion to God is productive of the being no less than its procession from him. Since procession and reversion are in reality the same relation of dependence, a thing's being made to be by God is not in any sense prior to its desire for him. Rather, the generation of the being consists in its tending toward God no less than in its coming from him. Thus reversion, as the activity of the being, is the being's share in its own being made to be. As in Plotinus and Proclus, the product has an actively receptive role in its production, and if it does not exercise this activity it cannot exist. For Dionysius, God cannot make beings without their active cooperation,[20] for without that activity they would not be anything. In every being, including animals, plants, and inanimate things, there is an element of "interiority," of selfhood, an active share in its own being what it is and so in its own being. At the level of rational beings, this interiority takes the form of self-consciousness, of personhood and freedom. But the principle that any being's reversion is creative of it means that there is something analogous to freedom and personhood at every level of reality, even in inanimate things.[21] For without this active selfhood, a being would have no unifying identity, it would not be this one distinct thing, and so would not be at all.

As the Good, by receiving which all things exist, God is also the Beautiful, and Dionysius tends to use these names conjointly and interchangeably (e.g. DN IV.7, 704B; IV.8, 704D; IV.10, 705C–708A; IV.18, 713D). Dionysius' account of God as Beauty is grounded in Plotinus' identification of beauty with form.[22] Plotinus argues that sensible things are beautiful, i.e. attractive and delightful to consciousness, in so far as they have a share of form, which has this effect on us because, as intelligible, it is "akin" to the cognitive power in us: both the form in the sensible object and the soul in the subject derive from and are lesser presentations of Intellect itself. What is beautiful, then, is what is intelligible, i.e. form (I.6.1–2). Elsewhere Plotinus reaches the same conclusion by arguing that an artistically sculpted stone is more beautiful than a raw lump because form is more evident in it, in that it has been shaped according to the idea in the artist's mind (V.8.1). He then transfers this reflection to the beauty of natural things, which are also works of art in that they are sensible images or expressions of Intellect, and remarks, "Is not this beauty everywhere form, which comes from the maker upon that which he has brought into being?" (V.8.2.14–15).

Since the beauty in sensible things is the share of form in them, what is truly and primarily beautiful is form itself, i.e. being, the content of Intellect. This in turn means that beauty, in the sense of "that which is beautiful," is the differentiated, intelligible manifestation of the Good. The Good, then, is not that which is beautiful, but is rather "beautifulness" or Beauty itself, that by which being is beautiful. "These beautiful things [the forms] then, must be measured and limited, but not the really beautiful or rather the super-beautiful [τὸ ὑπέρκαλον]; but if this is so, it must not be shaped or be a form. The primarily beautiful, then, and the first, is without form, and beauty is that, the nature of the Good" (VI.7.33.19–22; cf. I.6.9.40–43).

Proclus preserves this distinction between intelligible form as what is beautiful and the Good, beyond form, as in this sense beyond beauty,[23] but also argues that "in us," i.e. in participating particulars, there is no distinction between their goodness and their beauty.[24] The general Neoplatonic doctrine, then, despite variations in expression, is that form or being, the intelligible, is what is beautiful, and the Good is Beauty itself, as that by which the forms are forms, are beings, are beautiful.

On this basis, Dionysius says that "this Good is hymned . . . as Beautiful and as Beauty" (DN IV.7, 701C). Since form is beauty, and the formal determination in each thing is God in it, therefore the beauty in each being is God in it. Dionysius explains that "the Beautiful beyond being [τὸ . . . ὑπερούσιον καλὸν] is called Beauty [κάλλος] on account of the beautifulness [καλλονὴν] distributed from it to all beings in the manner proper to each" (DN IV.7, 701C). Just as God is the Goodness of all good things, which is to say of all things, so he is the Beauty of all things. Hence God is called Beautiful "as pre-possessing in himself, supereminently, the fontal beautifulness of every beautiful thing. For in the simple and supernatural nature of the whole of beautiful things, all beautifulness and every beautiful thing pre-exists uniformly as cause [κατ' αἰτίαν]" (DN IV.7, 704A). The final phrase is a Procline technical term for the undifferentiated containment of effects in their cause (El. Th., prop. 65). In this one sentence, then, Dionysius says three times over, with the words "simple" (ἁπλῇ), "uniformly" (ἐνοειδῶς), and "as cause" (κατ' αἰτίαν), that God contains in himself without distinction the beauty of all things. And since the beauty in each thing is God in it as its causal determination, the beauty of each being makes it to be: "From this Beautiful is being to all beings [ἐκ τοῦ καλοῦ τούτου πᾶσι οὖσι τὸ εἶναι], each being beautiful according to its proper determination [λόγον]" (DN IV.7, 704A). Since to be is to be intelligible, and to be intelligible is to be beautiful, to be is to be beautiful. All being, therefore, qua intelligible or beautiful, is the unfolding or manifestation of Beauty itself, or God. For Dionysius, as for Plato and Plotinus, it is in its beauty that being manifests itself as the manifestation of transcendence.

Since Beauty is the same as Goodness, it is at once ἀρχή and τέλος for all beings. Thus Dionysius says that God is named Beauty not only as present in each being as its beauty, making it to be, but also as "calling [καλοῦν] all things toward itself, wherefore it is called Beauty [κάλλος]."[25] Both Beauty and Goodness indicate God as the end which makes things to be by providing them with determinate identity. "The Beautiful is the principle [ἀρχὴ] of all things, as making cause [ποιητικὸν αἴτιον] and moving and holding together the whole by the love of its proper beautifulness, and limit of all things, and cherished, as final cause [τελικὸν αἴτιον], since for the sake of the Beautiful all things come to be; and paradigmatic [cause] [παραδειγματικόν], in that all things are determined [ἀφορίζεται] according to it" (DN IV.7, 704AB). Here Dionysius identifies determination, final causality, and causality of being under the name of Beauty, in that the beauty of each being, as its defining determination, is identically its end and its cause of being.[26]

Dionysius' entire account of procession and reversion, of God as the Good and the Beautiful, culminates in his celebration of God as Love (ἔρως). "The cause of all things, through excess [ὑπερβολὴν] of goodness, loves [ἐρᾷ] all things, makes all things, perfects all things, sustains all things, reverts all things; and the divine love is good, of good, through the good. For love, the very benefactor of beings, pre-existing in excess in the Good, did not permit it to remain unproductive in itself, but moved it to productive action, in the excess which is generative of all things" (DN IV.10, 708AB). God is Love, then, in that he is "excess," i.e. is distributed to all things, making all things to be by being differently present in each. Dionysius' account of God as Love is therefore another expression of the doctrine of God as beyond being, not any distinct, determinate being but the universal determination or differentiation that constitutes all things. His presentation of God as Love is in fact closely parallel to his account of the divine name *Different*, which we have examined earlier.[27]

Dionysius' doctrine of God as productive love for all things is often regarded as a uniquely Christian aspect of his thought, in which it differs significantly from non-Christian Neoplatonism.[28] In fact, however, Dionysius' position differs only in expression, not in philosophical content, from that of Plotinus and Proclus. His entire account of divine love recalls and coincides in meaning with Plotinus' description of the "overflow" of the One, or rather of the One as Overflow, which is the production of being.[29] "[T]he One, perfect because it seeks nothing, has nothing, and needs nothing, overflows, as it were, and its superabundance makes an other" (V.2.1.8–10). For Plotinus, the One produces all things in that it provides them with all that they have and are, as differentiated presentations of itself. "We breathe and are preserved because that Good does not give [δόντος] and then go away but is always providing as long as it is what it is" (VI.9.9.10–11). Plotinus does not use the term ἔρως in this context, but this "overflow" or "giving," the One as the productive "power of all things," is exactly what Dionysius refers to as productive divine love.[30] And in Plotinus as in Dionysius, the immanence of the One which this implies in no way compromises, but rather coincides with, the One's transcendence. The One, as we have seen, is transcendent not in the sense of being self-contained and apart from all things, but rather in that it is not any thing but the power of all things, present to all beings as that by which they are beings.[31] Thus it is transcendent as constitutively immanent, which is exactly what Dionysius expresses in his account of God as overflowing Love.

Proclus' position on this point may seem to be further removed from Dionysius' because of his distinction between participated and unparticipated terms, between, at the highest level, the henads and the One. He attributes to a certain kind of gods a "providential love" (ἔρως προνοητικός) whereby they produce subordinate things by "filling all things with themselves," which corresponds closely to, and is no doubt largely the source of, Dionysius' account of love.

> What then is it necessary to say about the gods or the good daimons? Is it not that being present to all things they transcend all things, and having filled all things with themselves they are likewise ummixed with all things, and permeating everywhere they have placed their own life nowhere? But what should we say about the gods who are said to love their own offspring . . . ? Is it not that such love is providential and preservative of those beloved, and perfective and constitutive of them? . . . And gods indeed love gods, the senior their inferiors, but providentially, and the inferior their superiors, but revertively.[32]

But Proclus does not ascribe such providential love to the One itself, as unparticipated.[33] However, we must remember that Proclus' intent in making the distinction between participated and unparticipated terms is *not* to keep the unparticipated term aloof from its participating effects, but, on the contrary, to guarantee its universal *presence* to all alike, without its being conditioned or limited by them. It is precisely by and as the participated terms that the unparticipated is present to all its effects, and indeed the participated terms, and, in turn, all their consequent terms, are nothing but the differentiated presence of the unparticipated to the effects.[34] The gods, therefore, which by providential love fill and constitute all things, are the differentiated presences of the One in all beings. Thus we find in Proclus the same coinciding of transcendence and immanence that we find in Plotinus' doctrine of the One as productive overflow and in Dionysius' account of divine love. For Plotinus and Proclus, then, the One "loves" his products (although they do not use this term), in that he is constitutively present to them, providing them with all that they are as the differentiated manifestation of himself.[35] To be sure, Dionysius is the first to use the terms ἔρως and ἐκστατικός to express this doctrine, and this terminological innovation may well be inspired by his Christianity;[36] but the conception of God that it expresses is already present in the thought of Plotinus and Proclus.

Dionysius elaborates on the understanding of divine Love when he says,

> The very cause of all things, by the beautiful and good love of all things, through excess of erotic goodness, becomes out of himself [ἔξω ἑαυτοῦ γίνεται] in his providences toward all beings, and is as it were enticed by goodness and affection [ἀγαπήσει] and love and is led down, from above all things and beyond all things, to in all things [ἐκ τοῦ ὑπὲρ πάντα καὶ πάντων ἐξῃρημένου πρὸς τὸ ἐν πᾶσι κατάγεται], according to an ecstatic power beyond being, without going out from himself [ἀνεκφοίτητον ἑαυτοῦ]. (DN IV.13, 712AB)

Since God's presence "in all things" is his making them to be, this is another account of the productive procession or differentiation that establishes beings as beings. God goes "out of himself" without "going out from himself" in that he is, as it were, intrinsically ecstatic, not a self-contained self but always already "out of himself" and "in all things" as their constitutive differences. His being "in himself" consists in his being "out of himself" and "in all things," just because God is no thing, not any being, but the causal determination, the production, or in Plotinus' phrase the "power," of all things.

As the constitutive differentiation of beings, not any thing but the making of all things, God is pure exteriority, having no inner core of "selfhood," no "interior" that could be distinguished from his "outward" productive activity. God is not a "self" of his own, a being, but only the self, the determining identity, *of others*, of all things; and this is what Dionysius means by describing him as ecstatic love. But for precisely the same reason, because his "self" is nothing but productive giving, it is equally true that God is pure interiority, absolutely unconditioned by any relation to beings that would be an accident or an affect additional to his inner self. In God as Love, therefore, pure interiority coincides with pure exteriority.[37]

From this it follows that the divine name Love indicates not only procession, the movement of God to beings, but also reversion, the movement of beings to God. For the being's interiority, its reversion to or love for God, which is the characteristic activity by which it is itself and so is, is God himself at work in the being.[38] "Hence the skilled in divine matters call [God] also jealous, as the great good love toward beings, and as waking to jealousy his erotic desire, and as showing himself as jealous, to whom the things desired are objects of jealousy, and because the objects of providence are objects of jealousy to him" (DN IV.13, 712B). God can be said to desire his products erotically, not in that he "lacks" or "needs" them, but in that he providentially, or productively, moves or draws them to himself. As we have seen, there is no difference between the cause's reverting the effect to itself and the effect's reverting to the cause: both formulations express the same ontological motion of effect to cause. Hence, God's erotic love for the being, his moving or reverting it to himself, is the being's reversion to or erotic love for God. This motion, which is the proper activity by which the being is what it is, is God's "providential" presence in the being as its interiority, its selfhood, its being. For this reason, the being's active participation in its own being produced does not contribute anything additional to what it receives from God: the being's reversion to God, which is its constitutive, identifying activity, is God himself present and active in it.

God's love for the being, which makes it to be, is thus not only his procession to it but also his moving or reverting the being to himself.[39] The identity of God's love for the being and the being's love for God follows from, or indeed simply reiterates, the identity of procession and reversion. God's procession to the being, the being's procession from God, the being's reversion to God, and God's reversion of the being to himself, are all one, for all describe the being's dependence on God as its constitutive determination. This single metaphysical motion, by which all things are, is the full meaning of the divine name Love.

This is why, for Dionysius, there can be no distinction whatever between ἔρως and ἀγάπη, between love as acquisitive desire and love as beneficent giving (DN IV.11–12, 708C–709D). God's "agapic" procession to all things is his "erotic" moving all things to himself, and the "agapic" self-abandonment of all things to God is their "erotic" acquisition of him. As Dionysius explains, "The divine love is ecstatic [ἔστι . . . ἐκστατικὸς ὁ θεῖος ἔρως], not allowing lovers to belong to themselves, but to those beloved" (DN IV.13, 712A). Ἔρως is "ecstatic" in that, as desire for the other, it is an abandonment of oneself to the other, a movement of the lover "out" of himself and "into" the other. As we have seen, God is himself only as the self of others, of all things. Thus, as Dionysius says, God's erotic desire for the being (reversion) is his providential, constitutive presence in it (procession). Conversely, his constitutive presence to the being (procession) is his moving it to himself (reversion). Because there is no real distinction between procession and reversion, there is no distinction between giving to the other and taking the other to oneself.

So also, on the side of the being, its erotic desire for God is a self-abandonment to God, a reception of God as its being, as its self, so that it may be. "Wherefore the great Paul, having come to be in possession of divine love, and participating in its ecstatic power, says with inspired mouth, 'I live, and yet not I, but Christ lives in me,' as a true lover and, as he says, ecstatic to God, and living not his own life but the life of the beloved, as greatly cherished" (DN IV.13, 712A). The felicitously ambiguous phrase "in possession of divine love" (ἐν κατοχῇ τοῦ θείου . . . ἔρωτος) means at once that Paul is possessed by divine love and that he possesses it. And this is precisely the point: to possess, or acquire, God as one's being is to give oneself up to

him, to be possessed by him. Every being whatsoever must in effect say, "I
am, and yet not I, but God is in me," not as an obscure mystical paradox but
as a precise metaphysical truth. Here again, therefore, the "agapic" self-
abandonment to God is the "erotic" acquisition of God whereby a being is.

The conventional distinction and antithesis between ἔρως and ἀγάπη[40]
depends on a dualistic vision of God and the creature as two beings set over
against one another, so that there is an opposition between "selfish" desire for
the other and "selfless" giving to the other. But where, as in Neoplatonism, the
being is nothing but the manifestation or presentation of God, where its very
being is nothing but God-in-it, and God is not a self-contained self or being but
the self, the being of all things, there can be no such opposition. Rather, the very
life of the world consists in the erotic exchange or interchange between beings
and God, which is at once and on both sides a giving and a receiving.

Dionysius describes this exchange in his account of how God is at once
love or charity and the beloved or cherished. "What do the theologians
mean when they say now that he is love and charity, and then that he is
beloved and cherished?" He explains that "in one respect he is moved, but
in the other he moves [τῷ μὲν κινεῖται, τῷ δὲ κινεῖ];" that is, as love God
is moved, i.e. proceeds to or is present in all things, while as beloved he
moves, i.e. causes other things to move, reverting them to himself.[41] But
since procession and reversion are the same metaphysical motion, this distinction breaks down. Thus Dionysius continues,

> They call him cherished and beloved, as beautiful and good, and
> again love and charity, as the power which at once moves and leads
> beings up to himself . . . and as being the manifestation [ἔκφανσιν]
> of himself through himself and the good procession [πρόοδον] of
> the transcendent union, and the erotic motion, simple, self-moved,
> self-active, pre-existing in the Good, and overflowing from the Good
> to beings, and again reverting them to the Good. Herein the divine
> love eminently shows its endlessness and beginninglessness, as an
> eternal circle, whirling around through the Good, from the Good,
> and in the Good and to the Good in unerring coiling-up, always
> proceeding and remaining and returning in the same and by the
> same. (DN IV.14, 712C–713A)

Here Dionysius expressly identifies God as not merely that which proceeds
to and so makes beings, but as the very procession or manifestation which
is the making of all things. The "whirling circle" of divine love, then, is God
present in all things as their goodness, their beauty, their activity, their
being. Love is the procession and reversion which is the very existence of all
things, and hence Dionysius' entire account of divine love is a presentation
in dynamic terms of participation, the constitutive relation of the determined to its determination.

Dionysius' presentation of God as productive Love raises the much-vexed question of whether, for Dionysius, God makes all things "freely" or "by necessity."[42] The entire issue is almost always misconceived, because it is usually assumed that to say that God creates "freely" means that he "might not create," and that he "chooses" between possible alternatives of creating and not creating; while, conversely, to say that there is no such choice between possible alternatives, that God "cannot" not create, means that he is subject to some "necessity." This entire construction of the problem is a misconception, and to correct it we must go back once more to Plotinus, who is often misunderstood in the same way.[43]

Plotinus regularly insists that the One produces being "by necessity" (e.g. I.8.7.20; II.9.3.8–12; V.1.6.32). But just what does this mean? Clearly, it indicates that there is no alternative possibility. As we have seen, the One's production of all things is not additional to or other than the One itself (e.g. VI.8.13.5–8, 31; VI.8.20.14–19); rather, the One simply is the production of being, "the power of all things," the enabling condition by which beings are beings. Thus, in addressing the issue of the One's "free-dom," Plotinus explains that there is no distinction between the One and his activity or will (VI.8.7.47; VI.8.13.7–8, 31). Obviously, if the One is nothing but the production of beings, then he is not "free" not to produce, and in that sense all things proceed from him "by necessity."

But this does not mean that the One is subject to some principle or law, some "necessity" higher or more universal than himself, such that he "must" produce beings. Plotinus' metaphors of "emanation" are, indeed, often misin-terpreted as indicating that the necessity of production is a universal law to which all things, *including the One*, are subject. But this cannot be correct, since the One is not any being, even the highest, and cannot be subject to any principle above or more universal than itself. Plotinus' point, rather, is that the universal productive tendency of all things to "impart themselves" is their imitation of or participation in the One as Giving or Production itself.

> If the First is perfect, the most perfect of all, and the primal power, it must be the most powerful of all beings[44] and the other powers must imitate it as far as they are able. Now when anything else comes to perfection we see that it produces, and does not endure to remain by itself, but makes something else. This is true not only of things which have choice, but of things which grow and produce without choosing to do so, and even lifeless things, which impart themselves to others as far as they can: as fire warms, snow cools, and drugs act on something else in a way corresponding to their own nature—all imitating the First Principle as far as they are able by tending to everlastingness and goodness. How then could the most perfect and the first Good remain in itself as if it grudged itself or were impotent—the power of all things? (V.4.1.24–36)

The One, then, is not subject to a "law of emanation" more universal than itself, but rather, as Giving or Production, is itself the law or paradigm to which all things, in producing, conform. And as this passage shows, the metaphor of emanation does not assimilate the One to a lifeless or sub-rational object that acts by natural necessity without choice. Rather, self-impartation by necessity of nature is the lowest mode, and production by choice a higher mode, of imitating the One. The chosen activity of rational beings, as a mode of activity that proceeds more immediately from the agent itself, thus comes closer to the One as pure productive activity than does the "natural" activity of sub-rational beings.

Thus, when Plotinus says that beings proceed from the One "by necessity," he means not that the One is subject to a more universal condition, but, on the contrary, that the One, as the power of all things, is absolutely *unconditioned* by anything. "He does not then have from another either his being or his being what he is. He himself therefore is by himself what he is, related and directed to himself, that he may not in this way either be related to the outside or to something else, but altogether self-related" (VI.8.17.24–27). It is just because the One is in no way conditioned by or related to anything that there are no alternative possibilities for him. For if the One might not produce being, then his productive activity would be distinct from himself and he would be conditioned by a relation to his product. Only a God who is not a producer but Production itself can "produce" without entering into a relation with his products. The necessity of procession, therefore, is in no sense a limitation on the One, but rather an expression of his absolute freedom from any limiting condition whatsoever.

In fact, the disjunctive presupposition that *either* God chooses between possible alternatives *or* he is necessitated to create situates God within a total framework of possibilities, as though the logical conditions of possibility and impossibility were prior to and more universal than God, conditions to which even he is subject. This presupposition envisions God either as confronted with a multiplicity of logical possibilities among which he can choose, or as subject to a logical law such that there is only one possibility open to him. This is precisely the "ontic" conception of God that Plotinus, and Dionysius, are concerned to avoid by declaring him "beyond being." God is not a being, subject, as are all beings, to the conditions of logical possibility such as the principle of non-contradiction. This is not to say that God can violate that principle; on the contrary, it would be more accurate to say that for the Neoplatonists, God or the One *is* the principle of non-contradiction. For what is that principle but the very condition of intelligibility and therefore of being? "To be is to be intelligible" means that to be is to conform to the laws of thought, which necessarily apprehends its object as determined by certain attributes and (therefore) as excluding the contradictory ones. The unity, the identity, and therefore the being of any thing consists in its conformity to this law. That law, therefore, is an expression of God as the unity, the identity, the being of beings. God is not a being, contained within a framework of possibilities determined by an abstract logic independent of himself. Rather, he is that framework within which all beings are contained, and hence he cannot be considered *either* as a being who chooses among a multiplicity of logical possibilities, *or* as a being confined by principles more universal than himself to a single possibility.[45]

The point of Plotinus' insistence on the necessity of procession, then, is not to situate the One within a total system to whose laws he is subject, but, on the contrary, to preserve the One's absolute transcendence to the totality of beings. If the One might-or-might-not-produce, then he would be a being, with an activity distinct from himself; his producing would be an accident or affect of him; and he would not be absolute or transcendent but conditioned by a relation to his products (see e.g. VI.8.8.13–15). As Plotinus says, "The Good does not need the things which have come into being from him . . . but is the same as he was before he brought it into being.[46] He would not have cared if it had not come into being; and if anything else could have been derived from him he would not have grudged it existence" (V.5.12.41–46). This does not mean that he does not "love" or "care for" his products: on the contrary, he loves and cares for them in the only metaphysically meaningful sense, in that he provides them with all that they are and have.[47] It means simply that the One-producing is not different from the One *simpliciter*, that the One is not affected or conditioned by or in relation to his products, as he would be if his producing were distinct from himself.[48]

The necessity of procession, then, is not a condition to which the One is subject but is simply the One itself as pure generosity, as productive Overflow.[49] "How then could the most perfect and the first Good remain in itself as if it grudged itself or were impotent—the power of all things?" (V.4.1.34–36). Being proceeds "necessarily" from the One as nothing but "the power of all things." The One itself, not any motion, choice, will, or activity distinct from the One itself, is the reason why there are beings (see VI.8.14.32–33). As Plotinus says, "[T]he One did not in some sort of way want Intellect to come into being, with the result that Intellect came into being with the wanting as an intermediary between the One and the generated Intellect; for if this was so, the One would be incomplete . . . But it is clear that if anything came into existence after him, it came into existence 'while he remained in his own proper state'" (V.3.12.29–35). Because of the One, then, being cannot not be. But the necessity of being is not a condition imposed on the One, but is rather the One himself: "[The One] is not held fast by necessity, but is itself the necessity and law of the others" (VI.8.10.34–35). And since the One himself is the reason why there is no possible alternative, this "necessity" could equally well be construed as "freedom."

Since the conventional antithesis between "Neoplatonic necessary procession" and "Christian free creation" is a misconception, so too is any attempt to situate Dionysius within these categories. For Dionysius as for

Plotinus, God is nothing but the making of all things, so that the possibility of not making does not arise. As Dionysius says, "Since, as subsistence of goodness, by its very being [αὐτῷ τῷ εἶναι] it is cause of all beings, the good-founding providence of the Godhead is to be hymned from all the effects . . . And by its being [τῷ εἶναι] it is the production and origin of all things [τῶν ὅλων παραγωγὴ καὶ ὑπόστασις]" (DN I.5, 593D; cf. DN IV.1, 693B).[50] As in Plotinus, to produce all things is not a "choice" on God's part. But also as in Plotinus, this means not that God is subject to a constraining condition, but rather the very reverse, that he is subject to no conditions, so that all things proceed from nothing but himself. That God "cannot not create" is a consequence, not a limitation, of his absolute transcendence, his unrelatedness to that which proceeds from him.[51] Dionysius offers an excellent formulation of this principle when he says, "Love . . . pre-existing in excess in the Good, did not permit it [οὐκ εἴασεν αὐτὸν] to remain unproductive in itself, but moved it to production, in the excess which is generative of all things."[52] "Did not permit it": no alternative, then, is possible. Precisely as the Good, as the productive condition of beings, God cannot not produce. But the "cannot" lies purely in himself, as Love.[53] It is not imposed on him, as a condition to which he is subject. As not any being but the ecstatic Love by which all beings are beings, therefore, the God of Dionysius, like the One of Plotinus, transcends both choice and necessitation and the opposition between them.[54]

CHAPTER FOUR

THE PROBLEM OF EVIL

Upon completing his account of God as Goodness, Beauty, and Love, Dionysius immediately raises the inevitable question: "If the Beautiful and Good is beloved and desired and cherished by all things . . . how does the multitude of demons not desire the Beautiful and Good . . . and, in general, what is evil, and whence does it originate, and in which of beings is it?" (DN IV.18, 716A). As is well known, the ensuing discussion of evil draws very extensively on Proclus' treatise *On the Subsistence of Evils*,[1] although Dionysius does not follow Proclus' account without alteration.[2] His own position is that evil is not a positive attribute of any being, but rather a deficiency of goodness, and hence of being, in a thing which to some extent is and is good. This position aligns Dionysius with other Christian thinkers such as Gregory of Nyssa, Augustine, and Thomas Aquinas. But the very familiarity of this "privation theory of evil," especially in its Augustinian and Thomist versions, may tend to obscure its full meaning and depth. A careful philosophical consideration of this doctrine in its Dionysian form reveals that the identification of evil as non-being is not a shallow "cosmic optimism," an absurd denial of the obvious fact of evil in the world,[3] but a profound and compelling theory which is more philosophically satisfying than many other accounts of evil.

The doctrine of evil as privation of being follows as a necessary consequence from the production of all things by God. If absolutely all that is, with no exception whatsoever, is made to be by God, the Good, then evil cannot be included within the whole of reality as anything that is at all. But the derivation of all reality from a God who is Goodness itself is not a philosophically unjustified article of faith, which could easily be falsified by the evident presence of evil in the world. It is rather, as we have seen, a philosophical consequence of the intelligibility of being: *since* being is intelligible, *therefore* it has the Good beyond being as its first principle, and every being is a different manifestation of goodness. The traditional claim that

53

"every being, insofar as it is a being, is good"[4] is virtually a restatement of the
law that to be is to be intelligible, for the intelligibility of anything consists
in its goodness. That which is altogether devoid of goodness has no intelligibility, no unity, no identity, and hence is not anything at all. Nothing can
be and be evil, insofar as it is. A wholly evil being is a contradiction in terms,
for it would be a wholly unintelligible being, and so not a being. It is from
these fundamental considerations that the Neoplatonic doctrine of evil as
deficiency is developed.

The foundations for the privation theory of evil are established in
Plotinus. As is well known, Plotinus identifies evil with the matter which
underlies sensible things (e.g. I.8.5.8–10). But this matter, for Plotinus, is not
a positive metaphysical component of sensible things that is other than form.
Rather, since to be is to be intelligible, only form is, and sensible things are
not, strictly speaking, composites of matter and form but rather lesser, "dimmer" forms.[5] In opposition to Aristotle, therefore, Plotinus understands matter,
insofar as it is not form, as privation (see e.g. II.4.16), the ontological deficiency
of sensibles in relation to purely intelligible realities. Matter, or evil, then,
is the partial non-being which belongs to sensible things in that they are not
reality itself but images or appearances (see, e.g. II.4.16.3–5). For Plotinus,
therefore, matter is identified with evil not as anything which is, an evil
being, but rather precisely and only as non-being, as the deficiency of being
which constitutes sensibles as sensibles rather than pure forms (see esp.
II.4.12.1–7). Hence matter or evil, considered by itself in abstraction from
any and all form, is non-being. "But when something is absolutely deficient—
and this is matter—this is essential evil without any share in good. For
matter has not even being—if it had it would by this means have a share in
good; when we say it 'is' we are just using the same word for two different
things, and the true way of speaking is to say it 'is not' " (I.8.5.8–13).

This non-being, matter, or evil, this deficiency, is thus generated as a "by-
product" in the production of the sensible cosmos, without which the sensible
qua sensible, i.e. *qua* appearance, would not occur at all (see II.4.12.1–7). Hence
Plotinus argues that evil, understood in this way as privation, is a necessary
aspect of the sensible cosmos and that it proceeds from the Good. "But how
then is it necessary that if the Good, also evil? Is it because there must be
matter in the All? This All [i.e. the sensible cosmos] . . . would not exist at
all if matter did not exist . . . Since not only the Good, there must be the last
end to the process of going out past it . . . and this last . . . is evil. Now it is
necessary that what comes after the First should exist, and therefore that the
last should exist; and this is matter" (I.8.7.1–4, 17–22). But if this "evil"
comes from the Good and is a necessary aspect of the cosmos which is itself
good, it is hard to see how it is truly evil. Indeed, Plotinus also argues that
the "evils" which afflict particular members of the cosmos, such as the destruction and consumption of one by another, are in fact necessary contributions to the perfection of the whole: "This All is visibly not only one

living creature, but many; . . . when the many encounter each other they often injure each other because they are different; and one injures another to supply its own need, and even makes a meal of another . . . The coming into being and destruction and alteration for worse or better of all these individual things brings to its fulness the unhindered life according to nature of that one [universal] living creature" (IV.4.32.32–38, 44–47). In the cosmic perspective, therefore, these "evils" are not really evil at all (cf. III.2.15–16).

Plotinus distinguishes the evil which is matter, and which can only problematically be regarded as evil, from another kind of evil, which he calls evil "in the soul" (I.8.5.30), or what we might call "moral" evil. This is not matter but rather the particular soul's descent from intellectual contemplation to sense perception as its mode of cognitive activity. This evil, too, therefore, is a kind of privation, a privation of intellectuality in the soul. The soul's descent is a separation, a self-isolation, from the universal governance of the cosmos. "But they [i.e. particular souls] change from the whole to being a part and belonging to themselves . . . Now when a soul does this for a long time, flying from the All and standing apart in distinctness, and does not look towards the intelligible, it has become a part and is isolated and weak and busy . . . ; it is fallen, therefore, and is caught, and is engaged with its fetter [i.e. the body], and acts by sense because its new beginning prevents it from acting by intellect" (IV.8.4.10–28). Such self-isolation, as a defection from the intellectual possession of and communion with the whole of being, is therefore a lessening of the self: "Now it is because you approached the All and did not remain in a part of it, and you did not even say of yourself 'I am just so much,' but rejecting the 'so much' you have become all—yet even before this you were all; but because something else came to you after the 'all' you became less by the addition; for the addition did not come from being . . . but from non-being" (VI.5.12.17–22). The fall of the soul from intellectuality to sensuality is, as it were, played out in the particular evil deeds we perform as a result of sensual desire, fear, and other passions: "[T]he sin of the soul can refer to two things, either to the course of the descent or to doing evil when the soul has arrived here below" (IV.8.5.17–18). Moral evil, then, consists for Plotinus not in matter but in the soul's failure to be fully intellectual,[6] a failure which is an ontological diminution of the soul itself. Hence moral evil, too, is not a positive attribute or activity of the soul, but rather a privation, a partial lack of intellectuality and therefore of being in the soul.

In *On the Subsistence of Evils*, Proclus largely, but not completely, follows Plotinus' account of evil. He agrees with Plotinus that there can be no absolute evil: "And since [evil] is twofold, on the one hand only evil, on the other not unmixed with the good, the one in no way is . . . but the other we order among beings" (9.4–6). Nothing, therefore, can be completely evil. "All things, then, are good, in that there is no evil unadorned and unmixed" (10.18–19). Whatever is evil must also be in some way good, or it would not be at all. The evil in any thing, then, is not a positive attribute or form but only a partial privation of goodness. "It would appear to be the most difficult of all things to know, in itself, the nature and form of evil, if every knowledge is a touching of form, but evil is formless and as it were privation [ἀνείδεον καὶ οἷον στέρησις] . . . For as the primally Good is beyond all things, thus evil itself is without a share in all goods, I mean *qua* evil, and a lack and privation of them [ἔλλειψις ἐκείνων καὶ στέρησις] . . . What is altogether evil is privation and lack of goods" (51.1–8, 42). However, Proclus differs from Plotinus by expressly rejecting the doctrine that evil is matter and that, as matter, it is necessary. He argues, more consistently than Plotinus, that "if matter is evil, one of two things is necessary: either to make the Good the cause of evil, or [to make] two principles of beings." Either alternative is unacceptable. "Since matter is from the Principle, even this has its entrance into being from the Good . . . Nor is evil from the Good" (31.5–9, 13). To say, as Plotinus does, both that matter is evil and that it proceeds from the Good leads to absurdity: "Thus the Good will be evil, as the cause of evil, but evil will be good, as produced from the Good" (31.16–18). Proclus further argues that matter, precisely in that it is a necessary aspect of the sensible cosmos, cannot be evil: "But if matter is necessary for the All, and the cosmos would not be 'this all-great and blessed god' if matter were absent, how can the nature of evil still be referred to this? For evil is one thing, and the necessary another, and the latter is such that [the universe] could not be without it, but the former is privation of being" (32.1–5).[7] By denying Plotinus' identification of evil with matter, Proclus thus avoids the difficulty of claiming that evil is a necessary condition for the good cosmos.

Taking the various levels of reality in turn, Proclus explains that evil is found neither in gods, nor in angels, nor in daimons,[8] nor in heroes. Evil enters only when we come to the level of human souls, which "are in potency at one time to ascend, at another to be carried into generation and a mortal nature" (20.7–8). Evil in human souls, for Proclus as for Plotinus, consists in their falling from intellectual contemplation: "When [a soul] is unable . . . to imitate its presiding [divinity], it becomes devoid of the contemplation of being, but is drawn by other, secondary powers which revolve around the world . . . This, therefore, is the weakness of a soul, that is, failing [*peccantem*] from that vision to be borne downwards" (23.18–22, 24.1–2). Evil in the soul, then, is not any positive attribute or activity, but a weakness, a lack of power, a privation of contemplative activity (cf. 56.3–5). Finally, particular bodies are subject to evil in the sense of harm or corruption in that, since their natures are only parts of nature as a whole, they can be harmed by other partial natures: "For indeed, to nature as a whole, nothing is outside of nature . . . But to that [nature] which is in singular things, one thing will be according to nature, but another not according to nature . . . It belongs to this nature, therefore, to be affected [*obtineri*] and to act outside of nature" (27.11–18). This corresponds to Plotinus' account of particular members of the cosmos injuring and destroying one another. And for Proclus as for Plotinus, what is in this sense evil for the part is good for the whole: "But how is the evil in bodies at the same time also good, save as being according to nature for the whole, but contrary to nature for the part?" (60.1–2).

The Good, then, and the subordinate divinities derived from it, is the cause of evil things not insofar as they are evil but only insofar as they are good. "Plato, placing all things around the king of all things . . . calls him cause of all beautiful things, and does not call him [cause] of all things simply; for he is not [the cause] of evils. But he is both not cause of these things, and cause of every being; for [he is cause] even of these things as beings and in that each is good" (61.10–16).[9] What, then, is the cause of the evil, the partial privation of goodness, in a human soul or in anything else which is to some degree evil? Proclus says, "It must in no way be posited that there is one cause of evils in itself. For if the cause of good things is one, the causes of evils are many" (47.2–4). But as what they cause is not a perfection but a privation, so these "many causes" are themselves purely negative, absences, deficiencies. The causes of evil are not productive powers, but lack of power, of productive activity: "Therefore the generation of what is contrary [to good] comes about . . . on account of weakness of that which makes [debilitatem facientis]" (50.18–20). Again, "evil is alien and supervenient, an unattainment [ἀτευξία] of the befitting end for each thing. But the unattainment is through the weakness [ἀσθένειαν] of that which makes" (50.34–35). Since evil itself is a deficiency, its "cause" is a lack of efficiency, of productive power. "And as good, [an evil thing] is from the gods, but as evil, from another, weak cause; for every evil is generated through weakness and privation" (42.8–10). And since the "cause" of evil is in fact a lack of causal power, evil, as deficiency, can even be said to be "without cause" (ἀναίτιόν) (50.30).

Dionysius largely follows Proclus, above all in adhering to the Neoplatonic principle that no being can be wholly evil, but must possess some goodness, without which it would not be anything at all. "All beings, insofar as they are, are good and from the Good; and insofar as they are deprived of the Good, they are neither good nor beings . . . But what is in every way deprived of the Good neither was nor is nor will be nor can be in any way whatsoever" (DN IV.20, 720B). Evil, Dionysius explains, is like a disease: "Disease is a lack of order, not whole. For if this happened, neither would the disease itself exist."[10] Just as a disease which kills its host destroys itself, so too, if a being were completely evil, totally devoid of goodness, it would not be an evil being, but would simply not be at all, and so would be neither evil nor good. Evil can be found, then, only as a deficiency in a being which, in that it is a being, must have some goodness whereby it is intelligible and so is.

The greatest change Dionysius makes in Proclus' theory is to extend the doctrine of evil as a partial privation of goodness to all levels of reality.[11]

He follows Proclus' procedure of looking for evil at every level, from angels, or intellects, down to matter. But whereas Proclus finds evil, as deficiency, only at the level of human souls and of natural bodies, Dionysius uses this procedure to explain, on the one hand, that evil is no positive reality in anything, and, on the other, that it can occur as a deficiency of proper perfection at any level of being whatsoever. Thus he argues that evil is no reality in angels (DN IV.22, 724BC); in demons (DN IV.23, 724C–725C);[12] in souls (i.e. human souls) (DN IV.24, 725D–728A); in irrational animals (DN IV.25, 728B); in nature as a whole (DN IV.26, 728C); in bodies (DN IV.27, 728D); and in matter (DN IV.28, 729AB). On this last point he expressly follows Proclus in denying Plotinus' "notorious" position that "evil is in matter, as they say, in that it is matter" (DN IV.28, 729A).[13] Dionysius argues, first, that "if [matter] is in no way whatsoever, it is neither good nor evil. But if it is somehow a being [πως ὄν], and all beings are from the Good, this too would be from the Good" (DN IV.28, 729A). He goes on to take up Proclus' cogent argument that if matter is necessary, it cannot be evil: "If they say that matter is necessary for the completion of all the cosmos, how is matter evil? For evil is one thing, and the necessary another" (DN IV.28, 729A). Whatever is necessary for the perfection of the whole is not evil but good. If, as Plotinus argues, matter is necessary, then it cannot be evil. This argument is effective not only against Plotinus' doctrine that matter is both evil and a necessary consequence of the Good, without which the (good) cosmos could not be produced, but also against all attempts, such as have been made from antiquity to the present, to explain the evils that occur in the world as necessary contributions to the perfection of the whole. Any such theory, as Dionysius here points out, does not explain evil but rather explains it away by claiming, in effect, that it is not really evil at all.

Nothing, then, is evil insofar as it is a being. Conversely, anything is evil insofar as it fails to be. Dionysius' doctrine of evil as non-being must be understood in light of the principle that any being is in virtue of its proper determinations or perfections, which are its way of being good and therefore its mode of being. Anything is evil, i.e. not good, then, insofar as it lacks the proper goodness which is its constitutive determination, and to that extent fails to be itself and so to be. Such a failure can occur not only in the human soul but at any level of reality, including that of angelic intellects. Thus Dionysius says, for example, that "the demons are not evil by nature" (DN IV.23, 724C) and are called "evil" "not insofar as they are, for they are from the Good and received a good reality, but insofar as they are not, by being weak (as the Oracles say) in preserving their principle [ἀρχήν]. For in what, tell me, do we say they are evil, except in the cessation of the possession and activity of divine good things?" (DN IV.23, 725A). He then says, still more clearly, that "they are not evil by nature, but by the deficiency [ἐνδείᾳ] of angelic goods" (DN IV.23, 725B). They are evil, then, insofar as they lack the perfections proper to and constitutive of them as angels. And since these perfections are their very being, to the extent that an angel lacks them (i.e. is a demon), to that extent it fails to be. Dionysius goes on to point out that the demons do have some perfections, for otherwise they would not exist at all, and to this extent they are good: "They are not altogether without a share in the Good, insofar as they both are and live and think" (DN IV.23, 725B), and again, "In that they are, they both are from the Good and are good . . . and by privation and fleeing away and falling away from the goods that are appropriate to them they are called evil" (DN IV.23, 725C).

Exactly the same principle applies to human souls: "In what are they made evil, except in the failure of good conditions and activities . . . ? . . . Neither, then, in demons nor in us is evil as an evil being [ὂν κακόν], but as failure and absence of the perfection of our proper goods" (DN IV.24, 728A). Dionysius thus explicitly extends the doctrine of evil as partial lack of goodness to cover not merely human souls and natural bodies but all beings whatsoever, including intellects, which for Plotinus and Proclus are incapable of evil: "This is evil, in intellects and souls and bodies: the weakness and falling away from the condition of their proper goods" (DN IV.27, 728D).[14] And in lacking its "proper goods," a being lacks the very unity and identity whereby it is, and to that extent it fails to be.

The "proper goods" of any being, as we have seen, are the constitutive determinations whereby it is itself and so is. But these determinations, at once its goodness and its being, are the presence of God in it, making it to be. How then can any being fail, to some degree, to possess them? Here we must return to the doctrine of reversion, which as we have seen means that a being actively takes part in its own being made to be. Its possessing its proper determinations, and so its being, is not a passive reception but an active performance of its nature, so that, as we saw, God cannot make it to be without its active cooperation or participation. To be is the activity of a being; and herein lies the possibility of evil. For the being may fail fully to exercise this activity, to appropriate the divine processions proper to and constitutive of it, to enact its nature, and so to be. A being is evil, then, insofar as it does not perform the proper activities which are its mode of being, and to that extent it fails to be.

As a being's partial lack of its proper perfections, evil is ultimately a failure of reversion, the being's failure to appropriate, to desire, to love God as the Goodness whereby it is. Since, as we have seen, to be is to love God, and anything can be only in and by desiring God, then insofar as anything does not desire God, it falls short of complete being. Thus Dionysius says that the demons "are not altogether without a share in the Good, insofar as they are and live and think, and in short, there is some motion of desire in them. But they are called evil through the weakness in their activity according to nature" (DN IV.23, 725B).[15] The natural activity of any being is its reversion, its mode of being, of desire for God. A thing's lack of its proper perfections, which qualifies it as evil, is a failure of this desire, and therefore a deficiency of being.

On Dionysius' view, there can be no actual desire for evil and therefore no positive activity which is evil. Following a common tradition of Greek thought, he argues that all desire is for some good. "And if beings desire the Beautiful and Good, and do all the things they do on account of what seems good, and every goal of beings has the Good as its principle and end, for nothing does what it does with a view to the nature of evil, how will evil be among beings?" (DN IV.19, 716C).[16] In other words, whatever is desired is by definition regarded as good, for to desire something means to take it as one's good. "No one does what he does with a view to evil" (DN IV.31, 732C).[17] As the scholastics would say, anything is desirable only *sub specie boni*. Evil *qua* evil, as what is not good, has no attractive or motivating power and cannot be a goal, a purpose, an object of desire for anything. Evil, therefore, cannot be the cause of any activity. Rather, as we have seen, all the activities of all beings take place in desire for the Good: "All things, by desiring the Beautiful and Good, do and wish all things that they do and wish" (DN IV.10, 708A). In the absence of any good at which to aim, there is no desire and hence no activity whatsoever.

No activity, *qua* activity, then, is evil. Evil, therefore, lies not in a being's acting contrary to its nature but only in its not acting according to its nature, and so not fully being. "Evil then is privation and failure and weakness . . . and purposeless . . . and inactive and ineffective . . . For that which is altogether without a share in the Good neither is nor is capable of anything" (DN IV.32, 732D–733A). And this inactivity stems not from a desire for evil, which is impossible, but only from a lack of desire for the Good. Since anything is good insofar as it is, to desire evil would be to desire nothing. "And desiring that which is not, [the demons] desire evil [τοῦ μὴ ὄντος ἐφιέμενοι τοῦ κακοῦ ἐφίενται]" (DN IV.23, 725C). But this means that insofar as anything desires evil, it is really just not desiring at all: "And insofar as [the demons] do not desire the Good, they desire that which is not. And this is not desire, but a missing of genuine desire" (DN IV.34, 733D). At bottom, then, evil as deficiency of being is a failure to revert to, to love, to desire God, who as the Good is the sole cause and end of all desire.

Evil, then, is fundamentally passivity, the failure in a being of the reversion, the agency, the interiority which is its taking part in its being made to be. This interiority, as we saw in chapter 3, is the freedom which is analogously present at every level of reality. A being is evil, then, insofar as it fails to act, to exercise its freedom. But that agency or freedom, we also saw, is God himself at work in the being, making it to be. Hence, insofar as anything is evil, i.e. insofar as it is not, God is not productively present in it. All reality is (nothing but) the manifest presence of goodness, i.e. of God. Where reality is lacking, goodness is deficiently present. But this deficiency is due to the being's failure to appropriate the love which is God as its own being and activity. The less the being acts, the less God acts in it,[18] and so the less it is. In these terms we can understand Dionysius' account of why there is no contradiction between universal divine providence and the freedom of beings, which includes the possibility of evil:

> And if none of beings is without a share in the Good, but evil is a lack of the Good, none of beings is altogether deprived of the Good, divine providence is in all beings, and none of beings is without providence . . . Therefore we will not accept the vain saying of the many, who say that providence ought to draw us to virtue against our will; for to corrupt nature does not belong to providence. Wherefore, as providence is preservative of the nature of each, it provides for the self-moved as self-moved. (DN IV.33, 733B)

Because God and the being which he makes are not two beings or selves defined over against each other, but rather God is the very selfhood of the being, there is no contradiction between being self-moved, or free, and being moved, or provided for, by God. The being's self-motion, its freedom, is its participation in God, the "providential" presence of God in it. So, conversely, the being's failure to move itself, to enact its nature, is its failure to be moved by God, i.e. to desire God, and so to be.

Dionysius' examples from the realm of human behavior illustrate this account of evil as passivity:

> For instance, the intemperate man, although he is deprived of the Good with regard to his irrational appetite, in this respect he neither is nor desires beings; but he participates somehow in the Good with regard to the obscure echo itself of union and friendship. And anger participates in the Good with regard to moving and desiring to straighten and turn around seeming evils to seeming goods. And he who desires the worst life, in wholly desiring life, and that which seems best to him, by the very fact of desiring, and desiring life, and looking to a best life, participates in the Good. (DN IV.20, 720BC)

Each of these men, in desiring anything at all, is therefore necessarily desiring something good, and to that extent is not wholly evil. Dionysius continues, "And if you take away the Good altogether, there will be neither reality nor life nor desire nor motion nor anything else" (DN IV.20, 720C). A man is vicious, then, not in that he desires evil but insofar as he does not desire the Good. But to that extent he is not desiring, not acting, not moving himself but being moved by passions, which means precisely that which we undergo (πάσχειν) as opposed to that which we ourselves do. Dionysius' account of the fall of man in the *Ecclesiastical Hierarchy* is thus fully in accord with the metaphysics of evil developed in the *Divine Names*: "The life of many passions [ἡ πολυπαθεστάτη ζωὴ] received human nature which in its beginning unintelligibly slipped away from the divine goods ... Thence it miserably exchanged the eternal for the mortal ... But also, having willingly fallen from the divine and upward-leading life, it was drawn to the opposite extreme, the alteration of many passions [τὴν πολυπαθεστάτην ἀλλοίωσιν] ... It pitiably fell into danger of non-existence [ἀνυπαρξίας] and destruction" (EH III.3.11, 440C–441A). Here Dionysius repeatedly links the fall, as a fall toward non-being, with the passions in their multiplicity.[19] For to the extent that a man is subject to passions he is failing to be a self at all, a center of unity that exists in and by performing its own activity. Largely passive, driven about not by himself but by the passions, by what happens to him from without, he is vicious in his lack of unity, of interiority, of selfhood, failing to take part in his own being and to that extent failing to be. Nothing can be wholly passive, for that would mean having no unity, no identity, no activity, no selfhood, and so not being at all. But to the extent that anything is passive, it fails to be one, to be itself, and so to be, and to that extent it is evil.

Having come this far in the discussion of evil, we inevitably ask: Why do some beings not fully desire God? What is the cause of this failure? By raising this question we reach the very heart of Dionysius' doctrine of evil: as non-being, as inactivity, evil is without cause (ἀναίτιον) (DN IV.30, 732A; IV.32, 732D). For it is only beings and their activities, things that are and that take place, that must have causes, without which they would not be or happen. To look for the cause of evil is to ask why it occurs. But evil is not something that occurs, but not-something that does not occur. It is not an act of non-love, but a non-act of love. As we have seen, whatever any being does, it does for some cause, and that cause is a good. As non-activity, evil is precisely what is *not* caused to happen and hence does not happen. Hence there can be no reason why a being fails fully to love God, i.e. to be. If there were such a reason, the "failure" would not be a failure but an activity, and as such not evil but good. "Everything which is according to nature comes about from a definite cause. If evil is without cause and indefinite, it is not according to nature" (DN IV.30, 732A).[20] Everything that is, insofar as it is, is according to nature, is caused, and is good. The causelessness of evil, conversely, is one with the identification of evil as a thing's not fulfilling its nature and so not fully being.

The claim that evil, as non-activity, has no cause, may seem highly unsatisfactory, a facile evasion of an unsolvable problem which in fact vitiates Dionysius' entire doctrine of evil, or indeed the privation theory of evil in any form. To see why, on the contrary, it is in fact a truly profound and philosophically insightful treatment of the problem, we must return to the fundamental connection between goodness and intelligibility. In demanding to know the cause of whatever we are trying to understand, we are in fact demanding intelligibility. Anything is intelligible, able to be understood by thought, only in virtue of the "why" for it. As Aristotle says, "We do not think that we know until we grasp the 'why' [τὸ διὰ τί] about each thing, and this is to grasp its first cause" (*Physics* II.3, 194b19–21). This is why philosophy, the effort to understand reality as a whole, is for the ancients fundamentally a doctrine of causes. For the Neoplatonists, as we have seen, the One is the "cause" of all things precisely as the universal principle of intelligibility. But further, the cause in virtue of which anything is intelligible is always its good, so that the end, the τέλος of anything is its cause of being or ἀρχή. To understand anything, to grasp the "why" of it, is to see how it is good, and therefore the Good is the universal principle of intelligibility and so of being. Consequently, if evil, the failure to desire the Good and so to be, took place for some reason, if it had a cause in terms of which it could be explained, that cause, that reason, would be a good. Evil itself, then, would not be evil but good, and explainable only because and insofar as it was good. Conversely, evil is evil exactly in that it is not good and therefore not intelligible, not understandable in terms of any reason or cause. When we describe something as evil, we mean that it is to some degree not good and to that extent does not make sense, that we can see no reason, no "why" for it. We may recall Dionysius' statement in the *Ecclesiastical Hierarchy* that man "unintelligibly [ἀνοήτως] fell from the divine goods" (EH III.3.11, 440C).[21] To be intelligible, to have a cause [αἰτία], and to be good, are one and the same. Unintelligibility, or causelessness, is therefore the very meaning of evil; and it is as unintelligibility that evil is non-being. The following passage thus summarizes Dionysius' entire doctrine of evil as causeless non-being:

> Evil, then, is privation and lack and weakness and asymmetry and failure [ἁμαρτία, usually translated as "sin" but literally having the negative meaning "missing" or "failing"] and aimless and beautyless and lifeless and mindless [ἄνουν] and irrational and purposeless [ἀτελές] and unstable and causeless and indeterminate and unproductive and inactive and ineffective and unordered and unlike and limitless and dark and insubstantial [ἀνούσιον] and itself no being whatever in any way whatsoever [μηδαμῶς μηδαμῆ μηδὲν ὄν]. (DN IV.32, 732D)

Dionysius' inability, or rather refusal, to assign a cause to evil, then, marks not the failure but the success of his treatment of the problem. To explain evil, to attribute a cause to it, would necessarily be to explain it away, to deny that evil is genuinely evil at all.[22] For to explain something is to show how it is in some way good. "Tout comprendre, c'est tout pardonner." Only by *not* explaining evil, by insisting rather on its radical causelessness, its unintelligibility, can we take evil seriously as evil. This is why most "theodicies" fail precisely insofar as they succeed. To the extent that they satisfactorily account for or make sense of evil, they tacitly or expressly deny that it is evil and show that it is in fact good. Dionysius' treatment of evil, on the other hand, succeeds by failing, recognizing that the sheer negativity that is evil must be uncaused and hence inexplicable, for otherwise it would not be negativity and would not be evil.[23]

It has been wisely remarked that any satisfactory account of evil must enable us to retain our outrage at it. Most theodicies fail this test, for in supposedly allowing us to understand evil they justify it and thus take away our outrage. For Dionysius, however, evil remains outrageous precisely because it is irrational, because there is no reason, no justification for it. The privation theory of evil, expressed in a radical form by Dionysius, is not a shallow disregard or denial of the evident evils in the world. It means rather that, confronted with the evils in the world, we can only say that for no reason, and *therefore* outrageously, the world as we find it does not perfectly love God, the Good, the sole end of all love. And since the Good is the principle of intelligibility and hence of being, to the extent that anything fails to partake of that principle it is deficient in being. The recognition of evils in the world and in ourselves is the recognition that the world and ourselves, as we find them, are less than fully existent because we do not perfectly love God, the Good.

CHAPTER FIVE

THE HIERARCHY OF BEING

In the *Divine Names*, Dionysius consistently presents the whole of reality as a hierarchically ranked sequence, descending from angels, or pure intellects, to inanimate beings. Although he applies his neologism ἱεραρχία only to the angelic and ecclesiastical ranks, the concept of hierarchy is at work throughout his understanding of reality, and all the related terminology, such as order, rank, higher/coordinate/lower, superior/inferior, superordinate/subordinate, is found in the *Divine Names* with regard to the structure of reality as a whole.[1] In articulating the metaphysical principles of this hierarchy of being, we shall see how these same principles are at work in the angelic and ecclesiastical ranks. Dionysius' understanding of hierarchy, whether ontological, celestial, or ecclesiastical, is a development of his account of the divine processions, of the constitutive perfections of beings, and hence of the whole of reality, as the differentiated presence of God.

The divine names which Dionysius presents as a ranked sequence in *Divine Names* V.1 and discusses in chapters IV, V, VI, and VII of the *Divine Names* respectively, are Good (i.e. Goodness), Being, Life, and Wisdom. These "names" or processions are the modes in which God is constitutively present in the various ranks of beings: inanimate things, or mere beings; plants, or living beings; irrational animals, or sensitive beings; humans, or rational beings; and angels, or intellectual beings. Animals, humans, and angels are here grouped together as cognitive beings, participants in God as Wisdom. The divine processions, then, are ordered on the basis of the degrees of universality in which they are participated or present in beings. "For the divine name of the Good, manifesting the whole processions of the cause of all things, is extended both to beings and to non-beings, and is above beings and above non-beings. That of Being is extended to all beings and is above all beings. That of Life is extended to all living things and is above living things. That of Wisdom is extended to all intellectual and rational and sensitive beings and is above all these things" (DN V.1, 816B). The Good is first, then, because as Goodness God is present in all beings and non-beings. (The meaning of this odd statement will be considered shortly.) Being comes next, because as Being he is present in all beings; next comes Life, for as Life God is present in all living things; and finally Wisdom, as which he is present in all cognitive beings.[2] The order of the divine processions is thus a mirror image of the ranks of beings:

> Good
> Being
> Life
> Wisdom
>
> cognitive living beings
> living beings
> (mere) beings
> non-beings

In ordering the divine processions on the basis of their degrees of universality, Dionysius is once again closely following Proclus. Proclus distinguishes Being, Life, and Intellect,[3] in that order, as the three aspects of intelligible reality, subordinate to the Good beyond being. "Unparticipated Intellect leads all things which participate in intellect, and Life all things which participate in life, and Being all things which participate in being; and of these Being is prior to Life and Life prior to Intellect . . . There must be Intellect prior to intellectual things and Life prior to living things and Being prior to beings." These terms are ranked on the basis of the relative universality of their causal presence: "Among these Being will be first; for it is present to all things in which there are Life and Intellect (for everything which lives and participates in intellection, by necessity is) but the converse is not true (for not all beings live and think) . . . If, then, Being is cause of more things, Life of fewer, and Intellect of still fewer, Being is first, then Life, then Intellect" (El. Th., prop. 101). Thus Proclus explains that animals (i.e. cognitive living things) are caused by the One, Being, Life, and Intellect; plants by the One, Being, and Life; and inanimate things by the One and Being.[4] Since whatever has a less universal perfection must also have the more universal ones, Proclus describes a series of "layers" of participated perfections, in which the more universal serves as a "substratum" for the less universal: "All that in the originative causes have more universal and higher rank become somehow in the resultant things, according to the illuminations from them, substrata for the impartations of the more specific . . . And thus some participations precede others" (El. Th., prop. 71).

Dionysius' hierarchy of causal determinations is thus fundamentally the same as that of Proclus. Proclus, however, "hypostasizes" all these terms, and in his philosophical apologetic for traditional polytheistic religion identifies them as "gods" of various types and levels.[5] Dionysius, on the other hand, obviously with Proclus and his school in mind, expressly and repeatedly rejects this position, taking care to explain that the various divine processions are not "demiurgic substances or hypostases," a multiplicity of divinities or quasi-divine entities in between God and his products (DN XI.6, 953D), but are nothing but the differentiated presence of God in different beings: "The treatise . . . does not say that the Good is one thing and Being another and Life or Wisdom another, nor that the causes are many and that there are different divinities, higher and lower, productive of different things; but that all the good processions and divine names hymned by us are of one God; and one [i.e. the name Good] manifests the complete providence of the one God, but the others, his more universal and more specific [providences]" (DN V.2, 816C–817A). This repudiation of Proclus' polytheism is often regarded as one of Dionysius' most significant "Christianizations" of Proclus and one of the most profound differences between them. Instead of positing a multiplicity of productive divinities subordinate to the One, Dionysius regards the constitutive perfections of all things as the immediate differentiated presence of God himself.[6] But is the difference really so great? As we have seen, Proclus' elaborate reifications are best understood as "aspects,"[7] and terms such as Being, Life, and Intellect are in fact various levels of manifestation of the One, its differentiated constitutive presence to all things at different levels of specificity. To say, for example, that living things are caused not only by the One but also by Life, and that they revert to the One through Life, means that life is the mode of unity proper to them, their specific way of being one. The hypostasis "Life," then, is the specific mode in which the One is causally present to living things *qua* living. The lower causal powers are specifications of higher, more universal ones, and as such are contained in and are differentiated presences of them (see e.g. *El. Th.*, props. 126, 140, 145).[8] Hence all these subordinate "hypostases" are contained in and are presences of the One, as the productive power of all things. All perfections of all things are modalities of unity, and hence all reality, for Proclus no less than for Dionysius, is the presence of the One, in differing modes and degrees: life is a higher degree of unity than mere existence, and consciousness a higher degree of unity than life. Thus all of Proclus' hypostasized causes are different modes in which unity is effectively present to beings. Proclus argues, for example, that the gods are henads *because* the One or Good, as "the 'whence' and the 'whither' of all things," is God, and the gods are "its proper manifold" of participated terms (*El. Th.*, prop. 113). As this argument makes clear, only the One or Good, as the total and absolute source of all reality whatsoever, is God in an absolute sense, and lesser terms are "gods" only because and insofar as they are distinct modes of unity. "Every god is a beneficent henad or a unifying goodness . . . but the primal God is the Good unqualified and Unity unqualified, whilst each of those posterior to him is a particular goodness and a particular henad" (*El. Th.*, prop. 133).[9]

Understood in terms of his own metaphysical principles, therefore, Proclus' position, subsuming lower divinities into higher and ultimately all into the One, might be more objectionable to a thoroughgoing polytheist than to a Christian.[10] The difference between Dionysius and Proclus at this point is thus more a matter of religious practice than of metaphysical content. Proclus hymns the many modes of unity as a multiplicity of gods; Dionysius hymns God as the many modes of unity. But for Proclus, no less than for Dionysius, these modes of unity are the differentiated presentations of divinity, and both philosophers worship that divinity as it is differently manifest in different beings.[11] What matters most is that beneath the superficial opposition between Dionysius and Proclus, they share the same fundamental vision, that of a world filled with and constituted by a multiplicity of divine powers at work differently in different things, all of which are presences or manifestations of the One, or God.

Dionysius' dependence on Proclus for the hierarchical ordering of the divine processions explains his initially puzzling statements that Goodness extends not only to beings but also to non-beings, and is therefore more universal than Being. We might expect that Goodness and Being, as the perfections by which all beings are beings, would be equally universal and simply identical, like Goodness and Unity or Goodness and Beauty. In any case, what can it mean to say that not only beings but even "things which are not" (τὰ οὐκ ὄντα) participate in Goodness? As Parmenides would point out, there are no "things which are not," and hence "they" cannot do anything or have any features. Further, Dionysius has just identified non-being with (what is not good but) evil. Nonetheless, he repeatedly claims that not only beings but also non-beings participate in, desire, or revert to the Good.[12] These statements can be understood only if we turn once more to Dionysius' Neoplatonic background.

An examination of the comparable passages in Proclus shows that what Dionysius means by the "non-beings" which participate in the Good is in fact simply matter, considered by itself in abstraction from form. As we saw in chapter 4, Plotinus, in opposition to Aristotle, identifies the matter of bodies as the ontological deficiency of sensibles vis-à-vis forms and in that sense as non-being. He further argues that this non-being which is matter proceeds, as do all things, from the Good. Proclus follows Plotinus in arguing that matter, understood in this way as privation, proceeds from and participates in the Good (*El. Th.*, props. 57, 72), and, more consistently than Plotinus, denies that it is evil. But since, considered by itself apart from form as that which underlies or is receptive to all form whatsoever, matter is not anything, having no intelligible content at all of its own, it does not proceed from or participate in Being; for to participate in Being is to be something, to have some definite intelligible identity, some form. Thus Proclus says, "[W]hat Intellect causes is also caused by the Good, but not conversely. For even privation of forms is from the Good (for all things are from it); but Intellect, being form, cannot give rise to privation" (*El. Th.*, prop. 57).[13] Matter, then, underlies Being as participated Being underlies Life and participated Life underlies Intellect. Thus Proclus concludes that the Good or the One is more universally productive than Being, since the Good produces even matter, considered in abstraction from form, while Being produces things only insofar as they have some form. "All those characters which in the participants have the relative position of a substratum proceed from more complete and more universal causes . . . From this it is apparent why matter, taking its origin from the One, is in itself devoid of form . . . For matter, which is the substratum of all things, proceeded from the cause of all things" (*El. Th.*, prop. 72). Thus we must complete the list given above by saying that animals are produced by the One, Being, Life, and Intellect; plants are produced by the One, Being, and Life; inanimate objects are produced by the One and Being; and matter is produced by the One.

This, then, is the position Dionysius is adopting when he says that even non-beings participate in God as the Good. The non-being in question is simply matter, which is not anything by itself, apart from form, but is found in things in that they possess, or receive, forms. The fundamental meaning of this doctrine, then, is that the very receptivity of beings, which constitutes them as beings rather than God, is itself a gift. The material aspect of beings, as their neediness or receptivity, could be regarded as their love, which is prior to their being in that they are constituted as beings only by loving, or actively receiving, God.[14] But this love itself, as God in them, is given to them. In this sense the matter of beings can be said to participate in the Good, but, considered as pure receptivity, not in Being. Understood in this way, Dionysius' statements that even non-beings participate in and desire the Good are fully in accord with his Neoplatonic sources and with the presentation of the Good as the source and principle of all form.

After presenting the hierarchy of divine processions, Dionysius addresses a hypothetical objection: "Yet someone might say, 'Wherefore is Being set above Life and Life above Wisdom, when living things are above beings, and sensitive things which live above these, and rational things above these, and the intellects are above the rational things and are more around God and closer to him?' " (DN V.3, 817A). In other words, since in the order of the world living things are higher than mere beings, animals higher than plants, and so on, it would seem to follow that the divine procession Life should be above Being, and Wisdom above Life. Dionysius replies that this would be case only if the more specific perfections excluded the more universal ones: "If someone supposed that the intellectual things were without being and without life [ἀνούσια καὶ ἄζωά], the saying would be sound" (DN V.3, 817B). But in fact, of course, plants have not only life, but also being; cognitive things have not only consciousness, but also being and life.

> But since the divine intellects also are [in a way] above other be-
> ings, and live [in a way] above the other living things, and think
> and know [in a way] above sense and reason . . . they are nearer to
> the Good, participating in it in an eminent way, and receiving from
> it more and greater gifts; likewise rational beings excel sensitive
> ones, having more by the eminence of reason, and the latter [excel
> other living things] by sensation, and [living things excel mere beings]
> by life. And . . . the things which participate more in the one and
> infinitely-giving God are closer to him and more divine than the
> rest.[15] (DN V.3, 817B)

As this account makes plain, the various processions are simply more and less
universal modes of the same divine presence, so that the more universal
contain the less universal as their specifications. Being is above Life, and Life
above Wisdom, because Life is nothing but a specification of Being, and
Wisdom nothing but a specification of Life.

Life, in plants, therefore, is not superadded to Being, but is the more
specific, intense mode of Being proper to them as compared to stones; Wisdom, i.e. consciousness, is not superadded to Life, but is the more specific,
intense mode of Life and Being proper to cognitive things.[16] Intellection, as
the highest mode of consciousness, is thus the highest mode of life and being.
Angels, as intellects, therefore possess in a higher way all the perfections of
lesser beings.[17] This accounts for what may seem to be Dionysius' excessive,
not to say obsessive, interest in angels, not only in the *Celestial Hierarchy* but
also in the *Divine Names* and the *Ecclesiastical Hierarchy*. Angels are not
merely the highest in a univocal series of beings; rather, they are *beings* in the
fullest, most complete, and therefore paradigmatic sense. "The holy ranks of
the celestial beings, then, are in participation of the thearchic impartation
[in a way] above things which merely are, and those which live irrationally,
and those which, like us, are rational" (CH IV.2, 180A). As in Plotinus,
intellect is being itself at its highest, most perfect level. Conversely, if life is
a higher mode of being and consciousness a higher mode of life, then the life
of plants is their lesser, more diffuse mode of what in animals is consciousness, and the "mere being" of inanimate things is a still lesser, more diffuse
mode of consciousness and life. Thus all things are in their lesser ways that
which angels are most fully. Angelology becomes ontology. This accords
with Proclus' and Dionysius' account of the modes of reversion, existential,
vital, and cognitive, where the characteristic activity, the reversion of each
order of beings, is the mode of being proper to them.

It is therefore one and the same constitutive divinity, the Good, that
is present in all things analogously, or in the manner proper to each. "The
Good is altogether not uncommunicated to any of beings, but shines forth
[ἐπιφαίνεται] the ray beyond being, established remainingly in itself, by
illuminations analogous [ἀναλόγοις ἐλλάμψεσιν] to each of beings" (DN

I.2, 588CD; see also DN IV.1, 693B). These "illuminations" are the participated determinations of creatures, and they are "analogous to each" in that
each being participates in God in the manner appropriate to and constitutive
of that being. Thus God, the Good, is present in each thing, as Dionysius
says, "according to its rank" (κατ᾽ ἀξίαν) (e.g. DN VIII.7, 893D–896C; DN
IX.10, 917A): in some as mere being, in others as life, in others as thought,
and so on. This is an "analogous" or "proportional" presence because it
means that being is to a stone as life is to a plant, as sensation is to an
animal, as reason is to a man, as intellection is to an angel: its proper mode
of goodness and unity, of interiority and selfhood, its participation in God.
Since the same divinity is present analogously at every level of reality, God
"is hymned from all beings according to the analogy of all things, of which
he is cause" (DN VII.3, 872A).

The principle Dionysius' doctrine of analogous participation in God is thus closely
parallel to Plotinus' teaching that the nature of all things is their share in
contemplation or intellectual activity (which itself is the manifestation of the
One), so that the life of plants is a "growth-thought" and that of animals a
"sense-thought" (III.8.8.14–15).[18] The same principle can be found in Proclus,
in the form of his well-known affirmation, "All things are in all things, but
properly in each." He goes on to explain: "In Being there is life and intellect;
in Life, being and intellect; in Intellect, being and life; but each of these exists
upon one level intellectually, upon another vitally, and on the third existentially" (El. Th., prop. 103). For him, too, the less universal perfections are
specifications of the more universal ones, so that, for example, living things
have intellect "vitally," i.e. in the mode of life, and intellectual things have life
"intellectually," i.e. in the mode of intellect. At bottom, for Plotinus, Proclus,
and Dionysius, this is because all orders of reality represent higher and lower
degrees of unity and goodness: Intellect or Wisdom, Life, and Being are simply
the diminishing degrees of unity and goodness found in cognitive beings, plants,
and inanimate things respectively.

The principle that in any hierarchy the same perfection or activity is
analogously present throughout all the levels is evident in Dionysius' accounts
of the angelic and the ecclesiastical hierarchies. In the Celestial Hierarchy, he
explains that the name of a higher level may be applied to a lower because
"just as the first [i.e. the higher ranks of angels] possess eminently the holy-
befitting properties of the lower, so the later possess those of the earlier, not
in the same way, but in a lesser way" (CH XII.2, 293B). He then uses this
principle to explain why the prophet Isaiah is said to have been purified by a
seraph, although according to the strict rules of hierarchy only the lowest rank
of angels should be in direct contact with men. As one possible account of this
apparent anomaly, Dionysius suggests that the angel in question was not really
a seraph but "ascribed his own purifying sacred activity . . . to God, and after
God to his prior-working hierarchy" (CH XIII.3, 300CD). This ascription,
however, was no mere courtesy but was in fact true, because

the thearchic power, coming to all things, spreads and extends ir-
resistibly through all things and again is unmanifest to all, not only
as transcending all things in a manner beyond being, but also as
hiddenly spreading its providential activities to all. But it is also
manifested analogously to all the intellectual things, reaching out
its own gift of light to the senior substances, through them, as first,
imparting it in good order to the subordinates, according to the
God-seeing measure of each rank. (CH XIII.3, 301A)

This clearly affirms that because the activity of every level in any hierarchy
is the presence of God in the mode proper to that level, therefore the activity of the lower is that of the higher, in a lesser, analogous way. Just as plants,
in living, are exercising thought in their lower mode, so the angel, in purifying, is exercising the seraphic activity in his lower mode. So also, in the
Ecclesiastical Hierarchy, Dionysius remarks that not only the angelic hierarchy
but "that and every hierarchy, and that which is now hymned by us, has one
and the same power throughout the hierarchical activity" (EH I.2, 372CD).
For this reason, all the sacramental activity in the church is in fact that of
the bishop: "Therefore the divine order of the hierarchs [i.e. bishops] is the
first of the orders which see God, but it is also the extreme and last, for in
it are perfected and fulfilled all the ordering of our hierarchy . . . The power
of the hierarchic [i.e. episcopal] order pervades all the sacred totalities, and
through all the sacred order effects the mysteries of its own hierarchy" (EH
V.1.5, 505AB). This is simply an application of the principle of analogy
articulated in the *Divine Names* for the hierarchy of being as a whole.

In light of this principle, there is no contradiction between the hierarchical structure of reality and the immediate constitutive presence of God
to all things. When Dionysius says that higher beings are "closer to [God]
and more divine than those that follow" (DN V.3, 817BC), this does not
mean that they stand between the lower orders and God. Rather, it means
that, having the more universal perfections in having the more specific ones,
they are "participating eminently in [the Good] and receiving more and
greater gifts from it" (DN V.3, 817B), or that they "participate in [God] in
many ways [πολλαχῶς]" (CH IV.1, 177D). All things participate in God as
Goodness and Being; living things participate in God as Goodness, Being,
and Life; cognitive things, as Goodness, Being, Life, and Wisdom. Thus all
things, at every level, participate directly in God in the manner appropriate
to them. Therefore the hierarchical structure of reality, far from separating
the lower orders of being from God, is itself the very ground of his immediate
presence in all things. Every being participates directly in God precisely in
and by occupying its proper place within the cosmic hierarchy: stones by
merely existing; plants by living; animals by sensing, humans by being rational, angels by being intellectual. It is not hierarchical order, but rather an
egalitarian leveling, that would violate the immediate participation of all
things in God by blurring the differences and ranks of beings which consti-

tute that very participation. Hence, in discussing the divine name *Righteous-ness* or *Justice* (δικαιοσύνη), Dionysius castigates the egalitarian view that rejects hierarchical order and identifies justice with equality:

> The divine righteousness orders and sets the bounds for all things, and, preserving all unmixed and unconfused with all, gives to all beings what is appropriate to each, attending to each of beings according to its rank. And . . . as many as rail against the divine righteousness are condemned unawares for their evident unrighteous-ness, for they say that immortality ought to be in mortal things, and what is complete in incomplete things . . . and identity in differing things, and perfect power in the weak . . . and altogether they at-tribute to things what belong to others [τὰ ἄλλων ἄλλοις ἀποδιδόασιν]. They ought to known that the divine righteousness in this is really true righteousness, because it assigns to all things what is proper according to the rank of each of beings, and preserves the nature of each in its proper order and power. (DN VIII.7, 896AB)

Justice, properly understood, means not equality but due proportion, "a place for everything and everything in its place."[19] All things participate equally in God by being unequal, by occupying different ranks in the hierarchical order of the whole.

The view that hierachical order separates the lower ranks of creatures from God depends on the mistaken conception of God as the "first and highest being," standing above the angels at the peak of the hierarchy of beings. If that were the case, then indeed only the highest beings would be in immediate communion with God. But since God is not any being but "all things in all things and nothing in any" (DN VII.3, 872A), he does not stand at the top of the universal hierarchy but transcends and permeates the whole. "The goodness of the Godhead which is beyond all things extends from the highest and most venerable substances to the last, and is still above all, the higher not outstripping its excellence nor the lower going beyond its con-tainment" (DN IV.4, 697C). The entire hierarchy of reality, therefore, from the highest seraph to the least speck of dust, is the immediate presence and manifestation of God, of unity and goodness, according to the different modes and degrees that constitute the different levels of being.

It is often said that in teaching that all things are immediately pro-duced by God, Dionysius departs from a Neoplatonic understanding of meta-physical hierarchy, in which each level produces, or causes to be, the next level down. According to this interpretation, for Dionysius, unlike the Neoplatonists, only cognitive "illumination," and not being, is transmitted through the created hierarchy.[20] Here again we encounter the supposed dif-ference between Dionysius and Neoplatonism that lies in Dionysius' denial of a multiplicity of productive divinities subordinate to the One. And here again the difference is more apparent than real. One the one hand, as we have seen, all of Proclus' productive divinities are modalizations of the One, so that all productivity is the One operative at higher and lower levels of universality. On the other hand, in Dionysius, there is no distinction between "direct" production and "hierarchically mediated" illumination. The making of all things is theophany, the manifestation or revelation of God, and the "rays" which God sends down into beings are explicitly identified as their constitutive determinations, their very goodness and being (see e.g. DN I.2, 588CD; IV.1–2, 693B–696D; V.8, 824BC).[21] *Light* is one of the universal divine names, discussed in chapter IV of the *Divine Names* along with *Good*, *Beauty*, and *Love*, naming God as he is present in all things whatsoever. As we have seen, knowing is the mode of being proper to cognitive beings, and all lesser modes of being are lesser modes of knowing. Hence it is impossible to distinguish between the transmission of knowledge and the transmission of being.[22] Illumination is production, and in both Dionysius and his Neoplatonic forebears it is at once direct and hierarchically mediated. An examination of how this is so will bring to light the full richness and metaphysical significance of Dionysius' doctrine of hierarchy.

In Plotinus' system, according to a conventional but superficial reading, the One generates Intellect, which in turn generates Soul, which in turn generates the sensible cosmos; and sensible things, on this view, are not produced directly by the One but stand at several removes from it. But in fact, as we saw in chapter 2, each level is not another being additional to its prior, as though the One were one thing, Intellect a second, Soul a third, and the sensible a fourth. Rather, each level down is the differentiated appearance, the expression, the unfolding of its prior, so that the content is the same thoughout all levels, in differing degrees of concentration and diffusion. In producing Intellect, therefore, the One produces all the lower levels, and Plotinus emphasizes that each level is not outside of but is contained in the next level up: "But Soul is not in the universe, but the universe in it: for body is not the soul's place, but Soul is in Intellect and body in Soul, and Intellect in something else [i.e. the One] . . . Where then are the other things? In it" (V.5.9.30–34). And therefore, as Plotinus says here and in many other places, all things, at all levels, are contained in the One: "The last and lowest things, therefore, are in the last of those before them and these are in those prior to them, and one thing is in another up to the first, which is the Principle. But the Principle, since it has nothing before it, has not anything else to be in; but since . . . the other things are in those which come before them, it encompasses all the other things" (V.5.9.6–10).[23]

All the levels of reality, therefore, are the continuous unfolding or presentation of the One: "All these things are the One and not the One; they are he because they come from him; they are not he, because it is in abiding by himself that he gives them. It is then like a long life stretched out at length; each part is different from that which comes next in order, but the whole is continuous with itself, but with one part differentiated from another, and the earlier does not perish in the later" (V.2.2.25–30). All reality, at every level, depends on unity and indeed is nothing but the differentiated presence of unity. "It is by the One that all beings are beings, *both* those which are primarily beings [i.e. intelligibles] *and* those which are in any sense said to be among beings [i.e. sensibles]" (VI.9.1.1–2; my italics). All that is given to cognition in any mode is nothing but the presence of the One, ever lessening as we descend from Intellect to the sensible. But where the One is not present, there is absolutely nothing there for cognition in any mode whatsoever and hence no slightest trace of reality. "[T]here is nothing in which it is not . . . [B]ecause it is free from everything it is not prevented from being anywhere. For if . . . it was prevented, it would be limited by something else, and what comes next would be without a share in it, and God would go just so far . . . But if it is not absent from anything and is not anywhere, it is everywhere independent. And one part of it is not here and another there . . . so that it is everywhere as a whole" (V.5.9.13–25). In the absence of the One there is simply nothing, not even matter, and the One is therefore immediately present to and productive of all things at every level, insofar as they can be said to be at all.

In Proclus, because of his proliferation of "mean terms" and more rigid distinctions of ontological items and levels from one another, we might superficially expect to find a greater sense of mediation and of the distance of sub-divine beings from the One. But in fact, Proclus no less than Plotinus affirms the One's immediate causal presence throughout all the levels of his elaborate metaphysical hierarchy. As we saw in looking at the hierarchy of universality of causal determinations, Proclus explains that absolutely every-thing, including matter, is caused by the One; all things insofar as they have any form are caused by the One and Being; all living things, by the One, Being, and Life; and so on. Thus it is not the case that anything is produced by a lower level *rather than* directly by the One itself. When we recall Proclus' argument that a transcendent cause is present to all its effects, it follows that the One is productively present throughout all the levels. "In order that as cause it [any transcendent cause] may be in all [ὑπάρχον ἐν πᾶσιν] that can participate in it while as a separate and independent principle it is prior to all the things that are filled from it [τῶν ἀπ' αὐτοῦ πληρουμένων], it must be at once everywhere and nowhere" (*El. Th.*, prop. 98).

Here again, the Neoplatonic principle that the lower level is contained in and is the manifestation of the higher is at work. Since a lower, more specific causal determination is simply a specification of a higher, more uni-versal one, the causal power of the former is not additional to or outside of, but is contained in and indeed simply is that of the latter, operating in a more specific way. "[I]n the activity of the secondary the higher co-operates [συνεργεῖ], because all that the secondary makes, the higher cause [τὸ αἰτιώτερον] co-generates [συναπογεννᾷ] with it" (*El. Th.*, prop. 70). Since the whole content of an effect, or lower level, is nothing but the participated presence of its cause, it follows that the effect's own causal activity is that of its cause at work in it. Hence, what is produced by a lower level is (not less but) *more* produced by the higher. Proclus' exposition of this principle is so clear that it is worth citing at length, especially since he has so often been misunderstood on this point.

> All that is produced by secondaries is more [μειζόνως] produced also from the prior and more causal terms [αἰτιωτέρων], from which the secondaries are also produced.
>
> For if the secondary has its whole being [ὅλην . . . τὴν οὐσίαν] from its prior, thence also it receives its power of further production, since productive powers reside in producers in virtue of their being and fulfil their being. But if it owes to the superior cause its power of production, to that superior it owes its character as a cause in so far as it is a cause . . . If so, the things which proceed from it are caused in virtue of its prior . . . If so, the effect owes to the superior cause its character as an effect.
>
> Again, it is evident that the effect is more from the superior principle. For if the latter has given to the secondary being the causality which enabled it to produce, it must itself have possessed this causality primitively . . . But if the secondary is productive by participation, the primal primitively and by communication, the latter is causative in a greater measure, inasmuch as it has communicated to another the power of generating consequents. (*El. Th.*, prop. 56)

From this it clearly follows that all things at every level are wholly and absolutely caused by the One, as the supreme and sole causal power, whereof the causal powers of all things are participations. Since all being, all power, all activity is from the One, nothing can be added to the One's productivity. The participated productivity of any lesser level is the One operating at that level of specificity. Hence the One is the only causal agency that is at work in all of the subordinate "causes." Consequently, all things proceed at once immediately from the One and from their own priors. Proclus' doctrine in this proposition might be expressed by the following diagram:

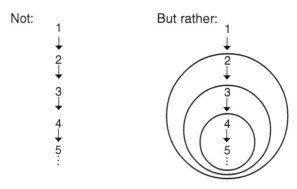

As this diagram shows, the One *immediately* produces and is present to the *entire* sequence of hierarchical mediation. As the productive power of the whole, it is present throughout the whole.[24]

Hence, as Proclus repeatedly insists, the gods or henads, which as the One's "participated terms" are the differentiated presences of the One to different beings,[25] fill all things: "All that is divine . . . has a potency which dominates the objects of its providence, a potency past all resisting and without all circumscription, in virtue of which the gods have filled all things with themselves" (*El. Th.*, prop. 121). Again: "[T]he divine from itself fills all things with the goods in it" (*El. Th.*, prop. 131). Again: " '[A]ll things are full of gods [μεστὰ δὲ πάντα θεῶν],' and what each has according to nature, it has from there" (*El. Th.*, prop. 145). And these "gods" or participated henads do not separate beings from the unparticipated One, for the very point of the distinction between the participated and the unparticipated is that the transcendent cause is not confined to any one of the participants but is "present [παρόν] to all alike" (*El. Th.*, prop. 23). In short, when Neoplatonic procession is properly understood in terms of manifestation or unfolding rather than as the making of additional things outside of and coordinate with the cause, the supposed opposition between immediate creative presence and mediated production disappears.

So also, in Dionysius, there is no opposition, or even distinction, between God's immediate productive presence to all things and the trans-mission of that presence through the hierarchy of creatures. Each thing's participation in God, its being, lies in its fulfilling its proper place within the hierarchical structure of reality. But this means that its participation in God consists in its rightly relating to other beings, above, below, and coordinate with it in the universal hierarchy. A being exercises its proper activities, its being, not in isolation but in relation to other beings. Hence, as Dionysius says, the love of all things for God, which is their reversion, their participation in him, and hence their very being, consists in their love for each other, according to the proper rank of each: "To all things, then, the Beautiful and Good is desired and beloved and cherished; and through it and for the sake of it also the lesser love the greater revertively, and those of the same sort [τὰ ὁμόστοιχα] their coordinates communally, and the greater the lesser providentially . . . and all things, by desiring the Beautiful and Good, do and wish all things that they do and wish" (DN IV.10, 708A) The higher being's love for or participation in God, its being, then, is its providence to the lower, and the lower being's love for or participation in God is its reversion, or receptivity, to the higher. Provid-ing to the lower and reverting to the higher is the very meaning of occu-pying a given position in the hierarchical structure of the whole. Dionysian hierarchy, therefore, has nothing to do with domination and subservience, but only with love, the love of all things for one another which is the love of God in them all.[26]

It is striking that Dionysius applies the terminology of procession and reversion not only to the relation of beings to God but also to the hierarchical interrelations among beings: the higher proceed or are providential to the lower, and the lower revert to the higher (DN IV.8, 704D; IV.10, 708A; IV.12, 709D; IV.15, 713AB). Beings, then, not only proceed from and revert to God but also proceed from and revert to each other. Thus, for example, angels providentially proceed to men, and men revert, not simply to God, but to angels. And since any being's proper activity is its mode of participation in God, its procession from and reversion to him, it follows that all things proceed from and revert to God in proceeding to their subordinates and reverting to their superiors. Thus the very being of all things, their procession from and reversion to God, consists in their hierarchical relations of procession and reversion to one another.

From this it follows that the being of all things consists in their taking part in God's making all things to be. Every being has an active role not only in its own production but in the production of all things. In that the identity and therefore the being of each thing lies in its hierarchical relations to other things, beings give determination to and receive determination from one another, and so contribute to one another's being. As in Proclus, the productive power which is God runs throughout the hierarchy of reality, exercised by each being as its own proper activity.[27] The "light" that is transmitted from one being to another in the hierarchy of beings is being itself, which is God in all of them. All things, in performing the proper activities which are their being, are participating in the making of the world, taking part in the constitutive divine ordering of the whole. But, as in the case of the being's role in its own being produced, this neither adds to nor detracts from God's immediate production of all things. For God, as Love or Difference itself, is the hierarchical, relational structuring of the whole. The proper and mutually constitutive activities of beings, their processions and reversions to one another, their love for each other, is the analogous presence of God in each of them.[28] Beings take part in the production of themselves and one another only by participation, which is to say that it is God who produces in them. As in Proclus, God himself is the only productive agency at work throughout the hierarchy. It is thus false to oppose Dionysius' doctrine of direct creation to a Neoplatonic doctrine of mediated production. For both Proclus and Dionysius, the One, or God, directly produces all things, in and through one another.[29]

Hence in the *Celestial Hierarchy* Dionysius says:

> Perfection for each of those appointed in hierarchy is to be led up according to its proper analogy to the imitation of God, and . . . to become a co-operator [συνεργὸν] of God and to show the divine activity revealed in itself [δεῖξαι τὴν θείαν ἐνέργειαν ἐν ἑαυτῷ . . . ἀναφαινομένην] as far as possible. As, since the order

of hierarchy is that some are purified and others purify, some are
illumined and others illumine, some are perfected and others perfect, the imitation of God is adapted to each in a certain mode.
(CH III.2, 165B)

Here Dionysius expressly indicates that the hierarchical activity of the being
is the divine activity manifest in it. This reflects Proclus' explanation that
the higher, more universal cause cooperates [συνεργεῖ] in producing whatever the lower cause produces, because the lower is itself nothing but a
specification of the higher. Thus in Dionysius' account of Isaiah and the
angel, the ascription of the angel's activity to the seraph is justified because
all the activities of all levels are the presence of God throughout the whole
structure. The being that beings give to and receive from one another in
hierarchy is the presence of God in each: "The purpose of hierarchy, then,
is likeness and union with God as far as possible . . . making the members of
his dancing company [τοὺς ἑαυτοῦ θιασώτας] divine images, clear and
spotless mirrors, receptive of the original light and thearchic ray and sacredly
filled with the granted [ἐνδιδομένης[30]] radiance, and ungrudgingly flaring it
up again to the next, according to the thearchic ordinances" (CH III.2,
165A). Here Dionysius likens the hierarchy of beings at once to a baccha-
nalian dance and to an array of mirrors, all receiving and passing on the
divine light, so that the same light is present throughout the entire structure
by means of the structure itself.

The central principle of Dionysian hierarchy, then, is *immediate mediation*:[31] it is by the hierarchical mediation of beings that God is immediately
constitutively present to all.[32] Acting in each thing as the activity of that
thing, God produces all things in and through each other. All things participate directly in God, i.e. possess being, in giving being to and receiving being
from one another, according to the rank of each. Thus Dionysius summarizes
his account of Isaiah and the angel:

God is by nature and really properly the source of being illumined
to all those who are illumined, as essence of light and cause of being
itself and of seeing; but by placement[33] and in a God-imitating way
that which is higher in rank [is the source] to each thing after, in
that the divine lights are derived to the latter through it . . . Wherefore they ascribe every sacred and God-imitating activity to God, as
cause, but to the first deiform intellects as the first effectors and
teachers of divine things. (CH III.3, 301D)

We may note that Dionysius here associates and indeed identifies "source of
being illumined" and "cause of being," and that "imitation," in a Neoplatonic
context, signifies not extrinsic copying but participation, the presence of the
archetype in the image. Hence the light, the being, derived (literally, poured

through a sluice) from the higher to the lower genuinely is God present in each. This is simply a particular application of the general principle laid out in the *Divine Names*: "This, the one Beautiful and Good, is singly cause of all the many beautiful and good things. From this are all the substantial existences of beings, the unions, the distinctions, the identities, the differ-ences, the likenesses, the unlikenesses, the communions of opposites, the unconfusions of united things, the providences of the higher, the mutual supports of the co-ordinates, the reversions of the inferiors" (DN IV.7, 704B). The processions of the higher to the lower, the communions of coordinates, and the reversions of the lower to the higher, are the Good, or Love, present thoughout all as the being of each.

Fundamentally, this is because what all things participate in, each according to its rank, is God who is Love, Ecstasy, Overflow itself. Since in God, as Love, interiority coincides with exteriority, so for any being, its interiority, its identity, its selfhood, which is the presence of God in it, coincides with its exteriority, its relations with other beings. The hierarchi-cal activity of beings, their love for one another, is the presence in them of Love itself. Since what all things receive, or participate in, as their being, is Giving itself, therefore to be, to participate in God, is to give. Hence it is in giving to each other that all things participate in God, or are.[34] Or again, since God is pure Openness, the donative openness of the higher to the lower and the receptive openness of the lower to the higher is the presence of God in each. The love of beings for each other, which is the activity of hierarchy, is the Love which is God whirling through all things as their being.

In Dionysius' metaphysics, then, there is no such thing as an indi-vidual, a being conceived as a closed, self-contained unit which extrinsically enters into relations with other beings. Because the principle of reality is pure Openness or Giving, the very identity, the being of each thing, God-in-it, is its giving to and receiving from others. Each thing, indeed, is noth-ing but its relations to others, its place within the structure of immediate mediation.[35] Hierarchy is thus, as its name signifies, the principle of sacred-ness, which is to say of being.[36] Nothing could be farther from the supposed "immovability" of Dionysian hierarchy[37] than this vision of being as περιχώρησις, as the Great Dance in which all beings are only in and through each other.[38] "The divine intellects are said to be moved cyclically, united to the illuminations, without beginning and without end, of the Beautiful and Good; but in a straight line, whenever they proceed for the providence of their inferiors . . . ; but spirally, because even in providing for the inferior they remain not gone out [ἀνεκφοιτήτως[39]] in identity around the beautiful and good cause of identity, ceaselessly dancing around [περιχορεύοντες]" (DN IV.8, 704D–705A). Although this is said specifically of the angels, it clearly applies to all things, since all things remain fixed in their identities in proceeding to their subordinates. Hence Dionysius describes hierarchy as a θίασος, a bacchic revel whose members ecstatically share in divinity.[40]

Dionysian hierarchy is none other than the communion of saints,[41] which, as a communion of intelligences, is itself the fullness of being. The hierarchical structure of reality is the articulated manifestation of the divine love that constitutes all things. Love itself, says Dionysius, is "a power unifying and connective and differentiatingly combining, pre-existing in the Beautiful and Good through the Beautiful and Good and given out from the Beautiful and Good through the Beautiful and Good, and holding together co-ordinates according to their mutual communion, moving the first things to providence for their inferiors, and establishing the inferiors in reversion to their superiors" (DN IV.12, 709C; cf. DN IV.15, 713AB).

CHAPTER SIX

THE CONTINUUM OF COGNITION

A sharp dichotomy and dualism between sense and intellect, as two different cognitive faculties apprehending two different kinds of objects, is conventionally regarded as perhaps the most fundamental feature of Platonic thought, elaborated in Neoplatonism and adopted by Dionysius.[1] But this is in fact a misunderstanding not only of Dionysius but of the entire Platonic tradition. A more careful examination reveals that in this tradition sense and intellect, with discursive reason as a mean between them, constitute a continuum of modes of cognition, articulated by the degrees of unity in which they apprehend reality. Thus Dionysius groups irrational animals, humans, and angels together as participants in Wisdom, i.e. cognition or consciousness in general, and then hierarchically subdivides Wisdom into intellection, discursive reason, and sense perception, loosely correlated with angels, human souls, and animals, respectively. The correlation is loose because, in Dionysius as in Plotinus, the human soul can, so to speak, move up and down the scale: although its proper cognitive activity is discursive reason, it also, obviously, engages in sense perception, and according to Dionysius it can ascend to the level of angelic intellection and beyond. This very elasticity on the part of the soul indicates that the different modes of cognition are a continuum of levels in what is fundamentally the same activity. In turn, Neoplatonic and Dionysian "mysticism," the passage beyond being and intellect, is the extension and completion of this continuum.

In Plato, the Parmenidean principle that to be is to be intelligible develops into an identification between levels of cognitive apprehension and levels of reality. Forms are real beings precisely in that they are what is perfectly intelligible; sensibles are less than really real in that they exhibit intelligible natures which they themselves are not, and hence are not beings but multiple, differentiated appearances of unitary forms.[2] But therefore, for Plato, the ascent of the soul from sense to intellect, illustrated by the chariot flight in the *Phaedrus*, the emergence from the cave in the *Republic*, the separation of soul from body in the *Phaedo*, is not a passage from one "world" or set of objects to another. It is rather, as Plato's references to "shadows," "puppets," and other "images" indicate, a passage from appearance to reality, and consists in a progressive unification of the content of consciousness, as the soul passes from the many different sensible presentations of a form to the one intelligible reality: "Man must understand what is said according to form, going from many sense-perceptions to a one gathered together by reasoning" (*Phaedrus* 249b6–c2). And because this ascent is a deepening communion of consciousness with reality, Plato expresses the soul's intellectual apprehension of the forms not only by the metaphor of vision but also by metaphors of sexual union and of eating, the soul's uniting with being and taking it into itself (*Phaedrus* 247e2–6; *Republic* 490a8–b7).

Aristotle's theory of knowledge can be seen as an extended reflection on such an understanding of consciousness as a communion of the soul with reality. Most basically, to be aware of something is to have it present to or in oneself. The things that I see or hear, the ideas that I think, are in me, as the content of my consciousness. Hence Aristotle argues that all cognition is an identity of some kind between subject and object. In the case of sense perception, the identity is not absolute but only qualitative (*On the Soul* II.5, 418a3–7): to sense a thing is to receive into oneself the sensible forms or qualities of the thing, without the matter (*On the Soul* II.12, 424a17–18). In the case of intellectual consciousness, however, the object itself is pure form or idea without matter, and therefore the identity between thought and its object is complete: "[I]n the case of objects which involve no matter, what thinks and what is thought are identical; for speculative knowledge and its object are identical" (*On the Soul* III.4, 430a3–5; cf. *Metaphysics* XII.9, 1075a2–4). Intellect is thus strictly identical with its intelligible object, having that idea as its content and hence as what the intellect itself is in that act of thinking.

Plotinus takes up this Aristotelian understanding of consciousness into the Platonic doctrine of being as form to arrive at the identity of being and consciousness which is a hallmark of his philosophy. If being is what is apprehended by thought, and thought is what it apprehends, then being is thought and thought is being. The sensible cosmos, Soul, and Intellect are therefore best understood not as a series of "worlds" or objects stacked one on top of another, but rather, to use Hadot's excellent phrase, "levels of the self," levels at which we, as consciousness, can be.[3] The standard translation of νοῦς in Plotinus as "Intellect" (with a capital "I") tends to obscure this, promoting an imagination of Intellect as a static "thing," located above the sensible world and Soul. But in fact, νοῦς for Plotinus is not a substance which exercises νόησις, the act of intellection, but is that activity itself. "If then [the intelligible] is activity [ἐνέργεια], and the first activity and the fairest, it is the first intellection and substantial intellection . . . but an intellection of this kind which is primary and primarily intellective will be the first Intellect; for this Intellect is not potential, nor is it one and its intellection another" (V.3.5.37–41; see also, e.g., V.9.5.1–10). Plotinian Intellect, then, is pure consciousness, consciousness itself at the highest level.

It is as pure consciousness, or thought, that Intellect is identical with being. For consciousness, as we have seen, means the communion or "togetherness" of subject and object. Hence consciousness is perfect only when they are one, and anything less than this unity is less than perfect consciousness. As Plotinus explains, "This is the reason, I think, why there is no truth in the senses, only opinion: opinion is opinion because it receives, and what it receives is different from that from which it receives it" (V.5.1.62–66). Because sense is not fully one with that which it perceives, sense perception is not strictly "true," and such consciousness is not perfect thought.[4] In the case of Intellect, therefore,

> if what are in it are impressions of [the objects contemplated], then it does not have them themselves; but if it has them themselves . . . the contemplation must be the same as the contemplated, and Intellect the same as the intelligible; for, if not the same, there will not be truth; for the one who is trying to possess realities will possess an impression different from the realities, and this is not truth . . . In this way, therefore, Intellect and the intelligible are one, and this is reality and the first reality, and also the first Intellect which possesses the real beings, or rather is the same as the real beings.[5] (V.3.5.19–29)

"We have here, then, one nature, Intellect, all realities, and truth" (V.5.3.1–2). This unity of thought and reality, consciousness in its purity and perfection, is what Plotinus means by Intellect.

Intellect, or intellection, is thus genuinely analogous to vision, as a bringing together of subject and object. In sense vision, the subject "reaches out," extends its gaze toward the object, and the object is taken into the subject's awareness. Sense perception, as a mode of consciousness, is a partial overcoming of the separation between subject and object, self and reality. In intellectual vision or intuition (νόησις), this is perfected, for there is no externality or "distance" between the self and reality, and so they are one. "For there is no longer one thing outside and another outside which is looking at it, but the keen sighted has what is seen within . . . But one must transport what one sees into oneself, and look at it as one and look at it as oneself" (V.8.10.33–42). And again, "If he sees it as something different, he is not yet in beauty [i.e. being, as form], but he is in it most perfectly when he becomes it. If therefore sight is of something external we must not have sight, or only that which is identical with its object" (V.8.11.20–23).

Intellect, therefore, is perfect consciousness in that it is the knowledge of being as its own content and therefore as itself. As such it is not an object fixed up above in metaphysical space but an activity that we ourselves, as consciousness, can be: "A man has certainly become Intellect when he lets all the rest which belongs to him go and looks at this with this and himself with himself: that is, it is as Intellect he sees himself" (V.3.4.25–32). The self, at the level of Intellect, *is* Intellect, which means that it is all things. Hence the ascent to Intellect is also an inward turn of consciousness, whereby we encounter reality not, as by sense, external to the self, but as the content of thought and thus within the self. "Let him who can, follow and come within, and leave outside the sight of his eyes and not turn back to the bodily splendours which he saw before" (I.6.8.4–6). But this inward turn is not a self-isolation, a cutting off of oneself from reality. Rather, by turning inward we have and know all of reality in and as the self, and we know the self in and as all things. By turning inward we are not less but more perfectly united with all things:

> If then we have a part in true knowledge, we are [the intelligibles] . . . So then, being together with all things, we are those: so then, we are all and one. So therefore when we look outside that on which we depend we do not know that we are one, like faces which are many on the outside but have one head inside. But if someone is able to turn around . . . he will see God and himself and the All . . . ; when he has nowhere to set himself and limit himself and deter-mine how far he himself goes, he will stop marking himself off from all being. (VI.5.7.3–16)

And again, "You will increase yourself then by rejecting all else, and the All will be present to you in your rejection" (VI.5.12.24–25). It is not the con-templative inward turn but rather the externality of sense that separates the self, as subject, from all else, as external object.[6]

As the vision of reality in and as itself, Intellect grasps all being, in its multiplicity, not piecemeal or sequentially but in a single complex intuition: "Intellect is the beings, possessing all things . . . as possessing itself and being one with them. 'All things are together' there, and none the less they are separate . . . Intellect is all things together and also not together, because each is a special power" (V.9.6.1–4, 8–9). All things as grasped in intellect are both "together" and "not together" in that the forms are distinct, and are intelligible only because they are distinct, but each one implies and therefore contains all the others (see e.g. V.9.8.3–7). Each being, therefore, is the whole of being in a distinct way, which is why Plotinus describes being or intellect, intelligible reality as a whole, as "one-many" (e.g. V.3.15.23). At the level of intellection, then, cognition knows all the forms in knowing each one of them: "[A]ll things there are transparent, and there is nothing dark or opaque; everything and all things are clear to the inmost part to everything . . . Each there has all things in itself and sees all things in every other, so that all are everywhere and each and every one is all . . . A different kind of being stands out in each, but in each all are manifest . . . [E]ach . . . is part and whole at once: it has the appearance of a part, but a penetrating look sees the whole in it" (V.8.4.6–12, 22–25). Intellection, then, is the apprehension of being, as a whole, in a complex but unified vision, and being itself is not a static series of lifeless forms but a communion of living intelligences.

Discursive reason, the lower mode of cognition that Plotinus associates with soul as distinct from Intellect, is an "unfolded" or extended vision of the same content, an apprehension of being not all at once and as a whole but sequentially: "For around Soul things come one after another: now Socrates, now horse, always some one of beings; but Intellect is all things" (V.1.4.20–22). Plotinus illustrates this difference by referring to ideogrammatic Egyptian hieroglyphs, which represent "the non-discursiveness of the intelligible world, that is, that every image is a kind of knowledge and wisdom . . . all together in one, and not discourse or deliberation. But [only] afterwards [others] discovered, starting from it in its concentrated unity, a representation in something else, already unfolded and speaking the same discursively [λέγον αὐτὸ ἐν διεξόδῳ]" (V.8.6.7–11). Discursive reason, then, apprehends the same content as intellection, but in greater multiplicity. As the unfolded representation of intellection in soul, discursive reason functions as a mean between the unity of the forms in Intellect and the still greater dispersion at the level of sense. "And the offspring of Intellect [i.e. soul] is a rational form and an existing being, that which thinks discursively; it is this which moves around Intellect . . . united to it on one side and so filled with it and enjoying it and sharing in it and thinking, but, on the other side, in touch with the things which came after it" (V.1.7.42–47), i.e. the sensible. Soul, as the locus of discursive reason, brings the multiplicity of sense impressions which it receives "from below" under the unity of the forms which it receives "from above" (see e.g. V.3.2.8–13). Soul makes discursive judgments, unifying its manifold of sense impressions into definite, identified objects by means of the impressions of the forms which it has from Intellect. Such cognition is thus more unified than mere sensation but less unified than pure intellection.

Sense, in turn, is a still more "unfolded" vision of being, the lowest, least unified mode of cognition. Each form is a single intelligible reality, but appears to sense "here and there," at many different points in space and time. "For it is sense-perception, to which we are paying attention when we disbelieve what is being said, which says that it is here and there, but reason says that the 'here and there' has not come about by its being extended but the whole of what is extended has participated in it, while it is not itself spaced out" (VI.4.13.2–6).[7] Just as it is the distinction of forms from one another in Intellect that constitutes them as not the One itself but appearances or manifestations of the One, so also it is precisely the multiplicity, the separation of sensible instances from each other, that constitutes them as not the forms themselves but appearances of them.

Intellect and sense, therefore, as modes of cognition, are not apprehensions of different "worlds" or sets of objects, but are more and less unified apprehensions of being, the only object of all cognition. The sensible cosmos as a whole is the sensuous apprehension of being, being as apprehended, most multiply, by sense, and the intelligible cosmos is the same content as apprehended, most unitarily, by intellectual intuition. The sensible and the intelligible are not two worlds, but rather the same reality, the manifestation of the One, apprehended in differing degrees of unity.[8] The ascent to intellection is thus not a passage from one set of objects to another, but a gathering of the content of consciousness into greater unity. To imagine this ascent, Plotinus says, we should "apprehend in our thought this visible universe, with each of its parts remaining what it is without confusion, gathering all of them together into one as far as we can . . . Let there be, then, in the soul a shining imagination of a sphere, having everything within it . . . Keep this, and apprehend in your mind another, taking away the mass: take away also the places, and the mental picture of matter in yourself" (V.8.9.1–13). That is, we must retain the same content and remove the dilution or distension in which it is apprehended at the level of sense. In ascending from sense to intellection, therefore, we do not abandon or lose anything. The notion that in rising to the intellection of the forms we leave sensibles behind is an aspect of the false dualism that views sensibles as real beings and therefore regards sensibles and intelligibles as two different sets of objects. Once we correctly understand sensibles as nothing but differentiated appearances of forms, we see that in rising from sense to intellect we leave nothing behind, just as in turning from a multiplicity of beautiful reflections to the one reality being reflected we lose nothing of what we saw in the mirrors.

Therefore in Intellect, or intellectual consciousness, we find more truly all the same content that is given to sense.

> And certainly the sky there [i.e. in Intellect] must be a living being, and so a sky not bare of stars, as we call them here below, and this is what being sky is. But obviously there is earth also, not barren, but much more full of life, and all animals are in it . . . and, obviously, plants rooted in life; and sea is there, and all water in abiding flow and life, and all the living beings in water . . . For as each of the great parts of the universe is there, so is of necessity the nature of the living beings in them. (VI.7.12.4–17)

Plotinus summarizes this account of Intellect by saying that it is "as if there was one quality which held and kept intact all the qualities in itself, of sweetness along with fragrance, and was at once the quality of wine and the characters of all tastes, the sights of colours and all the awarenesses of touch, and all that hearings hear, all tunes and every rhythm" (VI.7.12.26–30). This strikingly sensuous description of intelligible reality drives home the point that intellectual experience is far more rich, not less, than sense experience, because it apprehends in concentrated unity, although not without distinction, all the same content that sense apprehends in extended, "diluted" multiplicity.

The understanding of intellection and sense perception as higher and lower modes on a continuum of cognition emerges most clearly when Plotinus asks how sense perception could be present in the archetypal, intelligible man if there were no objects for it "there," in the intelligible (VI.7.3.22ff). His answer is that sense perception at the intellectual level "would be a power of perceiving the sense-objects there, and would correspond to the sense-objects there . . . For if there were bodies there, the soul [i.e. the higher, intellectual soul] had perceptions and apprehensions of them; and the man there, the soul of this kind, was able to apprehend these bodies" (VI.7.6.1–11). In some sense, then, there are sensibles or bodies at the intelligible level, and a corresponding faculty for apprehending them which can therefore be called "sense perception."[9] The meaning of this surprising claim becomes clearer in the conclusion of the discussion:

> [T]his man here below has his powers from that intelligible man and looks to those realities, and these sense-objects are linked to this man and those others to that; for those sense-objects [i.e., the ones at the intelligible level], which we called so because they are bodies, are apprehended in a different way; and . . . this sense-perception is dimmer than the apprehension there in the intelligible, which we called sense-perception because it is of bodies and which is clearer. And for this reason this man here has sense-perception, because he has a lesser apprehension of lesser things, images of those intelligible realities; so that *these sense-perceptions here are dim intellections, but the intellections there are clear sense-perceptions.* (VI.7.7.23–32; my italics)

In other words, intellection itself is the intelligible paradigm of which sense perception is the unfolded expression. This remarkable passage indicates that there are bodies in Intellect in that, since sensible bodies are images or appearances of forms, intelligible forms are genuine or archetypal bodies. Since the bodies perceived by sense are forms dimly apprehended, the forms grasped by intellect are bodies clearly apprehended. Correlatively, as lower and higher points on the continuum of cognition, sense perception is dim intellection, and intellection is clear sense perception.

This Neoplatonic understanding of consciousness in relation to being underlies Dionysius' gnoseology. For him, as for Plato, Aristotle, and Plotinus, all cognition is a union of subject and object: "Knowledge is unitive of those who know and the things known [ἡ γνῶσις ἑνωτικὴ τῶν ἐγνωκότων καὶ ἐγνωσμένων]" (DN VII.4, 872D).[10] The perfect case of this unity is found at the intellectual level, where, as in Plotinus, the subject is one with its

activity and with its object: "The unified divine intellects [i.e. angels] are
united to their intellections and to the things thought [τοῖς νοουμένοις]"
(DN XI.2, 949C). Such cognition is the most simple or unified mode of
consciousness, grasping its contents all at once, without the extension and
division found in discursive reason and sense:

> From [God as Wisdom] the intelligible and intellectual powers of
> the angelic intellects have their simple and blessed intellections.
> Not in parts or from parts or sense-perceptions or discursive reason-
> ings do they gather divine knowledge . . . but purified from every-
> thing material and multiple, intellectually, immaterially, uniformly,
> they think [νοοῦσιν] the intelligibles of divine things. And for
> them the intellectual power and activity . . . is synoptic [συνοπτικὴ]
> of the divine intellections. (DN VII.2, 868B)

Dionysius proceeds to present discursive reason, proper to human souls, as
inferior to angelic intellection precisely in that it is less unified: "Through
the divine Wisdom souls, too, have their rational faculty discursively, going
in a circle around the truth of beings, and by what is divided and manifold
of diversity falling short of the unified intellects, but, by the drawing together
of the many to the one made worthy, insofar as is proper and possible for
souls, of intellections equal to the angels' " (DN VII.2, 868BC). Finally,
Dionysius remarks that "one would not miss the mark in saying that even
sense-perceptions themselves are an echo of Wisdom" (DN VII.2, 868C).
This parallels Plotinus' account of sense perceptions as "dim intellections."
Sense perception is an "echo of Wisdom" in that, as a mode of cognition, it
is still a consciousness, however "dim" or diffuse, of being. Hence even the
lowest animal, in that it has sensation and thus some awareness of reality, is
a participant in God as Wisdom.

As Dionysius here indicates, however, human souls are not confined to
the level of discursive reason, but, as in Plotinus, can ascend to the level of
intellection and beyond. He repeatedly presents the angels as paradigms for
human cognition, describing our attainment of intellection as equality with,
imitation of, or union with the angels (DN I.4, 592C; DN IV.9, 705A; DN
VII.2, 868C).[11] Using a traditional Neoplatonic analogy, he ascribes to soul
three "motions," circular, spiral, and linear, corresponding to intellection,
discursive reason, and sense perception.

> The circular motion of soul is the entrance into itself from things
> outside and the uniform drawing together of its intellectual powers
> which gives it inerrancy, and reverting it from the many things
> outside, and gathering it first to itself, then uniting it, as having
> become uniform, to the uniformly united powers, and thus leading
> to the Beautiful and Good above all beings . . .

But soul is moved spirally insofar as it is illumined by divine knowledges in a manner proper to itself, not intellectually and uniformly but rationally and discursively and, as it were, by mixed and transitive activities.

But in a straight line, when it is moved, not entering into itself and in unitary intellectuality (for this, as I said, is circular), but proceeding toward the things around itself, and from the things outside, as from certain variegated and multiplied symbols, is gathered toward simple and unified contemplations.[12] (DN IV.9, 705AB)

Here intellection, as in Plotinus, is an inward turn, a concentration and unification of the consciousness, while sense perception is an externalization and multiplication of it, so that here again, the modes of cognition are distinguished by their degrees of unity. Hence human souls, by unification and interiority, can become intellects equal to the angels, and like them united to their intellectual acts and to their objects. It is only in union with the angels, as a community of intelligences like Plotinus' Intellect, that we are united with God.

For Dionysius as for Plotinus, then, sense, discursive reason, and intellection represent different points on a continuum of degrees of unity in the apprehension of reality. We can know and thus possess or be united with being most multiply by sense, in a more unified way by discursive reason, and in a more unified way still by intellection.[13] Here as in any Neoplatonic hierarchy, the same content and activity are found at every level, in higher and lower, more and less unified ways. Hence the higher level lacks nothing that the lower possesses but contains it in a higher way, while the lower has all that the higher possesses in a lower way. This is the basis of Proclus' doctrine that what is known is known according to the mode not of the object but of the knower: "For if the gods have all their attributes in a mode consonant with their character as gods . . . , it is surely manifest that their knowledge, being a divine property, will be determined not by the nature of the inferior beings which are its object but by their own transcendent majesty" (El. Th., prop. 124). Thus beings at a higher level of cognitive activity know all that falls below that mode in their superior cognition, just as, in Plotinus, intellect apprehends in a higher way all that is given to sense. So also, Dionysius explains that the angels, having intellection rather than sensation, are not therefore ignorant of sensibles, as if they were unable to apprehend them because they have no sense faculties. Rather, "the angels know . . . the things on earth, knowing them not by sense-perceptions (although they are sensible things), but by the proper power and nature of the deiform intellect" (DN VII.2, 869C). The higher power and activity includes, rather than excludes, the lower. By implication, then, for a human soul to ascend to the angelic or intellectual level is not for it to lose awareness of sensibles but know them in a higher, intellectual way. Here again, to ascend is not to leave some objects and go to others, but to know the same content, reality, in a superior mode.

For both Plotinus and Dionysius, then, all consciousness is the apprehension, at higher and lower levels, of being. But this means that the One, or God, is not the object of the highest mode of cognition, as if he were merely the highest being. Rather, the One is beyond all cognitive apprehension whatsoever, and, conversely, all consciousness is the reception of the One in differentiated multiplicity. This is in fact simply another side of the doctrine that being is the manifestation of the One. Manifestation, or appearance, necessarily takes place to and in consciousness as its constitutive content, what consciousness itself is. Being is not only the appearance but the apprehension of the One, and this is precisely what Plotinus means by Intellect. "That which is generated, when it has come into being, reverts to the One and is filled, and becomes Intellect by looking towards it. Its halt and turning towards the One constitutes being, its gaze upon the One, Intellect. Since it halts and turns towards the One that it may see, it becomes at once Intellect and being" (V.2.1.10–14).[14] But all other modes of cognition, and therefore of being, are lesser, "dimmer" intellections. "And every life is a thought [νόησίς τις], but one is dimmer than another, just as life [has degrees of clarity and strength]" (III.8.8.16–18). Hence all consciousness, including sense perception or even lower levels such as the "growth-thought" which is the life of a plant, or even the analogous life of minerals, is the differentiated vision and manifestation of the One at higher and lower levels.[15]

The doctrine, strongly implicit throughout Neoplatonism, that all cognition is the apprehension, at higher and lower levels, of the One or God, becomes fully explicit in Dionysius. For Dionysius as for Plotinus and Proclus, it is emphatically not the case that God is inaccessible to sense but accessible to intellectual contemplation. Rather, Dionysius says, God is the object of all cognition, even sense perception, and of none, even intellection. Since all cognition is the apprehension of being, and God is not any being, he is inaccessible to intellect no less than to sense: "It is necessary to ask how we know God, who is neither intelligible nor sensible [οὐδὲ νοητὸν οὐδὲ αἰσθητὸν] nor any of beings whatsoever" (DN VII.3, 869C). And conversely, since all cognition is the apprehension of being, and being is theophany, God is accessible to sense no less than to intellect:

God is known both through knowledge [γνώσεως] and through unknowing. And of him there is both intellection and reason and knowledge [ἐπιστήμη] and touching and sense-perception and opinion and imagination and name and all other things; and he is neither thought [νοεῖται] nor spoken [λέγεται] nor named. And he is not any of beings, nor is he known in any of beings. And he is all things in all things and nothing in any, and he is known to all from all and to none from any.[16] (DN VII.3, 872A)

Because God is all things in all things, to see anything is to see God in that thing. All knowledge is knowledge of God because all being, all that is given to consciousness in any mode, is nothing but the finite, differentiated presentation of God. Since all things are nothing but God-in-them, there is nothing to be known in anything but God-in-it.[17]

"Of God there is sense-perception": this stunning but wholly consistent affirmation cannot be overemphasized. It overturns all conventional misrepresentations of Neoplatonism in general, and Dionysius' thought in particular, as a "gnostic" repudiation of the senses and the sensible world. Since sense perception is an apprehension, a taking into oneself, of reality, however multiple, dim, or echoic it may be, it is an apprehension of theophany, of God as given to consciousness, for that is what reality is. This is why Dionysius revels in the contemplation of colors, shapes, sounds, scents, tastes: in all that we perceive, in our every sense-experience, we are encountering God,[18] and the same content, the same glorious theophany, is found not less but more intensely as we ascend to higher modes of cognition.[19] The claim that there is sense perception of God cannot be separated from Dionysius' account of God as Beauty, of the beauty seen in all things as the manifest presence of God in them. As he says a few lines later, "The knowledge of God . . . can be known, as I said, from all things; for it is . . . the cause, productive of all things and always fitting all things together, of the indissoluble adaptation and order of all things, and always conjoining the ends of the first things to the beginnings of the second, and beautifying [καλλιεργοῦσα] the one agreement and harmony of all" (DN VII.3, 872B). If, as Aristotle says, all men naturally take delight in sense perception (Metaphysics I.1, 980a23), this is because it is our first and most basic encounter with being. And being, for Dionysius, is theophany, or we might say "agathophany," the presentation to consciousness of the Good, and as such is delightful and attractive, that is, beautiful.

The knowledge of God, then, is given to sense no less than to intellect. Conversely, since God is the object of all cognition and of none rather than merely the object of the highest cognition, the cognitive ascent does not end with intellect. It extends beyond intellect to culminate in "the darkness of unknowing" (MT I.3, 1001A) or "the union above intellect" (DN VII.3, 872B; XI.2, 949D), a vision of or union with God which transcends all cognition whatsoever. Hence an account of Dionysius' gnoseology must extend from sense perception at one extreme to "mysticism" at the other. But here we must remember that in Dionysius, as in Plotinus and throughout the Neoplatonic tradition, "mysticism," the passage beyond thought and being, must be understood as an aspect of philosophical metaphysics and gnoseology, not an extrinsic, non-philosophical addition to them.[20] Understood in this way, Plotinian and Dionysian "mysticism" emerges as the completion of the progressive ascent from sense to discursive reason to intellect.

Since the One is not any being and therefore, as Plotinus says, to attain the One we must "not think" (V.3.13.33),[21] it might seem that for

Plotinus the "mystical" union with the One is discontinuous with the cognitive ascent. To see the One we must "take away everything [ἄφελε πάντα]"
(V.3.17.39), i.e. all beings, the objects and content of thought. This might
seem to indicate that we must abandon being, leave it behind, and turn
instead to the One as another object encountered in a super-cognitive mode.
But this is a misunderstanding strictly analogous to the mistaken notion that
in ascending to Intellect we must abandon the sensible. Just as to ascend
from sense to Intellect is not to leave the content of sense behind but to
gather it into greater unity, so to ascend from Intellect to the One is to
gather the same content into still greater unity. But since Intellect, as at
once thought and being, necessarily involves distinction and therefore multiplicity, to gather its content into absolute unity is to pass beyond thought
and being. Just as the intelligible is the *complicatio* of the sensible, so the One
is the *complicatio* of the intelligible: not another object over against being,
but the same content in absolute concentration, all things without distinction (see V.3.16.6–16).[22] As the sensible is the image, in the sense of the
differentiated appearance, of the intelligible, so the intelligible, or being, is
the image or differentiated appearance of the One. Thus the ascent from
sense to Intellect to the One is a continuous passage from appearance to that
which appears, from "image to original" (VI.9.11.45), in which nothing is
left behind. To pass from the intellectual apprehension of being to the
"mystical" encounter with the One is, once again, like turning from a multiplicity of reflections to that which is being reflected. Since being, as the
content of thought, is appearance, to transcend appearance altogether, to go
absolutely from "image to original," is to transcend being and cognition.

It is significant that when Plotinus enjoins us to "take away everything," "everything" is in fact in the plural, not πᾶν but πάντα, literally "all
things." It is all things in their plurality, as a multiplicity of distinct, intelligible beings, that must be transcended. But this going beyond all things in
their plurality, and hence as beings, is therefore the completion of the inward turn, the peak of the ascending unification of consciousness that we
have traced from sense to discursive reason to intellection. Even Intellect,
the most unified mode of cognition, necessarily demands and consists of
distinctions, and so still involves a looking "outward" into the multiplicity
of beings. But since the One is not any thing but the enfolding of all things,
Plotinus instructs us to "contemplate it without casting your thought out-
wards. For it does not lie somewhere leaving the other things empty of it, but
is always present to anyone who is able to touch it" (VI.9.7.3–5). To rise
from Intellect to the One, therefore, "the soul must let go of all outward
things and turn altogether to what is within, and not be inclined to any
outward thing, but unknowing all things (as it did formerly in sense-perception,
but then in the realm of forms, and even unknowing itself, come to be in
contemplation of that One" (VI.9.7.17–21). Here Plotinus makes the analogy explicit: as intellection is to sense perception, so the "vision" of the One

is to intellection, and hence the ascent from Intellect to the One is a continuation, an intensification of the inward turn of consciousness into unity. The
ascent might be likened to hearing a sound that gradually increases in pitch
until it passes beyond the range of hearing. In one sense, there is discontinuity:
we go from hearing to not hearing, from sound to silence. So also, in ascending
from Intellect to the One, we go from thinking to not thinking, from being to
not any being. But, as with the sound, in another sense there is continuity, for
the transition takes place through the continuation of the process by which we
reached the highest level of cognition.

Since the levels of reality are levels of the self, the One, as the enfolding of all things, is the highest and inmost level, the absolute enfolding of
the self (see V.1.10.1–7, V.1.11.7–11). Hence the mystical union with the
One is the complete unification of the self, as a cognitive subject. Thus
Plotinus says that in using the name *One* we are "wanting to unify our souls"
(VI.9.5.41–42) and that if someone fails to attain the One it is because he
is "not yet brought together into unity" (VI.9.4.24). Therefore, the "vision"
of the One is "an ecstasy and simplification and giving up of the self [ἔκστασις
καὶ ἅπλωσις καὶ ἐπίδοσις αὑτου]" (VI.9.11.23).[23] This "simplification" of
the self is an ecstasy or standing outside of the self and a giving up of the
self because form, or distinction, is the essence of thought and being, so that
in overcoming all distinctions in its content, the self is no longer consciousness and being. To achieve absolute unification is to pass beyond being:
"[O]ne becomes, not being, but 'beyond being' by this converse" (VI.9.11.42–
43). Since the otherness of being from the One is the otherness of beings
from each other, the complete unification of the self is the union of the self
with the One. "That One, therefore, since it has no otherness is always
present, and we are present to it when we have no otherness" (VI.9.8.34–
35). Although in its immediate context this refers to the otherness of the self
from the One, that otherness consists in the multiplicity or otherness of
consciousness within the self. The passage of the self beyond thought and
being into the One is thus not only discontinuous but also continuous with
the ascent from sense to Intellect, as the intensifying unification of the
content of consciousness and the progressively deepening inward turn.

In accord with the Neoplatonic understanding of being and cognition
as necessarily involving multiplicity, Dionysius frequently refers to the soul's
or mind's transcending of intellection as "the union above intellect," or
simply as "union." This refers at once to the union with God and to the
unification of the self, for these, as we have just seen in looking at Plotinus,
are identical.

> The unions, appropriate to angels, of the holy powers, whether they
> should be called applications or receptions [ἐπιβολὰς εἴτε
> παραδοχὰς] of the Goodness beyond unknowing and beyond light,
> are ineffable and unknown ... The deiform intellects, unified by

these in a manner imitating the angels as far as possible—since in the cessation of every intellectual activity such a union of the deified [ἐκθεουμένων] intellects to the super-divine light comes about— hymn it most properly through the taking away [ἀφαιρέσεως] of all beings.[24] (DN I.5, 593BC)

Here it is the minds (both angelic and human) which are themselves unified that are united to the light beyond divinity. The union of the mind itself, which as union transcends the act of intellection, is its union with God: "It is necessary to know that the intellect in us has on the one hand a power for intellection, through which it beholds intelligible things, and on the other hand the union exceeding the nature of intellect, through which it is joined with the things beyond itself" (DN VII.1, 865CD).[25]

But, as in Plotinus, this union which goes beyond intellect is continu-ous with the cognitive ascent. As the soul ascends from sense to discursive reason to intellect, it gathers its content into ever greater unity. At the peak, when absolute unification is achieved, intellectual knowledge passes over into the silence of unknowing: "Souls, uniting and gathering their manifold reasonings into one intellectual purity, go forth in the way and order proper to them through immaterial and undivided intellection to the union above intellection" (DN XI.2, 949D). Here Dionysius explicitly presents the ascent from discursive reason to intellection to mystical union as a continuous, progressive unification. Since God is not something else besides all beings but rather no thing as the *complicatio* of all things, the mystical unknowing of God as no thing is the inseparable completion of the knowledge of God, by every mode of cognition, as all things in all things. Thus Dionysius glosses his statement that God is the object of all cognition and of none by saying, "And there is, again, the most divine knowledge of God, that which is known through unknowing, according to the union above intellect, when the intellect, standing apart from all beings, then sending away also itself, is united to the rays beyond luminosity" (DN VII.3, 872AB). The "mystical" union with God in the "cessation of intellectual activities" is thus not opposed to the cognitive activity of knowing beings but is rather its goal and consummation.

Like Plotinus, Dionysius describes this union as an "ecstasy" from both the self and all things: "Leave behind sense-perceptions and intellectual activities and all sensible and intelligible things and all non-beings and beings, and be lifted up unknowingly toward the union, as far as possible, of that which is above all being and knowledge;[26] for by the irresistible and absolute ecstasy, purely, from yourself and all things, you will be led up to the ray beyond being of the divine darkness, taking away all things and being loosed from all things"[27] (MT I.1, 997B–1000A). It is an "ek-stasis," a stand-ing outside of oneself and all things, because, as the complete unification of consciousness, it is a passage beyond being as what is known and the self as a knower. Therefore, immediately after distinguishing between the mind's power of intellection and its transcendent union, Dionysius says, "According to this [union], then, divine things are to be thought, not according to us, but our whole selves standing outside of our whole selves [ὅλους ἑαυτοὺς ὅλων ἑαυτῶν ἐξισταμένους] and our whole [selves] becoming of God, for it is better to be of God and not of ourselves" (DN VII.1, 865D–868A).[28] The ecstasy in which we are "of God" rather than "of ourselves" is the complete unification of the self whereby we rise above being and knowledge.

This ecstasy, as the completion of the cognitive ascent, is the proper perfection of our nature as cognitive beings. Significantly, Dionysius speaks of ecstasy with regard to both love and knowledge. All beings are by loving, or reverting to, God, and this reversion, as a receptive self-abandonment, is an erotic ecstasy. But the mode of reversion proper to cognitive beings is knowledge. To be, for a cognitive thing, is to know, and since all knowledge is knowledge of God, to be is to know God. Consequently, for us as rational souls capable of ascending to intellect and beyond, the cognitive ascent is our reversion, and the culmination of the ascent in the ecstatic union above intellect is the fulfilment of our nature. The mystical ecstasy, as the end of cognition, is thus the mode of erotic, ontological ecstasy proper to and constitutive of rational beings.

But according to the principles of hierarchy and analogy, just as knowledge is the mode of being proper to cognitive things, so the being of things at lower levels is their lesser mode of knowledge. The mere existence of a stone, the life of a plant, and so on, is each thing's analogous knowledge of God. For any being at all, therefore, to be is, analogously, to know God. This, again, is simply the converse of the understanding of being as theophany. If to produce is to reveal, then to be produced is to receive that revelation, i.e. to know. If being is the manifestation of God, then it is also the knowledge of God. Indeed, the very content of all things, as the manifestation of God in them, is therefore the awareness, the knowledge of God, in them. The whole of reality is God made manifest as the intelligible content of all things, as what is given to cognition in all its analogous modes. The whole of reality, therefore, is the knowledge of God, just as, in Plotinus, being at higher and lower levels is consciousness at higher and lower levels, and all consciousness is the apprehension of the One in multiplicity.

This is why Dionysius uses the image of illumination to refer indifferently both to procession, God's making things to be, and to revelation, his making himself known. The "rays" or "illuminations" shed analogously on all things are rays at once of being and of knowledge, the manifestation of God that fills and constitutes all things (e.g. DN I.2, 588C–589D; IV.1, 693BC; IV.4, 697C). The "light" that beings, as mirrors, hierarchically transmit to one another, is the revelation, the knowledge of God which is all things in all things. Thus Dionysius says that the angels "are modeled on [God] as far as possible, and are boniform, and are communicative to those after them, as

the divine ordinance directs, of the gifts that extend to them from the Good"
(DN IV.1, 696A). These gifts, we know, include everything. In the *Celestial
Hierarchy* he indicates that the gifts which angels receive and transmit are
the knowledge of God, adding that by this ungrudging transmission "the
divine light extends analogously to all, by providence" and that through the
highest angels "the thearchic illumination is passed on to all, and to us" (CH
XIII.3, 301C–304A). Indeed, to receive and transmit the knowledge of the
unknowable God is what it is to be an angel: "The angel is an image [εἰκών]
of God, a manifestation of the unmanifest light [φανέρωσις τοῦ ἀφανοῦς
φωτός], a pure mirror, most transparent, unblemished, undefiled, spotless,
receiving whole, if it is right to say, the bloom of the good-stamped deiformity,
and unmixedly shining back in itself, as far as it can, the goodness of the
silence in the sanctuary" (DN IV.22, 724B). The light which the angels
reflect is the theophany, the received knowledge of God which constitutes
them as intellects.

But the intellectual nature of the angels is simply the highest, most
complete mode of being, enfolding in itself all lesser modes: the existence of
inanimate objects, the life of plants, the cognition of animals and humans.
Hence not the angels alone but all beings are mirrors, in lesser, dimmer ways.
What all beings reflect to one another are the gifts which they have received, and this is everything that they are. Hence the reflected light is the
knowledge of God which comprises all things. Since all that is in all things
is the manifestation of God in them, beings know God in and through each
other, and their revealing God to one another is their taking part in making
one another to be. The being of anything, therefore, consists at once in its
knowing God and in its making God known to others, in the manner proper
to it. The divine light which by means of hierarchy permeates the whole of
reality, is the knowledge of God which is the whole content of all things.

Having discussed the modes of cognition found in beings, we must
finally consider, with Dionysius, the cognition of God himself: "For how will
he think [νοήσει] any of the intelligibles, since he does not have intellectual
activities, or how will he know sensible things, being fixed above all sense
perception?" (DN VII.2, 868D). Dionysius replies that God knows all things,
not by any mode of cognition correlated and directed to beings, but in
knowing himself as their cause. "For the divine mind knows, not learning
beings from beings, but it pre-contains and pre-gathers the vision and knowledge [εἴδησιν καὶ γνῶσιν] and being of all things from itself and in itself,
as cause, not applying itself to each individually [οὐ κατ' ἰδίαν ἑκάστοις
ἐπιβάλλων], but in one encompassment of the cause knowing and comprehending all things" (DN VII.2, 869AB). Dionysius then paraphrases Proclus'
account of how the gods, or henads, know what is below themselves. "The
divine Wisdom, then, by knowing itself knows all things: material things
immaterially and divisible things indivisibly and multiple things singly, both
knowing and producing all things by himself, the One" (DN VII.2, 869B).[29]

Since the effects are nothing but appearances of the cause and the cause contains the effects without distinction, God is the undifferentiated containment of all things, and therefore in knowing himself knows all things at once: "For if as one cause God imparts being to all beings, as that single cause he will know all things, as being from him and pre-subsisting in him, and not from beings will he receive the knowledge of them . . . God, then, does not have a distinct knowledge of himself and another comprehending all beings in common . . . By this, then, God knows beings, not by the knowledge of beings, but by that of himself" (DN VII.2, 869BC).

This solution, however, raises the question of how God can even be said to know himself, since knowledge is confined to beings in that it necessarily involves distinction and multiplicity. The only possible answer is that God knows himself, not apart from all things—for apart from all things there is neither being nor knowledge—but only as cause, which is to say as all things in all things. There is thus no distinction between God's knowing himself, his knowing all things, and his making all things to be. Hence Dionysius repeatedly conjoins God's knowing all things with his making them: "Thus the divine intellect encompasses all things by the transcendent knowledge of all things, pre-containing the knowledge of all things in himself as the cause of all things, knowing and producing [εἰδὼς καὶ παράγων] angels before angels come to be, and within and from himself, so to speak, the source, knowing and bringing into being [εἰδὼς καὶ εἰς οὐσίαν ἄγων] all other things" (DN VII.2, 869A). God's knowing all things in himself, then, is his producing all things. God "knows things into being," making all things in knowing them by knowing himself in them. And since it is as all things in all things that God is their cause, God's knowing himself is not only the causing but the content of all reality, all things in all things. God's knowing himself, and in himself all things, is the procession into all things which is the making of all things and which is all things in all things.[30] As in Plotinus being and consciousness are identical as the manifestation and apprehension of the One, so in Dionysius all reality is the knowledge of God, in both the subjective and the objective sense of the genitive.

CHAPTER SEVEN

SYMBOLISM

Dionysius consistently uses the term *symbols* (σύμβολα) to refer to the sensible representations of God and of angels found in scripture and liturgy (e.g. DN I.4, 592B; IX.5, 913B; CH I.3, 121C–124A; II.5, 144CD; Ep. IX.1, 1104B). Such symbols, he says, are necessary for human beings, who must ascend to intellect from sense perception, but not for angels, as pure intellects (CH I.3, 121C–124A). On this basis he distinguishes the content of the *Divine Names* from that of the lost or unwritten *Symbolic Theology*: the former expounds the intelligible "names" of God found in scripture, while the latter interprets the sensible "symbols."[1] But just as sense and intellect are not opposed but in continuity, so the sensible symbols are continuous in kind with the intelligible names, and the distinction between them is relativized vis-à-vis God who infinitely transcends both. A philosophical examination of Dionysius' theory of symbols shows that being as such, not merely in its sensible aspect, is symbolic, and that there can be no non-symbolic knowledge of God. Therefore, as in the cognitive ascent from sense to intellect to mystical unknowing, to rise above symbols is not to discard them but to assume and penetrate into them. Dionysius' doctrine of symbolism thus represents the perfect unity of mystical unknowing and the cognitive apprehension of reality.

Since the symbols discussed by Dionysius, like the divine names, are those found in the scriptures, an account of his theory of symbolism might seem to belong to a study of his scriptural interpretation rather than to a study of the specifically philosophical content of his thought. But in fact, since the expressions of God found in the scriptures expressly include all things whatsoever, his exposition of both the intelligible names and the sensible symbols is not merely a matter of scriptural exegesis but a metaphysical account of being as theophany and hence of all sensible things as symbols of God.[2] Thus in the *Divine Names*, with regard to the representation of God as light, he quotes Romans 1:20, " 'The invisible things' of God 'from the creation of the world are seen, understood by the things that are made, his eternal power and divinity,'" and then adds, "But these things, in the *Symbolic Theology*" (DN IV.4–5, 700CD). Similarly in *Epistle* IX (which to some degree serves as an epitome of the *Symbolic Theology*), after giving an extensive list of scriptural symbols and explaining their use, Dionysius refers to the same scriptural text, saying, "And the world-ordering [κοσμουργία] itself of all that appears presents the invisible things of God, as Paul and the true word says" (Ep. IX.2, 1108B). Thus he explicitly grounds the scriptural use of sensible symbols in the metaphysics of being as theophany. This explains why, in describing the soul's three modes of cognition, Dionysius describes the outward, linear motion as an apprehension of "variegated and multiplied symbols," instead of referring directly to sense perception (DN IV.9, 705B). Because being is theophany, all sense perception is an apprehension of symbols of God.

In view of this metaphysical basis for his theory of symbols, Dionysius cannot and does not maintain the sharp distinction between intelligible "names" and sensible "symbols." In *Divine Names* I.6, explaining how "the theologians [i.e. the scriptural writers] . . . hymn [God] both as nameless and from every name," he passes with complete continuity from the series of names that will be discussed in the *Divine Names*, such as Being, Life, and Good, to a list of sensible names: "sun, star, fire, water, wind, dew, cloud, rock itself and stone, all beings and none of beings" (DN I.6, 596C). The theoretical ground of this continuity emerges explicitly in his account in the *Celestial Hierarchy* of "similar" and "dissimilar" representations, whether of angels or of God. "The mode of sacred revelation is twofold: on the one hand as like, proceeding through similar sacred-stamped images [ἱεροτύπων εἰκόνων], but on the other through dissimilar shape-makings, fashioned to what is altogether unlike and incongruous" (CH II.2–3, 140C). The "dissimilar" symbols are those that seem manifestly inappropriate or even repugnant in connection with the angels or God, such as wild beasts and inanimate things, while the "similar" ones are those that seem noble or exalted and hence appropriate to what they represent. This distinction thus to some degree parallels that between sensible and intelligible representations. But Dionysius goes on to explain that the seeming appropriateness of the "similar" symbols, including many of the intelligible names, is in fact a misleading appearance:

> Of course the mystical traditions of the revelatory oracles [i.e., the scriptures] at times hymn the blessedness of the thearchy beyond being as Word and Intellect and Being [λόγον καὶ νοῦν καὶ οὐσία] . . . and they shape it as Light and call it Life, such sacred formations being more reverent and seeming somehow superior to the shapings connected with matter [προσύλων μορφώσεων], but even so deficient in relation to the truth of the thearchic likeness. For it is above all being and life, no light characterizing it, every

word and intellect [λόγου καὶ νοῦ] incomparably [ἀσυγκρίτως] falling short of its likeness. (CH II.3, 140CD)

Since God is not any being or object of thought, it is as false, and false in the same sense, to say that God is Word, Mind, or Being as to say that he is lion, stone, fire, or worm.[3] All expressions of God, the exalted and intelligible no less than the lowly and sensible, are infinitely, and in that sense equally, inadequate, and hence all are "dissimilar."

For this reason Dionysius even says that the obviously "dissimilar" expressions are in fact more appropriate, as more clearly indicating the infinite otherness of all things from God: "If, then, the negations are true of divine things, but the affirmations are unsuitable to the hiddenness of ineffable things, the revelation concerning invisible things through dissimilar formations is rather more appropriate" (CH II.3, 141A). Even with regard to the angels, the seemingly "inappropriate" symbols are superior in that they are less likely to be taken literally as what the angels really are (CH II.3, 141AB).

Having explained that all expressions are infinitely inadequate to God, Dionysius then remarks, "Further, it is necessary to understand this too, that not even one of beings is altogether deprived of participation in the Beautiful, since as the truth of the oracles [i.e. the scriptures] says, 'all things are very beautiful' " (CH II.3, 141C, citing Genesis 1:31 [LXX]). Since all things exist only by participating in Beauty, or God, and thus are manifestations of God, nothing is absolutely to be despised and nothing is absolutely inappropriate or "dissimilar." That would be the case only if God were not genuinely transcendent but merely other, a different intelligible being set over against the rest of things. But since God is "all things in all things and nothing in any" (DN VII.3, 872A), it is as true, and true in the same sense, to say that he is lion, stone, fire, and worm as to say that he is Word, Mind, and Being. All expressions of God, the lowly and sensible no less than the exalted and intelligible, participate in him and are thus "similar."

Here, then, Dionysius explicitly overcomes any fundamental distinction between intelligible names and sensible symbols. All things, whether intelligible or sensible, are both "similar" and "dissimilar," and this is what it means to be a symbol. As beings, as finite, all things absolutely are not God himself, and thus are infinitely "dissimilar" or inappropriate; and as beings, as finite, all things are presentations of God and in this sense "similar" or appropriate. All the ways in which God is represented thus have the same ontological status. Although the word σύμβολον is confined to sensible representations, these are not fundamentally different in kind from the intelligible ones.[4] To insist on such a difference would be, once again, to regard God not as beyond being but as intelligible, as finite, as the proper object of some exalted mode of cognition. All things, then, are in effect symbols of God and are so used in the scriptures, and this is simply a restatement of the doctrine that being is theophany.

All symbols, in that they are both similar and dissimilar, at once reveal and conceal that which they symbolize, and this is the very nature of a symbol and hence of being as symbol. Not only does a symbol both reveal and conceal, but it does both in one: it conceals precisely in and as revealing, and reveals precisely in and as concealing. Every being, or symbol, is a differentiated expression, a presentation, a coming forth of God into openness, manifestness, availability. As such it reveals God, making him knowable in and as the content of that being. To know anything is to know God as manifest in that thing. The Platonic doctrine of participation, which Dionysius invokes in justifying the suitability of all things as symbols of God, makes it clear that the symbolized is not extrinsic to but present in the symbol,[5] that the symbol is a genuine presentation of the symbolized. But to reveal God in this way is to conceal him. For precisely as differentiated, as finite, and hence as available, as a presentation, every being, or symbol, is not God himself and thus conceals him, leaving him behind, inaccessible, in the dark. As Dionysius says, "Darkness becomes invisible by light, and more by much light; knowings [αἱ γνώσεις] make unknowing invisible, and many knowings more" (Ep. I, 1065A). Light, the content of all vision, by its presence conceals darkness, making it invisible. To apprehend a symbol, a manifestation, is to apprehend some being, and hence not God himself. The symbol or being, by providing content for thought, hides God from us. To know any thing is, *ipso facto*, not to know God. To engage in cognition at all is not to unknow, and the more multiple the cognition, as at the level of sense where we apprehend sensible symbols, the further removed it is from mystical union. Thus the revealing is the concealing.

But conversely, to conceal God in this way is to reveal him. Light makes darkness invisible; but then, the proper way, the only way to see darkness, is not to see. "We pray to come to [γενέσθαι][6] the darkness above light and through ungazing and unknowing to see and know the above seeing and knowing by not seeing and not knowing itself" (MT II, 1025A). Not to see *is* to see darkness. To leave darkness invisible, to conceal it, is thus to reveal it as darkness, and only so can it be revealed. A symbol, then, in being finite, available, in not being God and thus in leaving him behind, in concealing him, reveals him as beyond being and thought.[7] "For it is not possible that the thearchic ray illumine us otherwise than as anagogically cloaked in the variety of the sacred veils [Καὶ γὰρ οὐδὲ δυνατὸν ἑτέρως ἡμῖν ἐπιλάμψαι τὴν θεαρχικὴν ἀκτῖνα μὴ τῇ ποικιλίᾳ τῶν ἱερῶν παραπετασμάτων ἀναγωγικῶς περικεκαλυμμένην]" (CH I.2, 121B). It would be easy to overlook the paradox of this statement, taking it to mean merely that God is presented to us by means of symbols. What Dionysius actually says here, however, is that God *cannot* "illumine" us, i.e. be revealed, be known to us, except *by* being symbolically "veiled," i.e. hidden from us. Only by being concealed in symbols can God be revealed. For if he were not concealed, then what is revealed would be not God but some being, something which is and can be known. If we are truly to know God, if what is revealed is to be God himself, then what we know must be the unknowable, what is revealed must be concealed, for otherwise it would not be God that is known and revealed. Only by symbols is this possible. Hence, as Dionysius here indicates, there can be no non-symbolic knowledge of God, no knowledge of God without the concealment of symbolism. Only a symbol, in that *qua* symbol it conceals what it reveals, can make God known without objectifying him as a being, enabling us to know God without violating his unknowability, and thus truly to know God. The concealing is the revealing. Dionysius' doctrine of symbols is thus another expression of the principle that God is given to every mode of cognition, including sense perception, and is inaccessible to all cognition whatsoever.

There is no question, then, of stripping away all symbols so as to arrive at a direct, non-symbolic knowledge of God unveiled. Whatever is unveiled is not God. All knowledge involves symbols, having as its content being, not God. To transcend symbolism altogether, to remove all the veils, the beings, whereby God is revealed, would not be to know God directly, but to unknow, for apart from beings, or symbols, there is no content for knowledge. "We take away all things [τὰ πάντα ἀφαιροῦμεν], so that we may unhiddenly [ἀπερικαλύπτως] know that unknowing which is hidden [περικεκαλυμμένην] by all that is known in all beings, and may see the darkness beyond being which is concealed by all light in beings" (MT II, 1025B).[8] We might compare this "taking away all things" so as to "see" the divine darkness to unwrapping the Invisible Man of science fiction, who is rendered visible only by the coverings that give him determinate shape. When all the coverings have been removed and the man himself is laid bare, there is nothing left to see. The removal of all symbols is not a knowledge of God unveiled, as if God could be an object of knowledge, but the cessation of intellectual activities, the union above intellect, the darkness of unknowing.

The identity of concealing and revealing which is the essence of symbolism is captured in Dionysius' use of the word προβάλλειν.[9] Etymologically, this means "to throw forth," and so comes to means both "present, put forward, expose" and also "shield, screen, set up a defense."[10] The word thus carries two opposite meanings in one. Plotinus seems to use it in this way at least once, when he identifies the forms as the beautiful and then says, "That which is beyond this we call the nature of the Good, having the beautiful held as a screen [προβεβλημένον] before it" (I.6.9.37–39). It is not entirely clear that Plotinus intends the double meaning, for he may simply mean that the beautiful is "presented" or "projected" from the Good; but such a reading would accord with his doctrine that the forms, or the beautiful, at once manifest the Good and, since they are not the Good itself, conceal it.[11]

Dionysius repeatedly uses this word to express the two-in-one function of creatures as symbols, at once revealing and concealing God. In *Epistle* IX, after listing the many symbols of God found in scripture—which, let us remember, ultimately include all things—he says that these are

> sacred compositions of daring God-formation, manifest presenta-tions [φαινόμενα . . . προβεβλημένα] of hidden things, and multi-plications and divisions of single and indivisible things, and multiform shapings of formless and shapeless things; if anyone is able to see their hidden inner comeliness, he will find them all mystical and deiform and filled with much theological light. For let us not think that the appearances of the compositions [συνθημάτων[12]] are formulated for their own sakes, but that they screen [προβεβλῆσθαι] the knowledge of the unspoken and invisible to the many, lest the all-sacred things be accessible to the profane; but they are unhidden to only the genu-ine lovers of divinity, who do away with all childish imagination about the sacred symbols and are able to cross over, by simplicity of intellect and fittingness of contemplative power, to the simple and supernatural and exalted truth of the symbols. (Ep. IX.1, 1105BC)

A common reading of this passage takes it to mean, as on the surface it suggests, that the symbols present the knowledge of God to an intellectual elite ("the genuine lovers of divinity") and screen it from the many ("the profane").[13] This reading, however, does not do justice to Dionysius' use of the same word, within the space of six lines, to mean *both* "present" *and* "screen": we could as well say that the symbols are "manifest screens of hidden things," screening the hidden and simple precisely by being manifest and multiple, and that they "present the knowledge of the unspoken" to the many, keeping it from being profaned in that by presenting, they hide it. It is intrinsic to symbols to reveal and conceal in one; they do not simply reveal to some and simply conceal from others. All are called to "cross over" to the "truth" of the symbols, to ascend toward unknowing in receiving all things as symbols, and the distinction between "genuine lovers of divinity" and "the profane" simply recognizes different degrees in this ascent.[14] Shortly after-wards Dionysius uses 'προβάλλω' again to say that "the world-ordering itself of all that appears presents [προβέβληται] the invisible things of God (Ep. IX.2, 1108B)." The reference to Romans 1:20 may incline us to say "pre-sents" rather than "screens," but, in view of the already established identity of revealing and concealing, and the use of the word just above to indicate hiding as well as presenting, both meanings are present here: the things that appear at once present and screen the invisible things of God.[15]

The twofold meaning of 'προβάλλειν' is even more prominent in the *Divine Names*. Here Dionysius, explaining like Proclus that whatever pos-sesses a more specific perfection must first possess being, says that "before all the other participations of [God] being [τὸ εἶναι] is presented [προβέβληται]" (DN V.5, 820A). Therefore, "the beyond-goodness-itself is hymned . . . as presenting [προβαλλομένη] the first gift of being itself" (DN V.6, 820C). The very being of all things, then, and hence all their intelligible content, is a presentation which screens and a screen which presents God. In addressing the question of how we know God, therefore, Dionysius says that

> it is never true to say, then, that we know God; not from his nature, for this is unknowable and surpasses all reason and intellect; but from the order of all beings, as presented-as-a-screen [προβεβλημένης] from him, and having certain images and likenesses of his divine paradigms, we go up, by way and order according to our power, to the beyond all things, in the taking away and transcendence of all things[16] and in the cause of all things. Wherefore both in all things God is known and apart from all things. (DN VII.3, 869C–872A)

Here again, the order of all things is a presentation which screens God from us. It is immediately after this that Dionysius says that God is known by every mode of cognition and by none, that he is "known to all from all and to none from any." All beings, then, are προβεβλημένα, at once presentations and screens of God, and thus are symbols, revealing and concealing in one. Since "the being of all things is the divinity beyond being,"[17] every being is at once a presentation and a concealment of God.

The symbolic nature of being is most fully realized in the angels, because, as we have seen, they are beings in the fullest sense. From the Good, Dionysius says, it is given to them "to reveal in themselves the hidden Goodness, and to be angels as annunciative of the divine silence, and as presenting clear lights interpretive of that which is in the sanctuaries [τὸ ἐκφαίνειν ἐν ἑαυταῖς τὴν κρυφίαν ἀγαθότητα καὶ εἶναι ἀγγέλους ὥσπερ ἐξαγγελτικὰς τῆς θείας σιγῆς καὶ οἷον φῶτα φανὰ τοῦ ἐν ἀδύτοις ὄντος ἑρμενευτικὰ προβεβλημένας]" (DN IV.2, 696BC). Translation cannot fully capture the series of paradoxes contained in this sentence. The angels *reveal* what is *hidden*; they *announce*[18] the divine *silence*; they *present-as-screens* lights which *interpret* what is *inaccessible*. These paradoxes capture the very essence of symbolism: to hide what it reveals by revealing it and to reveal what it hides by hiding it. Any interpretation, in that it is not the meaning itself but an interpretation of it, leaves behind, renders inaccessible, the meaning which it presents. But in view of Dionysius' understanding of all being as theophany, and the doctrine that the angels possess in an eminent way all the perfections of lesser beings, this is true not only of the angels but, analogously, of all things. To be a being is to be a symbol, to interpret the inaccessible, to announce the divine silence.

Because of the identity between revealing and concealing in symbolism, there is no opposition between the symbolic knowledge of God in and from beings and the union with God in unknowing by the taking away of all beings. The ascent from sense to intellect to the union above intellect, in which unknowing is the culmination and enfolding of all knowledge, is also the ascent from sensible symbols to intellectual contemplation to unknowing: "Now [i.e. in the present age as distinct from the eschaton],[19] as far as is possible for us, we use proper symbols for divine things, and from these again we are drawn up analogously to the simple and unified truth of the intellectual visions, and, after every intellection of deiform things in us, ceasing our intellectual activities, we apply ourselves, so far as is right, to the ray beyond being" (DN I.4, 592CD). In this ascent, the sensible symbols are not merely left behind. For the very nature of a symbol is such that to know it is to unknow it. To understand a symbol as a symbol is to ignore it, to attend not to the symbol as an object in itself but rather to the meaning it concealingly reveals. Conversely, to attend to a symbol as an object in its own right is to fail to know it as a symbol. To a person who cannot read, for example, a written word is an object consisting of ink on paper. But a reader, in the very act of perceiving the word, is oblivious to the word as such and attentive only to its meaning. The more he ignores the word as an object, the more deeply immersed he is in the meaning, the more perfectly he is reading and the better he is knowing the word as what it really is, as a symbol. The non-reader might argue that the reader is simply disregarding the word in favor of something else; this is precisely the attitude of those who see in the Dionysian ascent from sensible symbols to intellectual contemplation to mystical unknowing a rejection or abandonment of sense and symbol. But in fact, of course, it is the reader, who in perceiving the word unknows it in itself, who truly knows and appreciates the word as word.

Therefore, as Dionysius says, "It is necessary, then, for us, contrary to the popular assumption about them, to cross over into [εἴσω . . . διαβαίνειν] the sacred symbols in a way befitting the sacred, and not despise them, because they are the offspring and impressions of the divine characters, and manifest images of the unspoken and supernatural visions" (Ep. IX.2, 1108C).[20] The ascent from symbols is the penetration into them. To rise to unknowing, to remove all the veils, to take away all things, is most fully to enter into the symbols, or beings. At the peak, therefore, we find the perfect union of knowing and unknowing, in which all beings are most perfectly known in being wholly unknown just as a word is most perfectly known in being ignored, because all beings are nothing but symbols of God.[21] The mystical union is not a non-symbolic encounter with God as an object other than all things. It is rather a penetration into all things to God who, as "all things in all things and nothing in any," is at once revealed and concealed by all things. To ascend to unknowing is to see the darkness hidden and revealed by all light, to hear all things "announce the divine silence."

Although we have for the most part left aside the specifically Christian aspects of Dionysius' thought in order to highlight its philosophical dimension, we may note in conclusion that Dionysius recapitulates his understanding of being as theophanic symbol in his account of the incarnation:

Concerning the love for man in Christ, even this, I think, the theology suggests: that out of the hidden the beyond-being has come forth into manifestation according to us [ἐκ τοῦ κρυφίου τὸν ὑπερούσιον εἰς τὴν καθ' ἡμᾶς ἐμφάνειαν], becoming a being [οὐσιωθέντα] in a human way. But he is hidden even after the manifestation, or, that I may speak more divinely, even in the manifestation. For even this of Jesus is hidden, and the mystery in him is brought forth to no reason or intellect, but what is said remains ineffable and what is thought, unknowable. (Ep. III, 1069B)

The incarnation, then, is the coming forth of God into manifestness. But this, as we have seen, is what all reality is. So also, by saying that God is "hidden . . . in the manifestation," Dionysius restates his doctrine of being as symbol, at once revealing and concealing God. Here as elsewhere Dionysius expresses the incarnation with the formula "the beyond-being becomes a being." "From the substance of men the beyond-being is made a being [ὁ ὑπερούσιος οὐσιωμένος] . . . Truly coming into being in a manner above being he is made a being [εἰς οὐσίαν ἀληθῶς ἐλθὼν ὑπὲρ οὐσίαν οὐσιώθη]" (Ep. IV, 1072B; see also DN II.9, 648A). This formula assimilates the incarnation to Dionysius' Neoplatonic metaphysics, in which God is manifest in and as each and every being, "all things in all things," and thus could be said to be made a being in them.[22]

The incarnation is thus seen to be fully consonant with, and indeed the fullest expression of, the Neoplatonic philosophical conception of God as not any being but the power of all things, as pure Giving, as Overflow, or, in Dionysius' terms, as Love.[23] In this sense it is true, as has often been remarked, that Dionysius understands the incarnation in terms of the Neoplatonic metaphysics of procession and reversion.[24] But this need not mean that the incarnation is merely another procession, additional to and parallel with the universal, creative procession of God to all things and all things from God. Rather, Dionysius' discussions of the incarnation suggest that the whole of being, as theophany, is to be understood in incarnational terms, and that God incarnate, as the "principle and perfection of all hierarchies" (EH I.2, 373B),[25] is the fullness of reality itself. Being as symbol, as theophany, and hence as being, is perfectly realized in Christ, in God incarnate, the finite being which is God-made-manifest.

CONCLUSION

The entire vision of reality articulated in this study arises from the single fundamental principle that may be called Parmenides' Law: τὸ γὰρ αὐτὸ νοεῖν ἔστιν τε καὶ εἶναι: to be is to be intelligible. The premise that being must conform to thought has sometimes been regarded as the central weakness of Neoplatonism, which is thus accused of building up an imaginary structure of reality as a mere projection of the workings of consciousness. As E. R. Dodds says of Proclus' system,

> [I]ts fundamental weakness seems to me to lie in the assumption that the structure of the cosmos exactly reproduces the structure of Greek logic. All rationalist systems are to some extent exposed to criticism on these lines; but in Proclus ontology becomes so manifestly the projected shadow of logic as to present what is almost a *reductio ad absurdum* of rationalism . . . [T]he cause is but a reflection of the 'because,' and the Aristotelian apparatus of genus, species and differentia is transformed into an objectively conceived hierarchy of entities or forces.[1]

Here Dodds puts his finger on the operative principle of Proclus' thought and indeed of all Neoplatonism. But what he fails to realize is that the structure of reality as understood by Neoplatonism matches not merely a culturally and historically specific phenomenon called "Greek logic," but the universal nature of thought as such, which necessarily apprehends its objects as beings, characterized and constituted by certain determinations in virtue of which they are what they are and so are beings at all. Dodds' argument is parallel to Nietzsche's remark that "we are not getting rid of God because we still believe in grammar":[2] the Neoplatonic ascent to the One as the transcendent ground of which reality is the manifestation, is a working out of the intelligibility of being, its conformity to the structure of thought ("grammar").

The alternative to the principle that to be is to be intelligible, therefore, is the nihilism which afflicts so much of contemporary thought and culture. For if being is not what is apprehended by thought, then thought does not apprehend being. This in effect means that there is no being, since whatever we call "being" is not being but a projection, interpretation, illusion—in short, nothing. If reality is not as thought must apprehend it, then there is no such thing as reality. Conversely, if thought is not the apprehension of being, then all thought, in that it never apprehends being, is illusory. Nihilism may indeed be said to consist most fundamentally in the denial of the intelligibility of being.[3] This is precisely the condition of much contemporary reflection, to the extent that it consists in the claim that we can never "break out" of our own language and thought to get at reality. As Plotinus saw, only if being is always already given in thought can we avoid the nihilistic conclusion that "there is no truth."[4] The Neoplatonic vision takes as its starting point the intelligibility, which is to say the reality, of being.

From the intelligibility of being follows its necessary multiplicity and determinateness, and consequently its status as dependent or derivative, as differentiated presentation, as manifestation. Hence Neoplatonism arrives at a God who is "beyond being" in a stricter, stronger, more absolute sense than is often recognized. This philosophy thus surpasses any "onto-theology," whether a crude form which conceptualizes God as the "first and highest being," or a more sophisticated and supposedly apophatic form which self-contradictorily identifies God as "a being beyond being," something which *is* albeit in a superior "way." In Neoplatonism, in Plotinus, Proclus, and Dionysius, divine transcendence is conceived so radically that it coincides with divine immanence. Transcendence and immanence are not opposed to each other, nor do they merely mitigate or even complement each other;[5] they are, rather, strictly identical.[6] Conceived Neoplatonically, transcendence in no way implies separation or duality between God and the world, which would leave the world itself godless and hence unworlded and thus lead to nihilism. Rather, the transcendent is precisely that which is given through, in, and as the world. The more transcendent God is, the more—not the less!—intimately present he is to the world; the absolutely transcendent God of Neoplatonism is therefore nothing but what is manifest in and as all things, "all things in all things and nothing in any" (DN VII.3, 872A). Thinking, therefore, must always look "beyond" the being which it apprehends to that which is never merely "present" either as a member of the world or as something separate from the world, but is always presented and so always equally and infinitely "absent."

As such formulations suggest, Dionysius' thought is worth examining not only for its intrinsic value and historical significance, but also for the contributions it can make to contemporary discourse. In the "postmodern" era, characterized by a salutary critique and even repudiation of the "modernity" that dominated Western culture from the later Middle Ages to the twentieth century and is still largely with us, Dionysius offers, from within the Western tradition itself, an alternative which is not proto-modern but rather radically pre-modern and un-modern. The togetherness of being and thinking and the interpretation of being as appearance, which is so central to Neoplatonism, including Dionysius, opens a major area of dialogue between Dionysius and recent phenomenological thought, overcoming the characteristically modern duality between subject and object. More specifically, Dionysius' philosophy can converse fruitfully with such Heideggerian themes as the critique of "onto-theology" and of "metaphysics of presence" and the dialectic of revealing and concealing. Heidegger shows how "metaphysics of presence," which on his view dominates the whole of Western thought, leads to a technological comportment toward being in which being is revealed only as *Bestand*, resources or stockpile, and how this technological instrumentalization of being makes possible modern science and leads inevitably to nihilism. As the alternative to this ultimately nihilistic, scientific-technological stance toward being, Dionysius offers a contemplative-liturgical stance in which being is not an object for mastery and exploitation but a gift which is received only in being given and a symbol which is known only in being unknown. His thought can thus also contribute to contemporary reflection on technology and the related area of "environmental philosophy." The Dionysian, Neoplatonic understanding of all things, including animals, plants, and minerals, as theophanies which analogously think, live, and love, may be set against the objectifying and reductionist view of nature which has led to its exploitation and destruction, and which is largely the result of a very different religious philosophy that opposes the natural both to the human and to the divine. In opposition to such a view, Dionysius and his Neoplatonic predecessors offer a compelling and philosophically grounded vision of all reality as the presence and manifestation of transcendent divinity.

NOTES

NOTE ON TRANSLATIONS

1. *The Works of Dionysius the Areopagite*, tr. John Parker (London: Parker, 1897).

2. *Pseudo-Dionysius: The Complete Works* (New York and Mahwah: Paulist, 1987).

3. Plotinus, ed. and tr. A. H. Armstrong, Loeb Classical Library (Cambridge: Harvard University Press, 1966–1988; London: William Heinemann, 1966–1988).

4. Proclus, *The Elements of Theology*, ed. and tr. E. R. Dodds, 2nd ed. (Oxford: Oxford University Press, 1963).

INTRODUCTION

1. I omit the prefix "pseudo-" on account of its verbal awkwardness and potentially pejorative connotations.

2. If I have disregarded Dionysius' background in earlier Christian thought, which has been recently and extensively investigated by Alexander Golitzin, *Et Introibo ad Altare Dei: The Mystagogy of Dionysius Areopagita, with Special Reference to Its Predecessors in the Eastern Christian Tradition* (Thessalonica: Patriarchikon Idryma Paterikon Meleton, 1994), this is not because it is unreal or unimportant, but because it does not contribute to the specifically philosophical understanding of Dionysius.

3. For Proclus' thought I have relied chiefly on the *Elements of Theology* because this work most clearly and systematically presents the fundamental structural principles of his metaphysics, and it is precisely these principles, rather than the detailed elaboration of his philosophy in the *Platonic Theology* and the commentaries, that contribute most to a philosophical understanding of Dionysius.

4. For the continuing life of this condemnation, see the survey of the literature on Dionysius in Golitzin, *Et Introibo*, 22–42.

5. A rare exception is Werner Beierwaltes, *Platonismus im Christentum* (Frankfurt am Main: Klostermann, 2001), 84, who expressly concludes "*Dionysius: Christianus simulque vere Platonicus.*" Nonetheless, even Beierwaltes says this only after arguing for a significant difference between Dionysius and his Neoplatonic predecessors. See below, 126 n. 33.

6. Notable examples of this approach are Bernhard Brons, *Gott und die Seienden* (Göttingen: Vandenhoeck and Ruprecht, 1976), and Jean Vanneste, *Le mystère de Dieu* (Paris: Desclée de Brouwer, 1959).

7. Examples of this approach include Endre von Ivanka, "Inwieweit ist Pseudo-Dionysius Neuplatoniker?" in *Plato Christianus* (Einsiedeln: Verlag, 1964), 262–89, and, to a lesser extent and with more sympathy for Neoplatonism, Golitzin, *Et Introibo*.

8. Golitzin, *Et Introibo*, 395, recognizes the difficulty here: "That element of the Dionysian synthesis which has been most to the fore in the scholarship of the past century is the matter of the CD's relationship to Neoplatonism. Here we confront a shibboleth that has long troubled the investigation of Christian thought from its beginnings down to the Middle Ages: that is, the assumption that the Platonic tradition and Christianity are mutually exclusive." He goes on to deny this assumption. Nonetheless, in reclaiming Dionysius as genuinely Christian, Golitzin still finds it necessary to argue that his thought is significantly different from Neoplatonism.

9. For a discussion of contemporary retrievals of Neoplatonism in relation to recent philosophy, see Wayne J. Hankey, "Why Heidegger's 'History' of Metaphysics is Dead," *American Catholic Philosophical Quarterly* 78 (2004): 425–43.

10. See, however, 122 n. 24, on the Trinity, and 108–109, on the incarnation.

11. For a recent theory of the philosophical structure of the *Divine Names* as a whole, and a discussion of earlier theories, see Christian Schäfer, *The Philosophy of Dionysius the Areopagite: An Introduction to the Structure and the Content of the Treatise "On the Divine Names"* (Leiden: Brill, 2006).

12. I refrain from speculation as to the author's "real" identity, both because such speculation is philosophically irrelevant and because it presumptuously assumes that the author must be someone who is independently known to history under another name. Cf. the apt remarks by Henri-Dominique Saffrey, "New Objective Links between the Pseudo-Dionysius and Proclus," in *Neoplatonism and Christian Thought*, ed. Dominic O'Meara (Albany: State University of New York Press, 1982), 65, and by Hans Urs von Balthasar, "Denys," in *The Glory of the Lord: A Theological Aesthetics*, vol. 2, *Studies in Theological Style: Clerical Styles*, tr. A. Louth et al. (San Francisco and New York: Ignatius, 1984), 146.

13. See Balthasar, "Denys," 147, on "the bad humour and resentment with which the CD [*Corpus Dionysiacum*] is often approached;" Alexander Golitzin, review of *Pseudo-Dionysius: A Commentary on the Texts and an Introduction to Their Influence*, by Paul Rorem, *Mystics Quarterly* 21 (1995): 29–30, on the thinly concealed "freight of venom" in Rorem's superficially neutral study; and, more generally, Golitzin, *Et Introibo*, 21: "[W]hether admitted or not, every attempt to date that has sought to deal with the CD as a single body of thought has . . . engaged the particular scholar's sympathies and presuppositions—most often in a negative manner—to a considerably greater degree than were he dealing with an ancient author whose purposes in writing (or even name) were clearly advertised."

CHAPTER ONE

1. This is due in large part to the Heideggerian critique of "onto-theology" and "metaphysics of presence," and the related deconstructionist assault on "logocentrism," as well as to a more generalized postmodern dissatisfaction with positive, closed "systems" in theology or philosophy and distrust of language and thought. For discussions of negative theology in general, and Dionysius in particular, in relation to deconstruction, see Jacques Derrida, "La différance," in *Marges de la philosophie* (Paris: Editions de Minuit, 1972), and "How to Avoid Speaking: Denials," tr. Ken Frieden, in *Languages of the Unsayable: The Play of Negativity in Literature and Literary Theory*, ed. Sanford Budick and Wolfgang Iser (New York: Columbia University Press, 1989). See also the essays in *Derrida and Negative Theology*, ed. Harold Coward and Toby Foshay (Albany: State University of New York Press, 1992). For a discussion of

Dionysius in relation to Heidegger, see esp. Jean-Luc Marion, *L'idole et la distance* (Paris: Editions Bernard Grasset, 1977); English translation *The Idol and Distance*, tr. Thomas A. Carlson (New York: Fordham University Press, 2001).

2. See *inter alia* Jan Miernowski, *Le dieu néant: Théologies négatives à l'aube des temps modernes* (Leiden: Brill, 1998), and Deirdre Carabine, *The Unknown God: Negative Theology in the Platonic Tradition: Plato to Eriugena* (Louvain: Peeters, 1995).

3. Parmenides, fr. 2.7–8 and fr. 3, in Hermann Diels and Walther Kranz, eds., *Die Fragmente der Vorsokratiker*, 7th ed. (Berlin: Weidmannsche Verlagsbuchhandlung, 1954), 1:231.

4. "Being, however, falls first in the conception of intellect . . . Wherefore being is the proper object of intellect." Thomas Aquinas, *Summa Theologica* Ia, 5, 2, resp.

5. Plato's point is exceptionally well expressed by J. N. Findlay, "Towards a Neo-Neo-Platonism," in *Ascent to the Absolute* (London: Allen and Unwin, 1970), 252: "[W]hile we may be inclined to look in the direction of particular embodiment for a paradigm of what is, we soon find that we cannot successfully pin down such particularity in its purity, or identify it in varying contexts and occasions. All that is substantial, invariant in it is a pattern, a character, a set of suches which we hail and name on every occasion of their appearance. This character or pattern is all that we can grasp and handle in thought on many occasions, and introduce to and consider with others: the existence of an individual seems to be no more than the fact that certain identifiable, recognizable universals are instantiated and reinstantiated."

6. Plato makes much the same point again at *Timaeus* 46e3–7.

7. The "forms of evils" that Plato often mentions, e.g. the unjust, the ugly, etc., can best be understood as included in their good opposites as possible modes of deviation from them. "It is necessary that the same person [who knows what is best] also know what is worse" (*Phaedo* 97d4). For this interpretation of the forms of evils, see J. N. Findlay, *Plato: The Written and Unwritten Doctrines* (London: Routledge and Kegan Paul, 1974), 43, 139, 375.

8. Τὸ ὄν here means not "that which is" but "beingness," the status or condition of being a being, just as, for example, τὸ καλόν can mean either "that which is beautiful" or "beauty." For another instance of this alteration in Plato's usage of τὸ ὄν, see *Sophist* 250b7 et seq. and the remark on this passage by F. M. Cornford, *Plato's Theory of Knowledge* (London: Kegan Paul, Trench, Trubner, 1935), 250–51.

9. The term means primarily "age" but comes to connote "dignity" or "rank." English "seniority" thus corresponds closely in meaning.

10. According to Aristotle and other ancient reports, Plato identified the Good with the One, and this identification is strongly suggested in the *Republic*. See Findlay, *Plato*, 184–85, and Giovanni Reale, *Toward a New Interpretation of Plato*, tr. John R. Catan and Richard Davies (Washington: Catholic University of America Press, 1997), 204–09.

11. The relation between Plato's Νοῦς or Demiurge and the forms is highly controversial. The current consensus, on the whole, is that they are separate; but see Eric D. Perl, "The Demiurge and the Forms: A Return to the Ancient Reading of Plato's *Timaeus*," *Ancient Philosophy* 18 (1998): 81–92. See also A. Diès, *Autour de Platon*, 2nd ed. (Paris: Belles Lettres, 1972), 549–51; Jean Pépin, "Éléments pour une histoire de la relation entre l'intelligence et l'intelligible chez Platon et dans le néo-platonisme," *Revue philosophique* 146 (1956): 39–44; and Cornelia J. de Vogel, *Philosophia I: Studies in Greek Philosophy* (Assen: Van Gorcum, 1970), 194–209.

12. Plotinus here speaks of the One constituting being as the definer of the "indefinite dyad"; but as he explains in II.4.5, this indefinite dyad or "intelligible matter" is nothing but the forms themselves, or being, considered *qua* receptive of determination from the One.

13. Cf. V.5.4.13–14: the One is "measure and not measured," i.e. provides determination to all things but itself has none.

14. Textually speaking, Plotinus' radically negative doctrine of the One is drawn to a considerable extent from the first hypothesis of Plato's *Parmenides*, as has been recognized ever since the seminal article by E. R. Dodds, "The *Parmenides* of Plato and the Origin of the Neoplatonic 'One,' " *Classical Quarterly* 22 (1928): 129–43. Philosophically speaking, however, Plotinus' doctrine is, as represented here, based on the argument that being *qua* intelligible is necessarily finite and hence derivative.

15. John Rist, *Plotinus: The Road to Reality* (Cambridge: Cambridge University Press, 1967), 24–37. Cf. Lloyd Gerson, *Plotinus* (London and New York: Routledge, 1994), 26: "[T]hat the One is beyond essence does not mean that it is beyond existence or being altogether. Suggestions to the contrary are just misunderstandings of Plotinus' so-called 'negative theology.' What Plotinus rejects in reference to the One is language that implies limitedness or complexity." But Plotinus' point is that existence or being necessarily implies both limitedness and complexity; and this is not simply a restriction on his use of the term 'being,' but a philosophical consequence of the identity of being and intelligibility.

16. Cf. A. H. Armstrong, "Negative Theology, Myth, and Incarnation," in *Neoplatonism and Christian Thought*, ed. Dominic O'Meara (Albany: State University of New York Press, 1982), 217: "It seems that the traditional terms 'beyond being,' 'nonbeing,' or 'nothing' applied to God are most significant when used in their proper Hellenic context in which being is closely correlated with intelligibility: real being is intelligible being. They mean, then, that God is not a somebody or something who can be discursively defined or discerned with intuitive precision. It is not that his intelligibility transcends our limited and fallen human intelligences, but that he has no intelligible content." For comparably radical (although not identical) readings of Plotinus' "negative theology" (or "negative henology," if "theology" is assumed to posit God as in any sense a supreme being), see Reiner Schürmann, "L'hénologie comme dépassement de la métaphysique," *Etudes philosophiques* 37 (1982): 331–50; Jean-Marc Narbonne, "Heidegger et le néoplatonisme," *Quaestio* 1 (2001): 55–82; and idem, *Hénologie, ontologie, et Ereignis (Plotin—Proclus—Heidegger)* (Paris: Les Belles Lettres, 2001).

17. See V.3.16.15–16: "There must therefore be a concentration into One, really outside all multiplicity and any simplicity whatsoever [ἁπλότητος ἡστινοσοῦν]." Contrast Gerson, *Plotinus*, 16, and Rist, *Plotinus*, 25: "Why does Plotinus generally call it 'the One'? Surely because it is exactly what it is, an entirely indivisible unity."

18. Vladimir Lossky, *The Mystical Theology of the Eastern Church* (Crestwood, NY: St. Vladimir's Seminary Press, 1976), 31, attempting to contrast the One of Plotinus with the God of Dionysius, fails to note this: "In his refusal to attribute to God the properties which make up the matter of affirmative theology, Dionysius is aiming expressly at the neo-platonist definitions: 'He is neither One, nor Unity.' " In fact, in negating the name 'One' Dionysius is simply following the precepts of Plotinus.

19. This is not to say that Plotinus' mysticism is in the least anti-intellectual. As we shall see in chapter 6, for both Plotinus and Dionysius the soul's meta-noetic union with the One is not a rejection or abandonment of intellection, but its proper culmination.

20. Dionysius' doctrine is, of course, drawn more immediately from Proclus and, in the case of his extreme negative formulations, from Damascius, than from Plotinus (although there is no doubt that he was directly familiar with the *Enneads*). For the influence of Damascius on Dionysius, see Salvatore Lilla, "Pseudo-Denys l'Aréopagite, Porphyre et Damascius," in *Denys l'Aréopagite et sa posterité en Orient et en Occident*, ed. Ysabel de Andia (Paris: Institut d'Etudes Augustiennes, 1977), 117–52. Here, however, we may pass directly from Plotinus to Dionysius because, while Dionysius' formulations may be drawn more from Proclus and Damascius than from Plotinus, the philosophical argumentation by which these doctrines are reached is already fully present in Plotinus. The examination of Damascius as a textual source for Dionysius would thus contribute little to a philosophical understanding of his position.

21. Contrast e.g. Paul Rorem, *Pseudo-Dionysius: A Commentary on the Texts and an Introduction to Their Influence* (New York and Oxford: Oxford University Press, 1993), 213: "Negation is a *human* concept, and thus cannot capture an infinite and transcendent God . . . Negation is negated and the *human* mind, befuddled, falls silent" (my italics). But in fact, for Dionysius as for Plotinus, human concepts and minds are unable to capture God, not because they are human, but because they are concepts and minds. Cf. n. 16 in this chapter.

22. See Derrida, "La différance," 31: "Negative theology [is] always concerned with disengaging . . . a superessentiality beyond the finite categories of essence and existence, that is of presence, and eager always to remember that if the predicate is refused to God, this is to recognize for him a superior, inconceivable, ineffable mode of being." This is simply an (all too common) misinterpretation of negative theology; see above, 11–12, and 118. If to be is to be intelligible, then an "inconceivable, ineffable mode of being" is a contradiction in terms. Cf. Derrida, "How to Avoid Speaking," 7–8: negative theology "seems to reserve beyond all positive predication, beyond all negation, even beyond being, some hyperessentiality—a being beyond being." This, again, is not true for the negative theology of Plotinus or of Dionysius.

23. Fran O'Rourke, *Pseudo-Dionysius and the Metaphysics of Aquinas* (Leiden: Brill, 1992), 203, sees this as a weakness in Dionysius and the whole Greek tradition: "For Dionysius, being has of necessity the status of a creature . . . That is to say, Dionysius did not have a fully developed appreciation of the absolute and transcendental nature of Being. Greek philosophy as a whole had not yet discovered the transcendent or universal and analogical value of Being, i.e. that as a concept unrestricted in itself, 'being' adequately expresses the reality both of creatures and of God while yet allowing their radical distinction. It failed, therefore, to harmonise faithfully within a unified order both the finite and infinite character of reality." But the Greek position is no mere inadequacy, but a strict consequence of the principle that to be is to be intelligible and hence finite. To embrace God and creation, the infinite and the finite, "within a unified order" is to render the infinite finite and violate divine transcendence. The very expression "the reality both of creatures and of God" is inadmissible, for it treats God as one member of a larger totality and subordinates God to a term more universal than himself, viz. "reality." This is precisely why Plotinus and Dionysius refuse to predicate "reality" or "being" of the One, or God.

24. Plotinus himself uses such a formula at V.3.14.7, but this must be qualified in light of his more careful statements that even negations must be negated so that we transcend thought altogether.

25. For this reason, nothing (i.e. no being) can be ineffable. Cf. Carl R. Kordig, "The Mathematics of Mysticism: Plotinus and Proclus," in *The Structure of Being*, ed. R. Baine Harris (Albany: State University of New York Press, 1982), 116–17: "Proclus and Plotinus claim that no descriptive predicate whatsoever applies to the One . . . Now let us introduce a new term 'Proclusian' in the following way: for any *x*, *x* is Proclusian if and only if *x* is such that no descriptive predicate applies to it . . . The One of Plotinus and Proclus is such that no descriptive predicate applies to it; therefore . . . the One is Proclusian. But since 'Proclusian' itself is a descriptive predicate, it also follows that the One is not Proclusian. But strictly speaking this is a contradiction, which is absurd. Proclus'—and Plotinus'—claim that no descriptive predicate whatsoever applies to the One leads to contradiction and must therefore be abandoned." This argument is flawed because the One is not "any *x*." Kordig fails to hear the silence in all that Proclus and Plotinus say about the One, *including* the claim that no descriptive predicate applies to it. He continues, "Proclus ends his *Commentary* [on Plato's *Parmenides*] with two sentences that succinctly express the principal theme and outlook of the Neoplatonic tradition: 'For by means of a negation Parmenides has removed all negations. With silence he concludes the contemplation of the One.' Now a silence justified by irrational means (i.e. by untenable claims and bad arguments) is not really justified. It is an irrational silence." The Neoplatonic silence, however, is not irrational, but is justified by Kordig's own argument. Precisely because nothing can truly be described as ineffable, the only recourse is silence.

26. For a comparable reading of Dionysius, see John Jones, "The Ontological Difference for St. Thomas and Pseudo-Dionysius," *Dionysius* 4 (1980): 119–32, and idem, "A Non-Entitative Understanding of Be-ing and Unity: Heidegger and Neoplatonism," *Dionysius* 6 (1982): 94–110.

27. Jean-Luc Marion, *Analogie et dialectique: Essais de théologie fondamentale* (Geneva: Labor et Fides, 1982), 20–21.

CHAPTER TWO

1. Cf. Jean-Luc Marion, *The Idol and Distance*, tr. Thomas A. Carlson (New York: Fordham University Press, 2001), 152: "If one means by *Aitia*, when applied to God, the modern 'cause of self and the world,' then one most certainly falls back among the idols of the divine. But the cause intervenes here in order to mark precisely the reverse: namely, that we have no naming suitable to God, not even in negation."

2. Cf. Plotinus, V.1.7.24–27, quoted above, 20: "Being . . . must be fixed by limit and stability; and stability in the intelligible world is limitation and shape, *and it is by these that it receives existence*" (my italics).

3. This phrase, although not the interpretation of Plotinus which I use it to express, is borrowed from Michael Wagner, "Vertical Causation in Plotinus," in *The Structure of Being*, ed. R. Baine Harris (Albany: State University of New York Press, 1982), 51–72.

4. Instrumental dative: *Greater Hippias* 287c1–d1, 289d2, 294b1–5; *Euthyphro* 6d11. δι᾽ ὅ: *Greater Hippias* 288a10; *Meno* 72c8. For both formulations together, see *Phaedo* 101a2–5.

5. On the transcendence-and-immanence of Plato's forms, see Eric D. Perl, "The Presence of the Paradigm: Immanence and Transcendence in Plato's Theory of Forms," *The Review of Metaphysics* 53 (1999): 339–62. See also Findlay, *Plato*, 36, and Reale, *New Interpretation*, 127–30.

6. The "receptacle" of the *Timaeus* is not another component of sensible things, but merely the "place" or "space" in which forms appear. Plato expressly identifies bodies, or sensible things, not as composites of form-appearances and the receptacle, but as nothing but likenesses or appearances of the forms. See *Timaeus* 50b6–c5, 52c2–4.

7. See R. Patterson, *Image and Reality in Plato's Metaphysics* (Indianapolis: Hackett, 1985), 3–4, 20–22.

8. Cf. John N. Deck, *Nature, Contemplation, and the One* (Burdett, NY: Larson, 1991), 124–25.

9. The image of being as "under pressure" suggests the One making being by providing "shape" or determination.

10. Dodds, *Elements of Theology*, 252, remarks that this doctrine "is accommodated to the more rigid theory of 'unparticipated' and 'participated' Forms (prop. 23)"; but this seems arbitrary. We could as well, or better, say that the "rigid" distinction between participated and unparticipated terms is "accommodated" to the simultaneity of transcendence and immanence.

11. Cf. John Dillon's remark in this context in the introduction to Proclus, *Commentary on Plato's Parmenides*, tr. Glenn R. Morrow and John M. Dillon (Princeton: Princeton University Press, 1987), xx: "The extreme realism of Proclus' philosophical position leads to his postulation of distinct entities answering to each aspect of an hypostasis, but things become clearer if we think of them as just aspects after all."

12. These terms are, of course, taken from medieval Latin Neoplatonism. But the anachronistic terminology is justified in that it provides a succinct and accurate articulation of Plotinus' thought. The concept of *complicatio-explicatio* is entirely Plotinian even if the words are not. See Thomas P. McTighe, "A Neglected Feature of Neoplatonic Metaphysics," in *Christian Spirituality and the Culture of Modernity: The Thought of Louis Dupré*, ed. Peter J. Casarella and George P. Schner (Grand Rapids: Eerdmans, 1998), 27–49.

13. See VI.9.2.44–47: "The [O]ne then cannot be all things, for so it would be no longer one; and it cannot be intellect, for in this way it would be all things since intellect is all things; and it cannot be being; for being is all things."

14. The concluding phrase could also be translated, "in the expression." For Intellect as the λόγος of the One, i.e. its expression in intelligible multiplicity, see V.1.6.45–46.

15. On this point see Eric D. Perl, " 'Power of All Things': The One as Pure Giving in Plotinus," *American Catholic Philosophical Quarterly* 71 (1997): 308.

16. Λόγος, in Plotinus, implies a more multiple and differentiated expression or presentation of a more simple and unified principle.

17. Proclus, *Commentary on Plato's Parmenides*, 1168–9, p. 520. Obviously "being one" is also a phrase taken "from the realm of beings."

18. The phrase "τὰ πάντα ἐν πᾶσι" is of course one of Dionysius' favorite scriptural citations (I Cor. 15:28), but Dionysius characteristically transposes the eschatological future into the metaphysical present.

19. "Powers": DN II.7, 645A; XI.6, 956A. "Participations": DN II.5, 644A; II.7, 645A; V.5, 820A. "Processions": DN I.4, 589D; II.4, 640D; II.11, 649B; V.1, 816B; V.2, 816D. "Providences": DN I.8, 597A; V.2, 817A. "Manifestations": DN II.4, 641A. "Distributions": DN II.5, 644A; II.11, 649C.

20. This Platonic term for the making of the world connotes making by giving intelligible determination.

21. The phrase "the measure of beings," derived from Plato (*Laws* 716c4) via Plotinus (e.g., V.5.4.14; VI.8.18.3) again implies the idea of God as the determination of all things.

22. This difference is the central thesis of E. Corsini, *Il trattato 'De Divinis nominibus' dello Pseudo-Dionigi e i commenti neoplatonici al Parmenide* (Turin: Giappichelli, 1962). See Gersh, *From Iamblichus to Eriugena*, 11. Gersh adds, "The transformation here . . . renders the First Principle of Christian Neoplatonism self-contradictory in a way that its pagan equivalent was not." But the verbal self-contradiction can be interpreted, as here, in a non-self-contradictory way.

23. Cf. the passage cited above, 29, in which Dionysius says that the λόγοι of all things preexist in God "uniformly," without distinction.

24. This "divine difference" which is constitutive of all things has nothing to do with the trinitarian differentiation of Father, Son, and Holy Spirit. Dionysius explains that all the "names" to be discussed in the *Divine Names*, the names of God drawn from beings, are common to all three Persons (DN II.1, 636C, 637C; II.3, 640B). The Godhead *simpliciter*—i.e. all three Persons indifferently, not the Father uniquely—corresponds to the Neoplatonic One. The production of being is common to all three Persons (DN II.5, 644A), and being proceeds from, or is the manifestation of, all three Persons indifferently. Unlike Augustine and Eriugena, Dionysius expressly does *not* introduce the trinitarian differences into his account of being as theophany. Cf. Balthasar, "Denys," 156: "Denys strictly denies any distinction between the functions and spheres of the three divine Persons in this world," and ibid., 184–85: "[A]ny theology of an *imago trinitatis* in the creature is strictly rejected . . . And this rejection is the work of a pupil of Proclus for whom the whole structure of being and the world has a triadic structure! One senses what sort of ascesis the Areopagite imposed on himself with this constant renunciation . . . Only by directing our gaze upwards to the transcendent unity do we look in the direction of the trinitarian mystery." This is not to say that Dionysius exalts divine unity or simplicity over the trinitarian distinctions, since Dionysius' God, like the One of Plotinus, is neither one nor many, neither simple nor complex. "The cause of all things is not one, one of the many, but before every one and multiplicity and determinative of every one and multiplicity" (DN XIII.2, 977CD), and hence, "while hymned as monad and triad [μονὰς . . . καὶ τριὰς], the divinity above all things is neither monad nor triad known among us or any other of beings" (DN XIII.3, 980D). Although trinitarian doctrine is fully present in Dionysius (see Golitzin, *Et Introibo*, 51–54), it does not enter into his philosophical understanding of being as theophany.

25. As Schäfer, *Philosophy*, 67 n. 26, points out, it is not in Dionysius but only in Eriugena that the term *theophany* (θεοφάνεια, *theophania*) becomes centrally important. Nonetheless, as Schäfer continues, "it quite neatly expresses what is meant here."

26. Cf. 25 and 121 n. 13.

27. Cf. Louis Dupré, *The Other Dimension* (New York: Doubleday, 1972), 129–30: "If the infinite is opposed to the finite, it is limited and thereby ceases to be infinite. Instead we must show that the finite is *in* the infinite. Which means that our initial affirmation of the finite must be followed by a negation of the finite's independent being. Such a negation cannot be provided by the argument which asserts the infinite as *also* existing and thereby juxtaposes it to the finite . . . True infinity, therefore, preserves the finite within itself."

28. Cf. Plotinus' statement, quoted earlier, 26, that the One "has no otherness." God as "not other" is of course the theme of Nicholas of Cusa's treatise *De non aliud*, which is strongly influenced by Dionysius.

29. Dodds, *Elements of Theology*, 217, commenting on Proclus' doctrine that the effect is contained, or remains, in the cause and that its going forth depends on a point of view, remarks, "If this be pressed, it must mean that the separateness of the lower is an illusion resulting from a partial point of view, and it follows that the sensible and the intelligible cosmos are both of them appearance, and only the One fully real." He adds, "This doctrine was never accepted by the Neoplatonists, but they often seem to be on the verge of falling into it." This comment exemplifies the failure to distinguish between *illusion* and *appearance*, and hence a failure to enter into the very heart of the Neoplatonists' thought about reality. It is true that for them "the sensible and intelligible cosmos are both of them appearance," but it does not follow that they are "an illusion."

30. Cf. Balthasar, "Denys," 164: In Dionysius we find "[m]anifestation conceived of in the Greek, not the Indian sense, as becoming visible in reality—not as *maya*, mere seeming illusion, but always as (real) manifestation of the unmanifest, of the ever greater God who can never be changed into simply comprehensible appearance." The reference to Indian thought may not be entirely just, for some forms of Hindu thought, notably that of Ramanuja, are strikingly similar to the Neoplatonic doctrine of participation and manifestation. See Fernand Brunner, "Une comparaison entre le néoplatonisme et le Viçishtadvaita," in *Néoplatonisme: Mélanges offerts à Jean Trouillard* (Fontenay aux Roses: Les Cahiers de Fontenay, 1981), 103–24.

31. See Fernand Brunner, "Création et émanation: Fragment de philosophie comparée," *Studia Philosophica* 33 (1973): 60–63.

CHAPTER THREE

1. For general treatments of this "motion" see Stephen Gersh, Κίνησις Ἀκίνητος, *A Study of Spiritual Motion in the Philosophy of Proclus* (Leiden: Brill, 1973), and Werner Beierwaltes, *Proklos: Grundzüge seiner Metaphysik* (Frankfurt am Main: Klostermann, 1965), 118–64.

2. This does not mean, of course, that Aristotle's doctrine is identical with Plato's. "The good," for Aristotle, is not a universal: each thing has its own distinct goodness. See esp. *Nicomachean Ethics* I.6, 1096a11ff.

3. For form in general as good, see *Physics* I.9, 192a17.

4. Jonathan Lear, *Aristotle: The Desire to Understand* (Cambridge: Cambridge University Press, 1988), 295–96, argues that for Aristotle "the desire which God inspires is *none other than the desire of each organism to realize its form* . . . [I]n trying to realize its form, the organism is doing all that it can do to become intelligible. It is

also doing the best job it can do to imitate God's thought—and thus to imitate God himself." (italics in original). The realized form in a thing is thus the result of its desire for God.

5. Armstrong in his note *ad loc.* rightly remarks, "This is one of the fundamental principles of Greek philosophical thought."

6. On this duality of expression see Gersh, *From Iamblichus to Eriugena*, 48 n. 102.

7. Dodds, *Elements of Theology*, 219–20, comments, "This is the converse of prop. 31. We saw there that, given the metaphysical ἀρχή, we can argue to the ethical τέλος: here we argue from the ethical τέλος to the metaphysical ἀρχή. Both arguments depend ultimately on the identity of the efficient with the final cause." This identity in turn depends on the identity of both with the formal cause.

8. See above 37. See also *El. Th.*, prop. 144, where Proclus argues that "even the last kinds in the realm of existence are consequent upon gods . . . who revert even these toward the Good; and so also are the intermediate and the primal kinds . . . [I]f anything fall away from the gods and become utterly isolated from them, it retreats into non-being and disappears, since it is wholly bereft of the principles which constitute it."

9. See above, 26.

10. This phrase could also be translated "subsisting by reversion," and the meaning would be the same: the effect's existing consists in its reversion.

11. Thus L. J. Rosán, *The Philosophy of Proclus* (New York: Cosmos, 1949), 74, characterizes reversion as "essentially the logical connection between the cause and its effect but viewed from the opposite direction." So also R. Beutler, "Proklos," in *Paulys Realencyclopadie der classischen Altertumswissenschaft* 23/1 (Stuttgart: Metzler, 1957), col. 212: "This reversion is dialectically indeed nothing other than the logical connection of cause and effect, but now viewed not from the cause but from the effect," and Dodds, *Elements of Theology*, 219: "Procession and reversion together constitute a single movement, the diastole-systole which is the life of the universe." The reference to "diastole-systole" is particularly illuminating, in that it indicates procession and reversion as another expression of the *complicatio-explicatio* structure of reality.

12. Dionysius uses the expressions τὸ ἀγαθόν or τἀγαθόν and ἀγαθότης interchangeably with reference to God. See e.g. DN IV.1–2, 693B–696D; IV.4, 697C–700B.

13. Or "subsist"; see above, 124 n. 10.

14. Since remaining, procession, and reversion are not sequential but ontologically simultaneous, the order in which they are expressed is unimportant.

15. See 38.

16. Following the traditional use of "love" to translate ἔρως and "charity" to translate ἀγάπη, I translate ἀγαπᾶν as "cherish," since this is the closest verbal form of *charity* in English. On the absence of any distinction in meaning between ἔρως and ἀγάπη, see 47–48.

17. See 70–71.

18. See 40.

19. Cf. Dodds, *Elements of Theology*, 223. We shall see in chapter 6 that intellection, discursive reason, and sensation are all subdivisions of "Wisdom," i.e. cognition or consciousness in general.

20. Thus the commonplace that God creates us without our cooperation but cannot save us without it is, from Dionysius' point of view, inadequate: God cannot even create without the active cooperation of the creature. This point will be prominent in his account of evil.

21. This insight is present in Plotinus in the form of his doctrine that all things contemplate (III.8), that the life of a plant is a "growth-thought" [φυτικὴ νόησις], that of an animal a "sense-thought," and so on. There is some form in everything, and every form is an act-of-thinking at some level. "How, then, are they thoughts? Because they are rational principles [λόγοι]. And every life is a thought, but one is dimmer than another" (III.8.8.13–17). Since for Plotinus even the earth is living, this principle extends below plants to the things that are ordinarily considered inanimate; see III.8.1.4, VI.7.11.18–35.

22. For a survey of Plotinus' doctrine of beauty, see Dominic O'Meara, "Textes de Plotin sur la beauté," in Art et vérité, ed. I. Schussler, R. Celis, and A. Schild (Lausanne: Suisse, 1996), 59–68.

23. Commentary on the First Alcibiades of Plato, ed. L. G. Westerink (Amsterdam: North-Holland, 1954), 221–22, 319–20.

24. Commentary on the First Alcibiades, 330.

25. DN IV.7, 701C. The pun on κάλλος/καλεῖν is derived from Proclus, Commentary on the First Alcibiades, 328.

26. In Neoplatonism the distinction between the paradigmatic cause and the formal cause or determination is the distinction between reality and appearance: the paradigmatic universal appears in the effect as its formal determination. Hence the formal perfection of the effect is an image, in the sense of manifest presence, of the cause.

27. See 32.

28. See, e.g., John Rist, "A Note on Eros and Agape in Pseudo-Dionysius," Vigiliae Christianae 20 (1966): 239; Cornelia J. de Vogel, "Greek Cosmic Love and the Christian Love of God," Vigiliae Christianae 35 (1981): 57–81; and Lisa Marie Esposito Buckley, "Ecstatic and Emanating, Providential and Unifying: A Study of the Pseudo-Dionysian and Plotinian Concepts of Eros," Journal of Neoplatonic Studies 1 (1992): 56.

29. See 27.

30. De Vogel, "Greek Cosmic Love," 70, argues that "the One of Plotinus is superabundant" and is "overflowing Goodness," but that unlike Dionysius' God "it cannot be said that it 'goes out of itself, seeking the other' " and that it "stays within itself." This is strange indeed. We may observe: (1) What can "superabundant" possibly mean if not that the One in some sense "goes out of itself"? (2) The words "seeking the other" are not found in Dionysius. His God can be said to "seek the other" only in the sense that he is in all things and reverts all things to himself; but this is true of Plotinus' One as well. (3) De Vogel fails to quote the end of the relevant passage in Dionysius, where he says not only that God "goes out of himself" but that he does so ἀνεκφοίτητον ἑαυτοῦ, "without going out from himself" (DN IV.13, 712B). Plotinus' One and Dionysius' God "goes out" "without going out" in that he is (nothing but) "overflowing Goodness." The idea that the One of Plotinus is "self-contained" is expressly contradicted by Plotinus himself, and depends on the misconception of the One as something, as a being, having some definite identity of its own and therefore limited by that identity.

31. See above, 22, 27.

32. Proclus, *Commentary on the First Alcibiades*, 55–56. See also the discussion of divine providence in *El. Th.*, props. 120, 122. The concept of divine 'ἔρως προνοητικός' indicates that in Proclus ἔρως no longer necessarily connotes a lack or need, such that it could not be ascribed to God. See A. H. Armstrong, "Platonic Eros and Christian *Agape*," *Downside Review* 79 (1961): 116–17, and Beierwaltes, *Platonismus im Christentum*, 72–73.

33. See Beierwaltes, *Platonismus im Christentum*, 73.

34. See above, 23–24.

35. De Vogel, "Greek Cosmic Love," 71, points out that "the term ἔρως . . . is absent from the *Elementa Theologiae* and hardly occurs in the *Theologia Platonica*, and this while the whole apparatus of such terms, as προνοητικός, ἀγαθοειδής, σωστικός, τελειωτικός and συνεκτικός, is fully present in those works," and concludes from this "that apparently the notion of *eros* was not essential to his theology." To argue from this that Dionysius is significantly different from Proclus on this point is to focus on terminology to the exclusion of meaning, for it admits that everything Dionysius *means* by ἔρως is centrally present in Proclus.

36. See Rist, "Note on Eros and Agape," 239, and Golitzin, *Et Introibo*, 68. Both Rist and Golitzin, however, see a real difference in content, not only in expression, between Proclus and Dionysius on this point.

37. For this doctrine in Plotinus, see Eric D. Perl, " 'The Power of All Things': The One as Pure Giving in Plotinus," *American Catholic Philosophical Quarterly* 71 (1997): 312.

38. Cf. Plotinus' remark that the soul in its erotic ascent to the Good is "lifted by the giver of its love" (VI.7.22.19–20). See Jean Trouillard, "Procession néoplatonicienne et création judéo-chrétienne," in *Néoplatonisme. Mélanges offerts a Jean Trouillard* (Fontenay-aux-Roses: Les Cahiers de Fontenay, 1981), 6: "Since the divine communication would lose its value if God did not remain the Absolute, the descent of God toward man is nothing other than the ascent of man toward God." In fact this applies not only to man but to all things.

39. Cf. the statement cited above, 44, that God "reverts all things."

40. Classically expressed by Anders Nygren, *Agape and Eros*, tr. P. S. Watson (London: SPCK, 1953).

41. In saying that as Love God not only causes other things to move but is himself moved, Dionysius directly targets the Aristotelian doctrine of God as the *unmoved* mover. This is not to say that Dionysius' God undergoes any change or actualization of potentiality (which is what Plotinus and Proclus mean when they deny that the One's production of being is a "movement") but rather that he is ecstasy or overflow, not a self-contained being but productively "out of himself" and "in all things." (See also DN IX.9, 916C, where Dionysius explains the sense in which God is unmoved as well as the sense in which he is moved.) Aristotle's God, as pure form, being (οὐσία), and intellect, keeps himself to himself. The God of Plotinus and Dionysius, as not any being but "all beings and not even one," "all things in all things and nothing in any," overflows, goes forth, or is differently present in all things. The shift from Aristotle's "unmoved" God to Dionysius' God who as Love "is moved" is thus a restatement of the shift from God as form or being to God as beyond being. Hence the difference between a God who is the object of love but does not love the world and a God who is not only beloved but also productively loves all things, is fundamentally a difference not between pagan and Christian but between Aristotelian and Neoplatonic conceptions of God.

42. On this problem in Dionysius see Golitzin, *Et Introibo*, 79, 82–83.

43. See K. Kremer, "Bonum est diffusivum sui: Ein Beitrag zum Verhältnis von Neuplatonismus und Christentum," in *Aufstieg und Neidergang der Romischen Welt*, ed. W. Haase and H. Temporini (New York: De Gruyter, 1987), II.36.1, 994–1032, for a discussion of the issue with extensive references to the literature on it.

44. Since the One is not a being, these superlative phrases should be interpreted to mean "more perfect than all" and "more powerful than all beings." As both the beginning and the conclusion of the passage indicate, the One is not "the most powerful being," but rather productive power itself. For this meaning of the superlative with a genitive, see Herbert Weir Smyth, *Greek Grammar*, rev. Gordon M. Messing (Cambridge: Harvard University Press, 1956), 334, §1434.

45. See Trouillard, "Procession," 8: "The processive movement, strictly speaking, is *neither necessary nor contingent*. Neither necessary, since it creates, along the way, its own laws. Nor contingent, since it invents at once the possible and the real. Which should not be surprising, since these modalities cannot regulate a radical production," (italics in original).

46. This temporal formulation indicates of course not temporal but ontological priority and hence means simply that the One is not conditioned by his production of beings.

47. Cf. Trouillard, "Procession," 6: " 'God is love' signifies 'God gives himself to his creatures.' "

48. It is ironic that Plotinus has been condemned by Christian thinkers *both* for saying that God does not "care for" his products *and* for saying that he is conditioned by a necessary relation to them, when in fact the sole meaning of the first claim is the denial of the second.

49. Cf. Gerson, *Plotinus*, 28: "[T]he putative necessity by which the One acts cannot be really distinct from the One or indeed from its will . . . So, to say that the One acts by necessity could mean nothing else but that it acts according to its will . . . [I]f the One acted by a necessity really distinct from it, then this would set up, counter to Plotinus' express argument, a real relation between the One and what it produces." Cf. also Trouillard, "Procession," 5: "What necessity is concerned here? Certainly *not a logical or dialectical necessity*. The absolute simplicity of the Good prevents establishing with regard to it any deduction whatsoever . . . *Nor* is the necessity of procession a *necessity of indigence*, as if the Absolute could add something to itself in manifesting itself . . . The only necessity to which the Neoplatonists give value here is the *necessity of superabundance* or of generosity" (italics in original).

50. Obviously Dionysius, like Proclus in a similar context, is using the term "being" loosely here, since properly speaking God does not have being.

51. For God as unrelated (ἄσχητος), see DN I.7. 596D; IV.16, 713C; V.6, 820DV.8, 824B; IX.9, 916C.

52. See above, 44.

53. For a less nuanced presentation of a similar position (apart from the unfortunate ascription of "Being" to God), see Philip Sherrard, *Human Image: World Image. The Death and Resurrection of Sacred Cosmology* (Ipswich: Golgonooza, 1992), 157: "[T]here is a higher form of freedom, a paradoxical 'determinative' freedom, which is not merely a liberty of choice. This freedom which is attained in apparent determinism is not a negative indeterminacy . . . ; it is a positive natural spontaneity. Non-compulsion from without may be one form of freedom; but compulsion from within is another and higher form. And it is this kind of compulsion that God is under when He creates.

"The creative act has its adequate ground in God's Being, and so is an essential and necessary self-determination of that Being: that God creates the world means that He could not not create it. The divine creative act belongs to the fulness of divine life, without any mechanical necessity or outer compulsion. God, with power to create, could not not be a Creator. God is love . . . The divine Lover—God—cannot not love at all, or love to a limited extent, or not extend His love to the farthest limits of possibility and so abstain from loving fully. He does not have that choice.

"It is the same with His creative power. He does not possess the possibility of not creating or of abstaining from creation. . . . Creation of the world is not a gratuitous extra. It is the expression of divine life with all the power of necessity, with all the absolute freedom and spontaneity of God's Being. God *qua* God is Creator and Creator *qua* Creator is God."

54. Cf. Golitzin, *Et Introibo*, 82–83.

CHAPTER FOUR

1. Proclus, *De malorum subsistentia*, in *Procli diadochi Tria opuscula, Latine Guillelmo de Moerbeka vertente et Graece ex Isaaci Sebastocratoris aliorumque scriptis collecta*, ed. H. Boese (Berlin: De Gruyter, 1960).

2. On Dionysius' alterations to Proclus' account of evil, see Carlos Steel, "Proclus et Denys: De l'existence du mal," in *Denys l'Aréopagite et sa posterité en Orient et en Occident*, ed. Ysabel de Andia (Paris: Institut d'Etudes Augustiennes, 1997), 89–116.

3. This is how Steel, "Proclus et Denys," 96, reads Dionysius' doctrine, which he therefore judges to be greatly inferior to that of Proclus.

4. See, e.g., Aquinas, *Summa Theologica* I, Q. 5, art. 3, resp.

5. See, e.g., V.8.7.23–24, where Plotinus says that "this universe is all form" and that even matter is "a sort of ultimate form," evidently meaning that matter is not a positive reality other than form and that it is a product of the Good.

6. On this point see also I.8.4.25–33 and I.8.15.13–15, 19–23.

7. The quoted words are from Plato, *Timaeus* 34b8.

8. Since Proclus' δαίμονες are wholly good spiritual beings, it would be extremely misleading to translate this term as "demons."

9. The reference is to Plato, *Letter* II, 312e1–3.

10. Cf. Proclus, *De malorum subsistentia* 7.48 and 38.14–18.

11. Cf. Steel, "Proclus et Denys," 101.

12. Here we may appropriately translate δαίμονες as "demons," for in Dionysius, contrary to Proclus, they are not wholly good but are fallen angels.

13. Dionysius does not indicate who says this, but "they" must certainly include Plotinus.

14. On the difference between Dionysius and Plotinus on this point, see Trouillard, "Le cosmos du Pseudo-Denys," 56: "Plotinus judges that souls are ill insofar as they are not sufficiently minds. Dionysius treats minds as souls."

15. This reflects Proclus' doctrine of evil in souls as weakness of activity.

16. Cf. Proclus, *De malorum subsistentia* 49.5–6, 12–13.

17. The principle that all activity aims at some good is found not only in Plato (e.g., *Republic* VI, 505e1, *Symposium* 204e–205d) but also in Aristotle (e.g., *Nicomachean Ethics* I.1, 1094a1).

18. Cf. the remarks of Trouillard, "Procession," 20, on the relation between divine and creaturely causality in Aquinas, in connection with the Neoplatonic doctrine of self-constitution: "The more man acts, the more God acts. Grace does not limit freedom, it is freedom itself (participation in the divine freedom), which is fundamentally something gratuitous. One would be not able to say: If man creates himself, he has not use for God. Quite the contrary, he manifests in that itself the power of God, capable of producing genuine causes and not beings which could affirm themselves only against him."

19. On the connection between multiplicity and non-being in this passage see Golitzin, *Et Introibo*, 178.

20. Cf. Proclus, *De malorum subsistentia* 44.11–12.

21. Perhaps significantly, he says not ἀνοήρως, "unintellectually" (which would merely be an expression of the common patristic tradition that the fall is a fall from a purely intellectual condition), but ἀνοήτως, "unintelligibly": the fall itself cannot be understood.

22. Cf. John Jones, *Pseudo-Dionysius the Areopagite. The Divine Names and Mystical Theology: Translated from the Greek with an Introductory Study* (Milwaukee: Marquette University Press, 1980), 86–87: "The question 'Why is there evil at all?' is a mistaken question; for, it seeks an ultimate cause where there is none. However, in denying the legitimacy of this question we do not seek to explain evil away; rather, we indicate that evil is uncaused and unexplainable."

23. Dionysius' view of evil as deficiency of being and hence as uncaused and unintelligible is thus closely comparable to Augustine's, although Augustine thinks more of efficient causality and Dionysius more of final causality. Having traced the origin of evil back as far as the will of a rational creature, Augustine then says, "Let no one, then, seek an efficient cause of an evil will. For its cause is not efficient, but deficient, because the evil will itself is not an effect of something, but a defect . . . Now to seek the causes of these defections, which are . . . not efficient causes, but deficient, is like wishing to see darkness or hear silence . . . Thus, too, our mind perceives intelligible forms by understanding them; but when they are deficient, it knows them by not knowing them; for 'who can understand his failings?' . . . [T]he will is made evil by nothing else than the defection by which God is forsaken: a defection of which the cause, too, is certainly deficient." Augustine, *The City of God against the Pagans*, ed. and tr. R. W. Dyson (Cambridge: Cambridge University Press, 1998), XII.7–9, 507–09.

CHAPTER FIVE

1. See esp. DN IV.4, 697C; IV.7, 704B; IV.8, 704D; IV.X, 708A; IV.12, 709D; IV.15, 713AB (a passage which explicitly extends the terminology associated with hierarchy beyond the angelic or intellectual to the psychic and natural levels); V.3, 817AB.

2. The divine procession Wisdom includes all modes of cognition, from angelic intellection down to the sensation of irrational animals. The distinctions of the various modes of cognition within Wisdom will be discussed in chapter 6.

3. Dionysius substitutes the biblical term Wisdom (σοφία) for the philosophical term Intellect (νοῦς), but the meaning remains the same. Σοφία was occasionally used in this sense by non-Christian Neoplatonists as well; see e.g. Plotinus, V.8.4.37, V.8.5.1–3, 15–20.

4. See Dodds, *Elements of Theology*, 232.

5. Strictly speaking, for Proclus, only the henads are gods, while terms such as Being, Life, and Intellect are lesser causes which derive their being and causal power from their proper henads. But Proclus also uses the term 'god' more loosely, to characterize various terms subordinate to the henads. See Dodds, *Elements of Theology*, 261.

6. On the supposed difference between Proclus and Dionysius on this point, see e.g. Roques, *L'univers dionysien*, 78–81, esp. 78 n. 3; Ivanka, *Plato Christianus*, 260–61; Gersh, *From Iamblichus to Eriugena*, 154ff.

7. See 121, n. 11.

8. Thus Dodds, *Elements of Theology*, 260, observes that "the principle of continuity in the vertical procession involved the splitting of each god into a series of gradually weakening forces, so that Zeus, for example, appears as five different gods each of whom symbolizes the 'jovial' principle on a different plane of reality." By the same token, we may say that every god "symbolizes" the One on a different plane of reality.

9. In view of the principle of continuity in Proclus' "series" (*El. Th.*, prop. 145), this is true not only of the henads themselves but of all the lower levels of divinity derived from them as well.

10. The real meaning of Proclus' many divinities is well expressed in Plotinus' reply to the Gnostics' denial of such "gods": "It is not contracting the divine into one but showing it in that multiplicity in which God himself has shown it, which is proper to those who know the power of God, inasmuch as, abiding who he is, he makes many gods, all depending upon himself and existing through him and from him. And this universe exists through him and looks to him, the whole of it and each and every one of the gods in it, and it reveals what is his to men" (II.9.9.36–42). Need Christians quarrel with this? It should rather be directed against the narrow "monotheism" which regards the world as by nature "profane" rather than as theophany and God as a unitary being rather than as "all things in all things and nothing in any." Just as the God of Dionysius and the Neoplatonists transcends the opposition between theism and atheism, so he transcends that between monotheism and polytheism, for he is strictly speaking neither one nor many in any positive sense.

11. Edward P. Butler, "Polytheism and Individuality in the Henadic Manifold," *Dionysius* 23 (2005): 83–103, argues persuasively for a more robust interpretation of Proclus' polytheism. He concludes, 98, "Procession by unity is not a matter of the manifold of the henads vanishing into the One, as if the henads were but 'aspect,' 'adumbrations' or 'perspectives' of the One. The One is not one, and its purpose is not the subordination of multiplicity. The characteristic the henads possess in common is none other than irreducible uniqueness and individuality . . . In accord, then, with the conclusion of the First Hypothesis of the *Parmenides* that the One neither *is*, nor is *one*, we should say that the One *is* as each henad, each God, rather than as the hypostasized entity that, for our own convenience, to be able to refer to divine activity in generic fashion, we refer to as 'the One itself.' " Nonetheless, as Butler admits, the henads do have "irreducible uniqueness" in common, and each god is a mode of unity (see *El. Th.*, prop. 133). It is precisely as a mode of unity that each god is the ground of being for all that falls below it. In this and only in this sense the henads are "aspects" of the One. As we have seen, to posit the One as the cause of beings means *only* that every being is a being by unity.

12. See also DN IV.3, 697A: "All beings and even non-being itself desire the Good."

13. Intellect here stands in the place of Being, as containing in itself all forms.

14. In this way the standard, and clearly correct, interpretation of Dionysius' "non-beings" as matter may be reconciled with the alternative reading offered by Jean-Luc Marion, *God without Being,* tr. Thomas A. Carlson (Chicago: University of Chicago Press, 1991), 77–78: "[T]he absence of all perfection, even ontic, already designates the place and the instance of a radical desire. The less the nothing has of perfection, the more it will desire perfection . . . The less than nothing aims at the Requisite [i.e. the Good] through its absolute desire itself."

15. The bracketed insertions are necessary to show that the prepositional phrases beginning with "above" (ὑπέρ) are adverbial, modifying "are," "live," and "think and know," rather than adjectival, modifying "the divine intellects."

16. Cf. again the Aristotelian dictum, "To be, for a living thing, is to live."

17. Cf. Dom Denys Rutledge, *Cosmic Theology: The Ecclesiastical Hierarchy of Pseudo-Dionysius the Areopagite: An Introduction* (New York: Alba House, 1964), 22–23 n. 2.

18. See above, 42 and 125 n. 21.

19. Dionysius' account of justice could thus be regarded as a universalization of Plato's account of justice as "every part doing its own work" in the soul and in the city: *Republic* IV, 443a–e.

20. So, e.g., Andrew Louth, *Denys the Areopagite* (London: Chapman, 1989), 84–85; Ivanka, *Plato Christianus,* 258–60, 271; Golitzin, *Et Introibo,* 142–45.

21. Cf. Semmelroth, "Θεολογία συμβολική," 4: "Where the Areopagite now by preference portrays God's creation as radiation of divine light, not only does the fact comes to light that the things are from God, but also that in the things something of the essence of the creating God shows through. From here on the Pseudo-Areopagite's entire theology of creation becomes a theology of light."

22. Cf. the response to Roques on this point by Jean Trouillard, "Le cosmos du Pseudo-Denys," *Revue de théologie et de philosophie,* Série 3, 5 (1955): 53: "Does Dionysius separate himself on this point from the Plotinian tradition? René Roques believes so . . . [Roques holds that] the God of Dionysius indeed communicates his power of unifying and illuminating, calls in mediations, he does not at all delegate his creative efficacy. But this restriction is something difficult to conceive within Neoplatonism. In this idealist context where the substance is in no way distinct from the operation, illumination comes back to creation. To produce a term different from himself, is for the One to create; but to assimilate this term to its principle, is again for this principle to create."

23. See also e.g. VI.8.18.1–3: "And you when you seek, seek nothing outside him [the One], but seek within all things which come after him . . . For he himself is the outside, the encompassment and measure of all things. Or within in depth." As this indicates, "All things in the One" coincides with "the One in all things."

24. Proclus' doctrine is exceptionally well expressed by Trouillard, "Procession," 11: "The continuity of procession rests therefore on a permanent *communication* of the processive power of the One. Every ontological focus participates in its fecundity to the point of engendering itself and engendering beings similar or inferior to itself." And again, ibid., 12: "According to Neoplatonism, the communication of

processive power is not such that the One would cease to act or that he would act only indirectly through his derivatives without being immediately present to them. In reality, *the One is always immediately operating*, because every efficacy is a modalisation of unity . . . Every subordinate cause plays within the more comprehensive causality which upholds it. The derived efficacy uses, in particularizing it, the operation which invests it. Thought determines life, the latter particularizes being, which itself is a mode of unity. Nothing has power except by the omnipresent power of unifying unity. The number of mediations changes nothing in this" (italics in original).

25. See above, 23–24.

26. Dionysius' doctrine of hierarchy could thus be read as an elaboration of Matthew 20:25–27: " 'You know that the rulers of the Gentiles lord it over them, and their great men exercise authority over them. It shall not be so among you; but whoever would be great among you must be your servant, and whoever would be first among you must be your slave.' " The higher any being is in the order of reality, the *more* it is in the service of—in Dionysius' terms, providentially proceeds to—all that is below it. Cf. the contrast of Dionysian hierarchy to the "vulgar" or "political" model of hierarchy by Marion, *The Idol and Distance*, 163–64, 170.

27. More clearly than any other interpreter of Dionysius, Rutledge, *Cosmic Theology*, 14 n. 1, sees how this overcomes the conventional opposition between direct and mediated production: "If the whole being and activity of each member is received it seems to matter little whether we say he or God creates the one immediately below. The immanence and transcendence of God . . . must be stated with *exactly* the same emphasis . . . If we say that God creates each member of the hierarchy immediately, then . . . we must add immediately that each member *is* God, at *exactly* this level of manifestation or creation" (italics in original).

28. Cf. Louis Bouyer, *Cosmos* (Petersham, MA: St. Bede's, 1988), 200.

29. Dionysius' doctrine of hierarchy thus constitutes an exception to Trouillard's claim, "Procession," 12: "Too often Christian thought about the universe goes from the parts to the whole and not from the whole to the parts . . . It declares God the author of things visible and invisible, and not of the visibles by the mediation of the invisibles . . . Except for Eriugena, we do not find a Christian doctor who overcomes this lack and here rejoins Neoplatonism." Such an exception should be no surprise in Dionysius, the student of Proclus and principal source of Eriugena.

30. The full connotations of this word cannot be captured in a single translation: "given into their hands," and in that sense entrusted to them (sc. to be passed on to others); "lent," and so not primally theirs, but God-in-them; and "shown" or "manifested" in them. See *A Greek-English Lexicon*, ed. Henry George Liddell and Robert Scott, 9th ed., s.v., ἐνδίδωμι.

31. See Marion, *The Idol and Distance*, 162–71. See also Louis Bouyer, *The Church of God*, tr. C. U. Quinn (Chicago: Fransiscan Heralds, 1982), 258–60. But Bouyer, 258–59, and to a lesser extent Marion, 165, erroneously contrast this to a conventionally caricatured Neoplatonism.

32. Such a doctrine should be the less troublesome to Christians in that it is simply the principle of sacramentality: the celebrant of any sacrament acts *in persona Christi*, and his sacramental activity is that of Christ. In Dionysius, this sacramental principle, in which the activity of the creature is the activity of God-in-it, is extended to all reality, which, as theophany, is sacramental in nature.

33. The contrast is between "by nature" (φύσει) and "by placement" (θέσει), the latter meaning "by participation."

34. Again see Marion, *The Idol and Distance*, 166: "[T]he gift cannot be received unless it is given, for otherwise it would cease to merit its name. The basin is not filled up by the cascade from above unless it ceaselessly empties itself into the basin below . . . To receive the gift of God, as gift, requires of man that he himself immediately welcome the gift in its essence—as a giving act . . . To receive the gift amounts to receiving the giving act, for God gives nothing except the movement of the infinite kenosis of charity, that is, everything . . . Receiving and giving are therefore achieved in the same act." See also Bouyer, *Cosmos*, 200: "[T]he various degrees . . . of the Dionysian hierarchies, are simply so many relays for communicating what the higher beings can keep for themselves only by sharing freely with others (as pseudo-Dionysius explicitly asserts). And . . . it is still the gift of God, i.e., not only something he gives, but in the final analysis his very self."

35. Balthasar, "Denys," 149, insightfully suggests that Dionysius' pseudonymity should be understood in terms of this aspect of his thought, "[o]n the level . . . of the specifically Dionysian humility and mysticism which must and will utterly vanish as a person so that it lives purely as a divine task and lets the person be absorbed (as in the Dionysian hierarchies) in *taxis* and function."

36. Cf. Marion, *The Idol and Distance*, 165.

37. See e.g. John Meyendorff, *Christ in Eastern Christian Thought* (Washington and Cleveland: Corpus Books, 1969), 82.

38. Dionysius does not develop the consequences of hierarchy with regard to evil; but it clearly implies that if any being fails to perform its proper function the order of the whole is impaired, just as, in a choral dance, if one dancer gets out of step the entire dance is disrupted. See Marion, *The Idol and Distance*, 168: "[T]hat which a redundancy does not manage to translate of the original gift . . . will be missed by all the other redundancies. This means that a failure defeats not so much the one who commits it as the one near him, and so on . . . This is also called sin."

39. Significantly, this is the same word Dionysius uses at DN IV.13, 712B to describe how God as ecstatic love goes out from himself "without going out from himself." See 46.

40. See above, 79.

41. For hierarchy as the communion of saints, see Balthasar, "Denys," 192; Marion, *The Idol and Distance*, 168–70. An illustration of Dionysian hierarchy as the communion of saints may be found in Dante's *Divine Comedy*, Inferno II, where Dante recounts Virgil's recounting of Beatrice's account of how she came to him. Beatrice says, "Love moved me," alluding to God as the Love that moves all things, and then explains that the Virgin Mary sent St. Lucy to send Beatrice to send Virgil to rescue Dante. Dante's salvation is thus effected by Love, or God, in Mary, Lucy, Beatrice, and Virgil.

CHAPTER SIX

1. E.g. Rorem, *Pseudo-Dionysius*, 92–94.
2. See above, 6–7, 20–21.

3. Pierre Hadot, *Plotinus or the Simplicity of Vision*, tr. Michael Chase (Chicago: University of Chicago Press, 1993), 23, 27. See also A. C. Lloyd, *The Anatomy of Neoplatonism* (Oxford: Oxford University Press, 1990), 126: "What makes a non-phenomenological description of any hypostasis inadequate is Neoplatonic idealism. The hypostases *are* experiences; they are types of consciousness; while, therefore, they have abstract and objective properties, they have also what we call phenomenological properties."

4. Cf. Gerson, *Plotinus*, 164: "The governing principle for the interpretation of the various modes of cognition of incarnate individuals in that they are all images and inferior versions of the form of cognition that is found in the ἀρχή, Intellect . . . Plotinus holds that intellection . . . entails an identification of subject and object. Inferior forms of cognition—images of the highest form—involve increasing qualifications of this identification in the direction of the externalization of the object in relation to the subject. Thus, a form of cognition is in proximity to the paradigm according to the extent to which it identifies with its object."

5. See also the more extended presentation of the same argument in V.5.1–2.

6. To interpret Plotinus' famous "flight of the alone to the alone" as a solipsistic self-isolation is thus a profound misunderstanding. When Plotinus says that the soul must ascend "alone," he means that it must free itself from the impurities which consist in its failure to be perfectly intellectual (see e.g. I.6.5.46–53). But it is precisely these impurities that isolate the soul from other beings, while the overcoming of them brings it into communion with all reality.

7. See above, 21.

8. Cf. Deck, *Nature, Contemplation, and the One*, 110: "Plotinus does not have two worlds, but only one. His world of true being is not, except metaphorically, a world above the everyday world. It *is* the everyday world, not as experienced by sense, by opinion, or by discursive reasoning, but as known by intellect, the Nous, the Knower." Deck's entire chapter here is an excellent exposition of this aspect of Plotinus' thought. See also Armstrong, "Introductory Note" to VI.7, 79: "In the end we are left with the very strong impression that for Plotinus there are not two worlds but one real world apprehended in different ways on different levels."

9. See also VI.2.21.52–53 for the presence of bodies in Intellect.

10. Cf. Semmelroth, "Θεολογία συμβολική," 9: "In [Dionysius], as for Greek thought in general, a communion of knowledge is, at an entirely level than in our thought, a kind of communion of being."

11. On the angels as "models" for human intelligence, see Golitzin, *Et Introibo*, 144–45.

12. The representation of intellection by circular motion goes back at least to Plato, *Laws* X, 898a3–b3. The comparison of sense to a line and intellect to a circle was evidently a stock analogy in the Platonic school by the time of Plotinus: see V.1.7.8 and Armstrong's note *ad loc*. The entire threefold analogy found in Dionysius occurs in Hermias, *Εἰς τὸν Πλάτωνος Φαῖδρον σχόλια*, ed. P. Couvreur (Paris: Librairie Emile Bouillon, 1901), 20–21. See Gersh, *From Iamblichus to Eriugena*, 75, n. 229.

13. Cf. Jones, *Divine Names*, 44: "[In Dionysius] there is not a plurality of worlds but one world which can be seen and known in different ways. Thus we can know all that is in the most unified and complete way, through contemplation of intelligible beings, or we can know things in the least unified and complete way through the sensation of sensible beings."

14. See above, 26.

15. Here we may remember Plotinus' comparison of the One to light, which cannot be seen by itself but which, in differentiated forms, is the only object of all sight.

16. The list of cognitive faculties is taken from Plato's *Parmenides* and Neoplatonic commentaries on it.

17. Cf. Jones, *Divine Names*, 44: "For Pseudo-Dionysius, in all knowledge we always see and know the divinity, for the divinity is all in all."

18. Cf. Balthasar, "Denys," 179: "Denys contemplates the divine symbols in creation and the Church with an aesthetic delight. Things are not simply the occasion for his seeing God; rather, he sees God in things. Colours, shapes, essences and properties are for him immediate theophanies." Again, ibid., 182: "One can only with difficulty resist the temptation to quote profusely the theological portrayals by this poet of water, wind and clouds, and particularly of the fragrance of God, the delightful interpretations that go right to the heart of such things as bodily eating and drinking and the assimilation of food, sleeping and waking." Nothing could be farther from the common view of Dionysius as a denigrator of the senses and the sensible.

19. See Rutledge, *Cosmic Theology*, 15–16, esp. 16 n. 1: "In this tradition bodily sight is but the lowest, the most superficial, 'material' aspect of a single activity in which all sight and knowledge, and indeed the very being of man and his world, is 'sight' and 'knowledge' of God."

20. The question of whether Dionysius' mysticism is based on "experience" is irrelevant here, where our purpose is to provide a philosophical account of its meaning. The interpretation of mysticism in terms of "experience" has in any case recently and rightly been subjected to criticism as distinctively modern. See Michael Sells, *Mystical Languages of Unsaying* (Chicago: University of Chicago Press, 1994), 214: "If the nonintentionality claims of apophatic mystics are taken seriously, and if experience is, by definition, intentional, it necessarily follows that mystical union is not an experience. All experience must have a grammatical object, but the prime motivation of apophatic language is to subvert or displace the grammatical object . . . If it is true that all experience is constructed, it is equally true that the concept of experience is a modern construct . . . The apophatic mystic speaks of the birth of the son in the soul, of annihilation, of an awakening without an awakener, but does not speak of 'the experience' of such birth, annihilation, or awakening." This is emphatically the case for Dionysius, with the substitution of "union," "darkness," "unknowing," for "birth," "annihilation," etc. See also Golitzin, *Et Introibo*, 31–32. On this issue with regard to Plotinus see John Bussanich, "Plotinian Mysticism in Theoretical and Comparative Perspective," *American Catholic Philosophical Quarterly* 71 (1997): 339–65.

21. See above, 12–13.

22. See above, 24–26.

23. Armstrong is unwilling to translate ἔκστασις as "ecstasy" because, he says in his note *ad loc.*, "there is no good reason for describing the mystical union according to Plotinus as an 'ecstasy.' It gives a very misleading impression of this austere and quiet mysticism." This seems unduly cautious in view of I.6.5.6–8; I.6.7.12–17; and VI.7.35.24–26, where Plotinus speaks of Intellect in contemplation of the One as "out of its mind" (ἄφρων), "drunk," and "in love."

24. The reference to ἐπιβολὰς or παραδοχὰς makes a clear allusion to Plotinus, VI.7.35.22–26: "Intellect also, then, has one power for thinking, by which it looks at the things in itself, and one by which it looks at what transcends it by a

direct awareness and reception [ἐπιβολῇ τινι καὶ παραδοχῇ] . . . And that first one is the contemplation of Intellect in its right mind, and the other is Intellect in love, when it goes out of its mind 'drunk with the nectar.' " In this context, Dionysius' use of "ἀφαιρέσεως" may also be an allusion to Plotinus.

25. Here Dionysius is paraphrasing the same passage in Plotinus referred to in the previous note. On the allusions to Plotinus in these passages see Michael Harrington, "The Drunken *Epibole* of Plotinus and its Reappearance in the Work of Dionysius the Areopagite," *Dionysius* 23 (2005): 131–32.

26. Literally "of the above all being and knowledge": the verb *is*, creating a manifest contradiction, is not present in the Greek.

27. Although the imagery of "divine darkness" is not found in Plotinus (see Werner Beierwaltes, *Denken des Einen* [Frankfurt: Klostermann, 1985], 149), the same meaning is present in phrases such as "You will not think" and "Take away everything."

28. Cf. MT I.3, 1001A, where Dionysius similarly speaks of Moses, in mystical unknowing, "being all of him who is beyond all things, and of nothing, neither of himself nor of another."

29. Cf. Proclus, *El. Th.*, prop. 124, and *De Malorum Subsistentia*, 61.18–20.

30. This formulation has a distinctly Eriugenian sound; but Eriugena's doctrine on this point is already present, although less explicit, in Dionysius.

CHAPTER SEVEN

1. On the *Symbolic Theology* see DN I.8, 597B; IV.5, 700D; IX.5, 913B; XIII.4, 984A; MT III, 1032A; Ep. IX.1, 1104B.

2. For a good account of the metaphysical basis of Dionysius' symbolic theology, see Semmelroth, "Θεολογία συμβολική," 1–11.

3. At CH II.5, 145A, Dionysius refers to the description of God as a worm in Psalm 22:6.

4. Cf. Semmelroth, "Θεολογία συμβολική," 6: "The conceptual expression still always itself remains a kind of symbol."

5. Cf. Semmelroth, "Θεολογία συμβολική," 8–9: "As a Neoplatonist the Pseudo-Areopagite certainly represents a strong realism of symbols . . . Between sign and signified in the symbol obtains not only a connection of knowledge, but also a connection of presence . . . In the thought of the Pseudo-Areopagite the symbol is realistically bound with the symbolized."

6. This could more literally and daringly be rendered "become," and such a reading would make sense on the basis of what we have seen in chapter 6: in the absolute unification of cognition we do not merely see but become the darkness beyond being.

7. Cf. Marion, *The Idol and Distance*, 140–43.

8. The phrase τὰ πάντα ἀφαιροῦμεν again recalls Plotinus' ἄφελε πάντα.

9. Cf. O'Rourke, *Pseudo-Dionysius*, 9: "Dionysius uses [*proballein*] in two closely related significations to convey the same fundamental reality from distinct viewpoints, namely both the veiling and the unveiling or unfolding of God through creation."

10. See *A Greek-English Lexicon*, s.v., προβάλλω.

11. On the latter point see VI.7.16.1 and esp. V.5.12.36–38.

12. The term σύνθημα is used interchangeably with σύμβολον in late Neoplatonic theurgical texts. See R. M. van den Berg, *Proclus' Hymns* (Leiden: Brill, 2001), 70, 79, 126.

13. See e.g. Rorem, *Pseudo-Dionysius*, 25.

14. In opposition to the "esoteric" reading of such passages see Golitzin, *Et Introibo*, 153–54: "[I]t does not appear to us that the Areopagite is doing much more than referring here to a basic fact of the spiritual life. There are degrees of knowledge, of receptivity to truth, and of advancement in it . . . The 'sacred veils' . . . embrace an ascending series of revelations adapted to the believer's progress in love, simplicity, purification from selfish imagination, and consequent capacity for contemplation."

15. O'Rourke, *Pseudo-Dionysius*, 9, taking 'προβέβληται' in the passive rather than the middle voice, translates this, " 'the creation of the visible universe is a veil before the invisible things of God (προβέβληται, literally, is placed before).' "

16. The phrase πάντων ἀφαιρέσει again recalls Plotinus' ἄφελε πάντα.

17. CH I.4, 177D.

18. According to *A Greek-English Lexicon*, s.v., ἐξαγγελία, an ἐξάγγελος is a "messenger who brings out news from within: hence, one who betrays a secret, informer," and, in the context of the stage, a "messenger who told what was doing in the house or behind the scenes (opp. ἄγγελος, who told news from a distance)." Dionysius' angel is thus not merely a "messenger," but one who reveals something which remains hidden, and indeed hides it by revealing it, in that narration takes the place of direct portrayal. Here as elsewhere, the precise connotations of Dionysius' carefully chosen term are essential to his philosophical meaning.

19. Immediately before this (DN I.4, 592BC) Dionysius has traced a parallel ascent within the eschaton itself from sense to intellect to "the union above intellect."

20. This passage again overturns the interpretation of Dionysius as a despiser of the sensible.

21. Cf. Balthasar, "Denys," 169: "The same knowledge of God demands both a deeper penetration *into* the image and also a more sublime transcendence *beyond* it, and the two are not separated one from another but are the more fully integrated, the more perfectly they are achieved" (italics in original).

22. Cf. Jones, *Divine Names*, 60: "Yet is it only in the God-man Christ that the divinity takes on being? Is only the God-man Christ an incarnation of the divinity in which it takes on being? For the procession and reversion of all beings is the procession and reversion of the divinity out of itself and about itself; in its procession and reversion the divinity itself stands out of itself . . . But, then, does not the divinity itself take on being in its ecstasis? Are not beings an 'incarnation' of the divinity?"

23. Cf. Philip Sherrard, *The Rape of Man and Nature. An Enquiry into the Origins and Consequences of Modern Science* (Ipswich: Golgonooza, 1987), 26: "[T]he humanization of God is fully in accord with the divine nature as such . . . God's transcending of His own transcendence in an outgoingness through which He becomes immanent in His creation . . . is an act of creative self-expression without which the divine itself would remain incomplete. There is a divine as well as a human form of ecstasy." Sherrard does not refer to Dionysius in this connection, but the parallelism, not only in concept but in terminology, is striking.

24. E.g., Roques, *L'univers dionysien*, 315–17.

25. In its immediate context this refers to the celestial and ecclesiastical hierarchies. But since the celestial hierarchy is the paradigm for all lesser reality, and all reality is hierarchical, it follows that God incarnate is the "principle and perfection" of all things.

CONCLUSION

1. Dodds, *Elements of Theology*, xxv. Dodds later, ibid., xxxiii, quotes Coleridge saying that what we find in Proclus is a "philosophy which endeavours to explain all things by an analysis of consciousness, and builds up a world in the mind out of materials furnished by the mind itself."

2. Friedrich Nietzsche, *Twilight of the Idols*, tr. R. J. Hollingdale (New York: Penguin 1972), 48.

3. Cf. Vittorio Possenti, *Terza navigatione: Nichilismo e metafisica* (Rome: Armando Editore, 1998), 28.

4. "If then [Intellect] does not possess the true reality . . . it will have falsities and nothing true . . . So if there is not truth in Intellect, then an intellect of this sort will not be truth, or truly Intellect, or Intellect at all. But then truth will not be anywhere else either." V.5.1.56–57, 66–69.

5. Cf. Sells, *Mystical Languages*, 21–22 and 228 n. 17.

6. Cf. A. H. Armstrong, "The Hidden and the Open in Hellenic Thought," in *Eranos* 54 (Frankfurt am Main: Verlag, 1987); repr. in *Hellenic and Christian Studies* (Aldershot: Variorum, 1990), V, 103: "That which is utterly beyond us and cannot be expressed or thought is by its very transcendence of distance and difference most intimately present. The Neoplatonists express this with particular force: it was from them that Christianity and Islam learnt their understanding of the unity of transcendence and immanence."

BIBLIOGRAPHY

THE DIONYSIAN CORPUS

Corpus Dionysiacum I. De Divinis Nominibus. Ed. Beate Regina Suchla. Berlin: Walter de Gruyter, 1990.

Corpus Dionysiacum II. De Coelesti Hierarchia, De Ecclesiastica Hierarchia, De Mystica Theologia, Epistulae. Ed. Günter Heil and Adolf Martin Ritter. Berlin: Walter de Gruyter, 1991.

OTHER ANCIENT SOURCES

Aristotle. *De Anima.* Ed. W. D. Ross. Oxford: Oxford University Press, 1956.

———. *Ethica Nicomachea.* Ed. L. Bywater. Oxford: Oxford University Press, 1894.

———. *Metaphysica.* Ed. W. Jaeger. Oxford: Oxford University Press, 1957.

———. *Physica.* Ed. W. D. Ross. Oxford: Oxford University Press, 1956.

Diels, Hermann, and Walther Kranz, eds. *Die Fragmente der Vorsokratiker.* 7th ed. Berlin: Weidmannsche Verlagsbuchhandlung, 1954.

Plato. *Opera.* Ed. John Burnet. Oxford: Oxford University Press, 1900–1907.

Plotinus. *Opera.* Ed. P. Henry and H.-R. Schwyzer. Oxford: Oxford University Press, 1964–1982. Reprinted with emendations in *Plotinus.* Ed. and tr. A. H. Armstrong. Loeb Classical Library. Cambridge: Harvard University Press, 1966–1988; London: William Heinemann, 1966–1988.

Proclus. *Commentary on the First Alcibiades of Plato.* Ed. L. G. Westerink. Amsterdam: North-Holland, 1954. Eng. tr. *Proclus: Alcibiades I.* Tr. William O'Neill. The Hague: Martinus Nijhoff, 1965.

———. *Commentary on the Parmenides of Plato.* Ed. V. Cousin. Paris: Durand, 1864. Eng. tr. *Commentary on Plato's Parmenides.* Tr. Glenn R. Morrow and John M. Dillon. Princeton: Princeton University Press, 1988.

———. *De Malorum Subsistentia.* In *Procli diadochi Tria opuscula, Latine Guillelmo de Moerbeka vertente et Graece ex Isaaci Sebastocratoris aliorumque scriptis collecta.* Ed. H. Boese. Berlin: De Gruyter, 1960.

———. *The Elements of Theology.* Ed. and tr. E. R. Dodds. Oxford: Oxford University Press, 2nd ed. 1963.

STUDIES

Alfind, M. R. "Plotinus on the Possibility of Non-Propositional Thought." *Ancient Philosophy* 8 (1988): 273–84.

Andia, Ysabel de. "Pathon ta theia." In *Platonism in Late Antiquity*. Ed. S. Gersh and
    C. Kannengiesser. Notre Dame: University of Notre Press, 1992.
―――. "Philosophie et union mystique chez le Pseudo-Denys l'Aréopagite." In *Sophies
    Maietores: "Chercheurs de sagesse." Hommage à Jean Pépin*. Paris: Institut d'Etudes
    Augustiniennes, 1992.
―――. "La divinisation de l'homme selon Denys." In *Premier congrès international
    Denys l'Aréopagite* (Athens, 29 juin-2 juillet 1993). Athens, 1995.
―――. *Henosis: L'union à Dieu chez Denys l'Aréopagite*. Leiden: Brill, 1996.
―――, ed. *Denys l'Aréopagite et sa posterité en Orient et en Occident*. Paris: Institut
    d'Etudes Augustiniennes, 1997.
―――. "Neoplatonismo y cristianismo en Pseudo-Dionisio Areopagita." *Anuario
    Filosofico* 33 (2000): 363–94.
Aquila, Richard E. "On Plotinus and the 'Togetherness' of Consciousness." *Journal of
    the History of Philosophy* 30 (1992): 7–32.
Armstrong, A. H. "Emanation in Plotinus." *Mind* 46 (1937): 61–66. Reprinted in
    Plotinian and Christian Studies, 2.
―――. *The Architecture of the Intelligible Universe in the Philosophy of Plotinus*. Cam-
    bridge: Cambridge University Press, 1940.
―――. "Plotinus' Doctrine of the Infinite and Its Significance for Christian Thought."
    Downside Review 73 (1955): 47–58. Reprinted in *Plotinian and Christian Stud-
    ies*, 5.
―――. "Platonic Eros and Christian Agape." *Downside Review* 79 (1961): 105–21.
    Reprinted in *Plotinian and Christian Studies*, 9.
―――. ed. *The Cambridge History of Later Greek and Medieval Philosophy*. Cambridge:
    Cambridge University Press, 1967.
―――. "Beauty and the Discovery of Divinity in the Thought of Plotinus." In
    *Kephalion: Studies in Greek Philosophy and Its Continuation Offered to Professor
    C.J. de Vogel*. Ed. J. Manfeld and L. M. de Rijk. Assen: Van Gorcum, 1975.
    Reprinted in *Plotinian and Christian Studies*, 19.
―――. "The Escape of the One." In *Studia Patristica 13: Papers Presented to the
    International Conference on Patristic Studies*. Ed. E. A. Livingston. Berlin:
    Akademie Verlag, 1975. Reprinted in *Plotinian and Christian Studies*, 23.
―――. "Negative Theology." *Downside Review* 95 (1977): 176–89. Reprinted in
    Plotinian and Christian Studies, 24.
―――. *Plotinian and Christian Studies*. London: Variorum, 1979.
―――. "Some Advantages of Polytheism." *Dionysius* 5 (1981): 181–98. Reprinted in
    Hellenic and Christian Studies, 1.
―――. "Negative Theology, Myth and Incarnation." In *Neoplatonism and Christian
    Thought*. Ed. Dominic O'Meara. Albany: State University of New York Press,
    1982. Reprinted in *Hellenic and Christian Studies*, 7.
―――. "Dualism Platonic, Gnostic, and Christian." In *Plotinus amid Gnostics and
    Christians*. Ed. D. T. Runia. Amsterdam: Free University Press, 1984. Re-
    printed in *Hellenic and Christian Studies*, 12.
―――. *Hellenic and Christian Studies*. London: Variorum, 1990.
Atherton, P. J. "The Neoplatonic 'One' and the Trinitarian 'Arche.' " In *The
    Significance of Neoplatonism*. Ed. R. Baine Harris. Albany: State University of
    New York Press, 1976.

Aubenque, P. "Plotin et le dépassement de l'ontologie grecque classique." In *Le Néoplatonisme. Colloque de Royaumont 9–13 juin 1969.* Paris: Centre Nationale de la Recherche Scientifique, 1971.

Baladi, N. *La Pensée de Plotin.* Paris: Presses Universitaires de France, 1970.

Bales, E. F. "Plotinus' Theory of the One." In *The Structure of Being: A Neoplatonic Approach.* Ed. R. Baine Harris. Albany: State University of New York Press, 1982.

Balthasar, Hans Urs von. "Denys." In *The Glory of the Lord: A Theological Aesthetics,* vol. 2: *Studies in Theological Style: Clerical Styles.* Tr. A. Louth et al. San Francisco and New York: Ignatius, 1984.

Barnard, Charles-André. "Les formes de la théologie chez Denys l'Aréopagite." *Gregorianum* 59 (1978): 36–69.

Beierwaltes, Werner. "Die Metaphysik des Lichtes in der Philosophie Plotins." *Zeitschrift für Philosophische Forschung* 15 (1961): 334–62.

———. "Der Begriff des 'Unum in Nobis' bei Proklos." *Miscellanea Mediaevalis* (vol. 2, *Die Metaphysik im Mittelalter*). Berlin: De Gruyter, 1962.

———. *Proklos: Grundzüge seiner Metaphysik.* Frankfurt: Klostermann, 1965, 2nd ed. 1979.

———. "*Exaiphnes* oder die Paradoxie des Augenblicks." *Philosophisches Jahrbuch* 74 (1966–67): 271–82.

———. "Andersheit: Zur neuplatonischen Struktur einer Problemgeschichte." In *Le Néoplatonisme. Colloque de Royaumont 9–13 juin 1969.* Paris: Centre Nationale de la Recherche Scientifique, 1971.

———. "Andersheit: Grundriss einer neuplatonischen Begriffsgeschichte." *Archiv für Begriffsgeschichte* 16 (1972): 166–97.

———. "Die Entfaltung der Einheit." *Theta-Pi* 2 (1973): 126–61.

———. "Plotins Metaphysik des Lichtes." In *Die Philosophie des Neuplatonismus.* Ed. C. Zintzen. Darmstadt: Wissenschaftliche Buchgesellschaft, 1977.

———. *Denken des Einen: Studien zur neuplatonischen Philosophie und ihrer Wirkungsgeschichte.* Frankfurt: Klostermann, 1985.

———. *Platonismus im Christentum.* Frankfurt: Klostermann, 2001.

Bell, D. N. "Esse, Vivere, Intelligere: The Noetic Triad and the Image of God." *Recherches de théologie ancienne et médiévale Louvain* 52 (1985): 5–43.

Beutler, R. "Proklos." In *Realenkyklopaedie der klassischen Altertumswissenschaft.* Ed. A. F. Pauly and G. Wissowa. Stuttgart: Druckenmüller, 1957.

Blumenthal, H. J, and R. A. Markus, eds. *Neoplatonism and Early Christian Thought: Essays in Honour of A. H. Armstrong.* London: Variorum, 1981.

Boss, G., and C. G. Steel, eds. *Proclus et son influence.* Zurich: GMB Editions du Grand Midi, 1987.

Bouyer, Louis. *The Church of God.* Tr. C. U. Quinn. Chicago: Franciscan Heralds, 1982.

———. *Cosmos.* Petersham, MA: St. Bede's, 1988.

Bréhier, Émile. *La Philosophie de Plotin.* Paris: Boivin, 1928.

Breton, Stanislas. "Le théorème de l'Un des Eléments de 'Théologie' de Proclos." *Revue des sciences philosophiques et théologiques* 58 (1974): 561–83.

———. "Difficile néoplatonisme." In *Néoplatonisme. Mélanges offerts à Jean Trouillard.* Fontenay-aux-Roses: Les Cahiers de Fontenay, 1981.

———. "L'Un et l'être." *Revue philosophique de Louvain* 83 (1985): 5–13.

Brons, Bernhard. *Gott und die Seienden. Untersuchungen zum Verhältnis von neuplatonischer Metaphysik und christlicher Tradition bei Dionysius Areopagita.* Göttingen: Vandenhoeck and Ruprecht, 1976.

———. "Pronoia und das Verhältnis von Metaphysik und Geschichte bei Dionysius Areopagita." *Freiburger Zeitschrift für Philosophie und Theologie* 24 (1977): 166–80.

Brontesi, A. *L'incontro misterioso con Dio. Saggio sulla teologia affermative e negative nello Pseudo-Dionigi.* Brescia: Morcelliana, 1970.

Brunner, F. "Création et émanation: Fragment de philosophie comparée." *Studia Philosophia* 33 (1973): 33–43.

Buckley, Lisa Marie Esposito. "Ecstatic and Emanating, Providential and Unifying: A Study of the Pseudo-Dionysian and Plotinian Concepts of Eros." *Journal of Neoplatonic Studies* 1 (1992): 31–61.

Bussanich, J. R. *The One and its Relation to Intellect in Plotinus.* Leiden: Brill, 1988.

———. "Plotinian Mysticism in Theoretical and Comparative Perspective." *American Catholic Philosophical Quarterly* 71 (1997): 339–65.

———. "Plotinus on the Inner Life of the One." *Ancient Philosophy* 7 (1987): 163–89.

Butler, Edward P. "Polytheism and Individuality in the Henadic Manifold." *Dionysius* 23 (2005): 83–103.

Carabine, Deirdre. *The Unknown God: Negative Theology in the Platonic Tradition: Plato to Eriugena.* Louvain: Peeters, 1995.

Carroll, William Joseph. "Participation in Selected Texts of Pseudo-Dionysius the Areopagite's *The Divine Names.*" Ph.D. thesis, Catholic University of America, 1981. Ann Arbor: University Microfilms International.

———. "Participation and Infinity in Dionysius the Areopagite." *Patristic and Byzantine Review* 2 (1983): 54–64.

———. "Unity, Participation and Wholes in a Key Text of Pseudo-Dionysius the Areopagite's *The Divine Names.*" *The New Scholasticism* 57 (1983): 253–62.

Chrétien, J.-L. "Le Bien donne ce qu'il n'a pas." *Archive de Philosophie* 43 (1980): 263–77.

Clarke, W. N. "Infinity in Plotinus: A Reply." *Gregorianum* 40 (1959): 75–98.

Combès, J. *Etudes néoplatoniciennes.* Grenoble: Editions Jérome Millon, 1989.

Corbin, M. "Négation et transcendance dans l'oeuvre de Denys." *Revue des sciences philosophiques et théologiques* 69 (1985): 41–76.

Corsini, Eugenio. *Il Trattato De Divinis Nominibus dello Pseudo-Dionigi e i commenti neoplatonici al Parmenide.* Turin: Giappichelli, 1962.

Couloubaritsis, L. "Le sens de la notion 'démonstration' chez le Pseudo-Denys." *Byzantinische Zeitschrift* 1982: 317–35.

D'Ancona Costa, C. "*Amorphon kai aneideon.* Causalité des formes et causalité de l'Un chez Plotin." *Revue de philosophie ancienne* 10 (1992): 69–113.

———. "Proclus, henads and archai in the superintelligible world." *Rivista di Storia della Filosofia* 47 (1992): 265–94.

———. "Separation and the Forms: A Plotinian Approach." *American Catholic Philosophical Quarterly* 71 (1997): 367–403.

Deck, J. N. *Nature, Contemplation, and the One. A Study in the Philosophy of Plotinus.* Toronto: University of Toronto Press, 1967. 2nd ed. Burdett, NY: Larson, 1991.

———. "The One, or God, Is Not Properly Hypostasis: A Reply to Professor Anton." In *The Structure of Being: A Neoplatonic Approach.* Ed. R. Baine Harris. Albany: State University of New York Press, 1982.

Derrida, Jacques. "La différance." In *Marges de la philosophie*. Paris: Editions de Minuit, 1972.

———. "How to Avoid Speaking: Denials." Tr. Ken Frieden. In *Languages of the Unsayable: The Play of Negativity in Literature and Literary Theory*. Ed. Sanford Budick and Wolfgang Iser. New York: Columbia University Press, 1989.

Dodds, E. R. *Proclus. The Elements of Theology: A Revised Text with Translation, Introduction and Commentary*. Oxford: Oxford University Press, 2nd ed. 1963.

Doherty, K. F. "Pseudo-Dionysius the Areopagite: 1955–1960." *Modern Schoolman* 40 (1962/63): 55–59.

———. "Toward a Bibliography of Pseudo-Dionysius the Areopagite: 1900–1955." *Modern Schoolman* 33 (1956): 257–68.

Douglass, J. W. "The Negative Theology of Dionysius the Areopagite." *Downside Review* 81 (1963): 115–24.

Duclow, Donald F. "Pseudo-Dionysius, John Scotus Eriugena, Nicholas of Cusa: An Approach to the Hermeneutic of the Divine Names." *International Philosophical Quarterly* 12 (1972): 260–78.

Dupré, Louis. *The Other Dimension*. New York: Doubleday, 1972.

Elorduy, E. "El problema del mal en Proclo y el ps. Areopagita." *Pensiamento* 5.9 (1955): 481–89.

———. "Ammonio Sakkas I, La doctrine de la creatión y del mal en Proclo y el Ps. Areopagita." *Estudios Oniensas*, ser. 1, vol. 7. Burgos, 1959.

Emilsson, E. K. *Plotinus on Sense-Perception*. Cambridge: Cambridge University Press, 1988.

Every, G. "Dionysius the Pseudo-Dionysius." In *One yet Two: Monastic Tradition East and West*. Kalamazoo: Cistercian, 1976.

Findlay, J. N. "Toward a Neo-Neo-Platonism." In *Ascent to the Absolute*. London: Allen and Unwin, 1970.

———. *Plato: The Written and Unwritten Doctrines*. London: Routledge and Kegan Paul, 1974.

———. "The Three Hypostases of Plotinism." *Review of Metaphysics* 28 (1975): 660–80.

Fischer, H. *Die Aktualität Plotins: Über die Konvergenz von Wissenschaft und Metaphysik*. Munich: Beck'sche Verlagsbuchhandlung, 1956.

Frei, W. "Versuch eines Einfuhrung in das areopagitische Denken." *Theologisches Zeitschrift* 16 (1960): 91–109.

Gandillac, M. de. *La sagesse de Plotin*. Paris: Librairie Hachette, 1963. 2nd ed. 1952.

Gersh, Stephen. Κίνησις Ἀκίνητος: *A Study of Spiritual Motion in the Philosophy of Proclus*. Leiden: Brill, 1973.

———. *From Iamblichus to Eriugena: An Investigation of the Prehistory and Evolution of the Pseudo-Dionysian Tradition*. Leiden: Brill, 1978.

———. "Ideas and energies in Pseudo-Dionysius the Areopagite." *Studia Patristica* 15 (1984): 297–300.

Gerson, L. P. *Plotinus*. London and New York: Routledge, 1994.

Golitzin, Alexander. " 'On the Other Hand': A Response to Father Paul Wesche's Recent Article on Dionysius." *St. Vladimir's Theological Quarterly* 34 (1990): 305–23.

———. "The Mysticism of Dionysius Areopagite: Platonist or Christian?" *Mystics Quarterly* 19 (1993): 98–114.

————. *Et Introibo ad Altare Dei: The Mystagogy of Dionysius Areopagita, with Special Reference to Its Predecessors in the Eastern Christian Tradition.* Thessalonica: Patriarchikon Idryma Paterikon Meleton, 1994.

————. Review of *Pseudo-Dionysius: A Commentary on the Texts and an Introduction to Their Influence,* by Paul Rorem. *Mystics Quarterly* 21 (1995): 28–38.

Goltz, H. *Hiera Mesiteia: Zur Theorie der hierarchischen Sozietät im Corpus Areopagiticum.* Erlangen, 1974.

Guérard, C. "La théorie des hénades et la mystique de Proclus." *Dionysius* 6 (1982): 73–82.

————. "La théologie négative dans l'apophatisme grec." *Revue des sciences philosophiques et théologiques* 68 (1984): 183–200.

Gurtler, G. M. *Plotinus: The Experience of Unity.* New York: Lang, 1988.

Haase, W., and H. Temporini, eds. *Aufstieg und Niedergang der Römishcen Welt,* pt. 2: *Principat,* vols. 36.1 and 2. New York: De Gruyter, 1987.

Hadot, P. "L'Etre et l'étant dans le néoplatonisme." *Revue de théologie et de philosophie* 23 (1973): 101–13.

————. "Les niveaux de conscience dans les états mystiques selon Plotin." *Journal de Psychologie* 77 (1980): 243–66.

————. *Plotin ou la simplicité du regard.* Paris: Institut des Etudes Augustiniennes, 3rd ed. 1989. Eng. tr. *Plotinus or the Simplicity of Vision.* Tr. Michael Chase. Chicago: University of Chicago Press, 1993.

Hankey, Wayne. "Denys and Aquinas. Antimodern Cold and Postmodern Hot." In *Christian Origins.* Ed. Lewis Ayres and Gareth Jones. London and New York: Routledge, 1998.

————. "Why Heidegger's 'History' of Metaphysics Is Dead." *American Catholic Philosophical Quarterly* 78 (2004): 425–43.

Harrington, Michael. "The Drunken *Epibole* of Plotinus and Its Reappearance in the Work of Dionysius the Areopagite." *Dionysius* 23 (2005): 117–38.

Harris, R. Baine, ed. *The Significance of Neoplatonism.* Albany: State University of New York Press, 1976.

————, ed. *The Structure of Being: A Neoplatonic Approach.* Albany: State University of New York Press, 1982.

————, ed. *Neoplatonism and Contempary Thought.* Albany: State University of New York Press, 2002.

Hathaway, Ronald F. *Hierarchy and the Definition of Order in the Letters of Pseudo-Dionysius.* The Hague: Martinus Nijhoff, 1969.

Hauken, A.I. "Incarnation and Hierarchy: The Christ according to Pseudo-Dionysius." *Studia Patristica* 15 (1984): 317–20.

Hodgson, Phyllis. "Dionysius the Areopagite and Christian Mystical Tradition." *The Contemporary Review* 176 (1949): 281–85.

Horn, Gabriel. "Note sur l'unité, l'union dans les noms divins du Pseudo-Aréopagite." *Archives de Philosophie* 2 (1924): 422–32.

————. "Amour et extase d'après Denys l'Aréopagite." *Revue d'ascetique et de mystique* 6 (1925): 278–89.

Hornus, Jean-Michel. "Quelques réflexions à propos du Pseudo-Denys l'Aréopagite et de la mystique chrétienne en géneral." *Revue d'histoire et de la philosophie religieuses* 27 (1947): 37–63.

———. "Les recherches récentes sur le Pseudo-Denys l'Aréopagite." *Revue d'histoire et de la philosophie religieuses* 35 (1955): 404–48.

———. "Les recherches dionysiennes de 1955 à 1960." *Revue d'histoire et de la philosophie religieuses* 41 (1961): 22–81.

Ivanka, Endre von. "Der Aufbau der Schrift 'De divinis nominibus' des Ps.-Dionysius." *Scholastik* 15 (1940): 386–99. Reprinted in *Plato Christianus*, 228–42.

———. "La signification historique du 'Corpus Areopagiticum." *Recherches de science religieuse* 36 (1949): 5–24.

———. "But et date de la composition du 'Corpus Areopagiticum." *Actes du 6e congrès international d'études byzantines* I. Paris, 1950: 239–40.

———. "Zum Problem des christlichen Neuplatonismus I: Was heisst eigentlich 'Christlicher Neuplatonismus'? 2: Invieveit ist Pseudo-Dionysios Areopagita Neuplatoniker?" *Scholastik* 31 (1956): 31–40, 384–403. Reprinted in *Plato Christianus*, 43–54.

———. "Pseudo-Dionysios und Julian." *Wiener Studien* 70 (1957): 168–78. Reprinted in *Plato Christianus*, 43–54.

———. *Plato Christianus. Übernahme und Umgestaltung des Platonismus durch die Väter.* Einsiedeln: Verlag, 1964.

Jones, John D. "The Character of the Negative (Mystical) Theology for Pseudo-Dionysius Areopagite." *Proceedings of the American Catholic Philosophical Association* 51 (1977): 66–74.

———. "The Ontological Difference for St. Thomas and Pseudo-Dionysius." *Dionysius* 4 (1980): 119–32.

———. *Pseudo-Dionysius the Areopagite. The Divine Names and Mystical Theology, Translated from the Greek with an Introductory Study.* Milwaukee: Marquette University Press, 1980.

———. "A Non-Entitative Understanding of Be-ing and Unity: Heidegger and Neo-platonism." *Dionysius* 6 (1982): 94–110.

Kélessidou-Galanou, A. "L'extase plotinienne et la problématique de la personne humaine." *Revue des études grecques* 84 (1971): 384–96.

———. "Plotin et la dialectique platonicienne de l'absolu." *Philosophia* 3 (1973): 307–38.

Kenney, J. P. "Mysticism and Contemplation in the Enneads." *American Catholic Philosophical Quarterly* 71 (1997): 315–37.

Kern, Cyprien. "La structure du monde d'après le Pseudo-Denys." *Irenikon* 29 (1956): 205–09.

Koch, Hugo. *Pseudo-Dionysius Areopagita in seinen Beziehungen zum Neuplatonismus und Mysterienwesen.* Mainz: Kirchheim, 1900.

Kordig, C. R. "Proclus on the One." *Idealistic Studies* 3 (1973): 229–37.

———. "The Mathematics of Mysticism: Plotinus and Proclus." In *The Structure of Being: A Neoplatonic Approach.* Ed. R. Baine Harris. Albany: State University of New York Press, 1982.

Krämer, H. J. "Epekeina tes Ousias." *Archiv für Geschichte der Philosophie* 51 (1969): 1–30.

Kremer, Klaus. "Das 'Warum der Schöpfung': 'quia bonus' vel/et 'quia voluit'? Ein Beitrag zum Verhältnis von Neuplatonismus und Christentum an Hand des Prinzips 'bonum est diffusivum sui.' " In *Parusia: Studien zur Philosophie Platons und zur Problemgeschichte des Platonismus.* Ed. K. Flasch. Frankfurt am Main: Minerva, 1965.

———. *Die Neuplatonische Seinsphilosophie und ihre Wirkung auf Thomas von Aquin.* Leiden: Brill, 1966. 2nd ed. 1971.

———. *Gott und Welt in der klassischen Metaphysik.* Stuttgart: Kohlhammer, 1969.

———. "Selbsterkenntnis als Gotteserkenntnis nach Plotins." *International Studies in Philosophy* 13 (1981): 41–68.

———. "Bonum est diffusivum sui: Ein Beitrag zum Verhältnis von Neuplatonismus und Christentum." In *Aufstieg und Neidergang der Romischen Welt,* ed. W. Haase and H. Temporini. New York: De Gruyter, 1987.

Lear, Jonathan. *Aristotle: The Desire to Understand.* Cambridge: Cambridge University Press, 1988.

Lilla, S. "The Notion of Infinitude in Ps.-Dionysius Areopagita." *Journal of Theological Studies* 31 (1980): 93–103.

———. "Introduzione allo studio dello Ps. Dionigi l'Areopagita." *Augustinianum* 22.3 (1982): 533–77.

Lossky, Vladimir. "La notion des 'analogies' chez Denys le Pseudo-Aréopagite." *Archives d'histoire doctrinale et littéraire du moyen age* 5 (1930): 279–309.

———. "La théologie négative dans la doctrine de Denys l''Aréopagies." *Revue des sciences philosophiques et théologiques* 28 (1939): 204–21.

———. *The Mystical Theology of the Eastern Church.* Crestwood: St. Vladimir's Seminary Press, 1976.

Louth, Andrew. *Denys the Areopagite.* London: Geoffrey Chapman, 1989.

Macharadse, Michael. "Die mystische Erkenntnis Gottes bei Plotin und Pseudo-Dionysius Areopagita." In *Selbst-Singularität-Subjektivität: Vom Neuplatonismus zum Deutschen Idealismus.* Ed. Mojsisch Burkhard. Amsterdam: Gruner, 2002.

Marion, Jean-Luc. *L'idole et la distance.* Paris: Editions Bernard Grasset, 1977. English translation *The Idol and Distance.* Tr. Thomas A. Carlson. New York: Fordham University Press, 2001.

———. *Analogie et dialectique: Essais de théologie fondamentale.* Geneva: Labor et Fides, 1982.

———. *Dieu sans l'être.* Paris: Fayard, 1982. English translation *God without Being.* Tr. Thomas A. Carlson. Chicago: University of Chicago Press, 1991.

McTighe, Thomas P. "A Neglected Feature of Neoplatonic Metaphysics." In *Christian Spirituality and the Culture of Modernity: The Thought of Louis Dupré.* Ed. Peter J. Casarella and George P. Schner. Grand Rapids: Eerdmans, 1998.

Meyendorff, John. *Christ in Eastern Christian Thought.* Washington: Corpus Books, 1969.

Moreau, J. "L'Un et les êtres selon Plotin." *Giornale di metafisica* 11 (1956): 204–24.

———. *Plotin ou la gloire de la philosophie antique.* Paris: Vrin, 1970.

Mortley, R. "Negative Theology and Abstraction in Plotinus." *American Journal of Philosophy* 96 (1975): 363–77.

———. "Recent Work in Neoplatonism." *Prudentia* 7 (1975): 47–52.

———. *From Word to Silence II: The Way of Negation, Christian and Greek.* Bonn: Athenäum, 1986.

Mossé-Bastide, R. *La pensée philosophique de Plotin.* Paris: Bordas, 1972.

Müller, H. F. *Dionysios, Proklos und Plotinos.* Münster: Aschendorffsche Verlagsbuchhandlung, 1918.

Narbonne, Jean-Marc. "Heidegger et le néoplatonisme." *Quaestio* 1 (2001): 55–82.

————. *Hénologie, ontologie, et Ereignis (Plotin—Proclus—Heidegger)*. Paris: Les Belles Lettres, 2001.

Neidl, Walter N. *Thearchia. Die Frage nach dem Sinn von Gott bei Pseudo-Dionysius Areopagita und Thomas von Aquin*. Regensburg: Habbel, 1976.

O'Daly, Gerard. "Dionysius Areopagita." *Theologische Realenzyklopädie* 7 (1981): 772–80.

O'Meara, Dominic. *Structures hiérarchiques dans la pensée de Plotin*. Leiden, 1975.

————. "The Problem of Omnipresence in Plotinus *Ennead* 6, 4–5: A Reply." *Dionysius* 4 (1980): 61–74. Reprinted in *The Structure of Being and the Search for the Good*, 6.

————. Ed. *Neoplatonism and Christian Thought*. Albany: State University of New York Press, 1982.

————. "Le problème du discours sur l'indicible chez Plotin." *Revue de théologie et de philosophie* 122 (1990): 145–56. Reprinted in *The Structure of Being and the Search for the Good*, 11.

————. "The Freedom of the One." *Phronesis* 37 (1992): 343–49. Reprinted in *The Structure of Being and the Search for the Good*, 12.

————. *Plotinus: An Introduction to the Enneads*. Oxford: Oxford University Press, 1993.

————. "Textes de Plotin sur la beauté: Initiation et remarques." In *Art et vérité*. Ed. I. Schüssler, R. Célis, A. Schild. Lausanne, 1996. Reprinted in *The Structure of Being and the Search for the Good*, 10.

————. "Evêques et philosophes-rois: Philosophie politique néoplatonicienne chez le Pseudo-Denys." In *Denys l'Aréopagite et sa postérité en Orient et en Occident*. Ed. Y. de Andia. Paris: Institut d'Etudes Augustiniennes, 1997. Reprinted in *The Structure of Being and the Search for the Good*, 19.

Oosthout, H. *Modes of Knowledge and the Transcendental: An Introduction to Plotinus Ennead 5.3 [49]*. Amsterdam: Grüner.

O'Rourke, Fran. "Being and Non-Being in the Pseudo-Dionysius." In *The Relationship between Neoplatonism and Christianity*. Ed. T. Finan and V. Twomey. Dublin: Four Courts, 1992.

————. *Pseudo-Dionysius and the Metaphysics of Aquinas*. Leiden: Brill, 1992.

Otten, Willemien. "In the Shadow of the Divine: Negative Theology and Negative Anthropology in Augustine, Pseudo-Dionysius and Eriugena." *Heythrop Journal* 40 (1999): 438–55.

Pépin, Jean. "Univers dionysien et univers augustinien." *Recherches de philosophie* 2 (Aspects de la dialectique) (1956): 179–224.

Perl, Eric D. "Hierarchy and Participation in Dionysius the Areopagite and Greek Neoplatonism." *American Catholic Philosophical Quarterly* 68 (1994): 15–30.

————. "Symbol, Sacrament, and Hierarchy in Saint Dionysios the Areopagite." *Greek Orthodox Theological Review* 30 (1994): 311–65.

————. "The Metaphysics of Love in Dionysius the Areopagite." *Journal of Neoplatonic Studies* 6 (1997): 45–73.

————. " 'The Power of All Things': The One as Pure Giving in Plotinus." *American Catholic Philosophical Quarterly* 71 (1997): 303–13.

————. "Signifying Nothing: Being as Sign in Neoplatonism and Derrida." In *Neoplatonism and Contemporary Thought*. Part 2. Ed. R. Baine Harris. Albany: State University of New York Press, 2002.

————. "Pseudo-Dionysius." In *A Companion to Philosophy in the Middle Ages*. Ed. Jorge J. E. Gracia and Timothy B. Noone. Oxford: Blackwell, 2003.

Pines, S. "The Problem of 'Otherness' in the Enneads." In *Le Néoplatonisme. Colloque de Royaumont 9–13 juin 1969*. Paris: Centre Nationale de la Recherche Scientifique, 1971.

Places, E. des. "Le Pseudo-Denys l'Aréopagite, ses précurseurs et sa posterité." *Dialogues d'histoire ancienne* 7 (1981): 323–32.

————. "La théologie négative du Pseudo-Denys." *Studia Patristica* 17 (1982).

Putnam, Caroline Canfield. *Beauty in the Pseudo-Denis*. Washington: Catholic University of America Press, 1960.

————. "The Philosopher-Monk according to Denis the Pseudo-Areopagite." In *Studies in Philosophy and the History of Philosophy*, vol. 5. Ed. John K. Ryan. Washington: Catholic University of America Press, 1970.

Reale, Giovanni. *Toward a New Interpretation of Plato*. Tr. John R. Catan and Richard Davies. Washington: Catholic University of American Press, 1997.

Riggi, C. "Il creazionismo e il suo simbolo nello Pseudo-Dionigi (*De divinibus nominibus* IV 8–9, IX 9)." *Salesianum* 29 (1967): 300–25.

Rist, John M. "Plotinus on Matter and Evil." *Phronesis* 6 (1961): 154–66.

————. "Mysticism and Transcendence in Later Neoplatonism." *Hermes* 92 (1964): 213–25. Reprinted in *Platonism and Its Christian Heritage*, 15.

————. "A Note on Eros and Agape in Pseudo-Dionysius." *Vigiliae Christianae* 20 (1966): 235–43.

————. *Plotinus: The Road to Reality*. Cambridge: Cambridge University Press, 1967.

————. "The Problem of 'Otherness' in the Enneads." In *Le Néoplatonisme. Colloque de Royaumont 9–13 juin 1969*. Paris: Centre Nationale de la Recherche Scientifique, 1971. Reprinted in *Platonism and Its Christian Heritage*, 8.

————. *Platonism and Its Christian Heritage*. London: Variorum, 1985.

————. "Pseudo-Dionysius, Neoplatonism and theWeakness of the Soul." In *From Athens to Chartres, Neoplatonism and Medieval Thought: Studies in Honor of Edouard Jeauneau*. Ed. H. J. Westra. Leiden and New York: Brill, 1992.

Roques, René. "Le primat du Transcendant dans la purification de l'intelligence selon le Pseudo-Denys." *Revue d'ascétique et de mystique* 23 (1947): 142–70.

————. "Note sur la notion de *Theologia* chez le Pseudo-Denys l'Aréopagite." *Revue d'ascétique et de mystique* 25 (1949): 200–12.

————. "De l'implication des méthodes théologiques chez le Pseudo-Denys." *Revue d'ascétique et de mystique* 30 (1954): 268–74.

————. *L'Univers dionysien. Structure hiérarchique du monde selon le Pseudo-Denys*. Paris: Aubier, 1954.

————. "Dionysius Areopagita." *Reallexikon für Antike und Christentum*, 3. Stuttgart: Hiersemann, 1957.

————. "Denys l'Aréopagite (Pseudo-)." *Dictionnaire de spiritualité*, 3. Paris: Beauchesne, 1957.

————. "Symbolisme et théologie négative chez le Pseudo-Denys." *Bulletin de l'Association Guillaume Budé* 1 (1957): 97–112.

————. "A propos des sources du Pseudo-Denys." *Revue d'histoire ecclésiastique* 56 (1961): 449–64.

————. *Structures théologiques de la gnose à Richard de Saint-Victor*. Paris: Presses Universitaires de France, 1962.

Rorem, Paul. "The Place of *The Mystical Theology* in the Pseudo-Dionysian Corpus." *Dionysius* 4 (1980): 87–98.

———. *Biblical and Liturgical Symbols within the Pseudo-Dionysian Synthesis.* Toronto: Pontifical Institute of Mediaeval Studies, 1984.

———. *Pseudo-Dionysius: A Commentary on the Texts and an Introduction to Their Influence.* Oxford: Oxford University Press, 1993.

Rosán, L. J. *The Philosophy of Proclus: The Final Phase of Ancient Thought.* New York: Cosmos, 1949.

Ross, Robert R.N. "The Non-existence of God: Tillich, Aquinas and the Pseudo-Dionysius." *The Harvard Theological Review* 68 (1975): 141–66.

Ruh, K. *Die Mystische Gotteslehre des Dionysius Areopagita.* Munich: Bayerischen Akademie der Wissenschaften, 1987.

Rutledge, Dom Denys. *Cosmic Theology: The Ecclesiastical Hierarchy of Pseudo-Denys, An Introduction.* New York: Alba House, 1964.

Saffrey, H. D. "Un lien objectif entre le Pseudo-Denys et Proclus." *Studia Patristica* 9 (1966): 98–105.

———. "New Objective Links between the Pseudo-Dionysius and Proclus." In *Neoplatonism and Christian Thought.* Ed. Dominic O'Meara. Albany: State University of New York Press, 1982.

———. *Recherches sur le néoplatonisme après Plotin.* Paris: Vrin, 1990.

Scazzoso, Piero. "Valore del superlativo nel linguaggio Pseudo-Dionisiano." *Aevum* 32 (1958): 434–46.

———. "Elementi del linguaggio pseudo-dionisiano." *Studia Patristica* 7 (1960): 384–400.

———. *Ricerche sulla struttura del linguaggio dello Pseudo-Dionigi Areopagita. Introduzione alla lettura delle opere pseudo-dionisiane.* Milan: Società Editrice Vita e Pensiero, 1967.

———. "La teologia antinomica dello Pseudo-Dionigi." *Aevum* 49 (1975): 1–35; *Aevum* 50 (1976): 195–234.

Schäfer, Christian. *The Philosophy of Dionysius the Areopagite: An Introduction to the Structure and the Content of the Treatise "On the Divine Names."* Leiden: Brill, 2006.

Schlette, H. *Das Eine und das Andere: Studien zur Problematik des Negativen in der Metaphysik Plotins.* Munich: Verlag, 1966.

Schürmann, R. "L'hénologie comme dépassement de la métaphysique." *Etudes philosophiques* 37 (1982): 331–50.

Scimè, S. "Transcendenza dell'assolute nello pseudo-Dionigi l'Areopagita." *Nuovo Didaskaleion* 3 (1949): 73–86.

———. *L'assoluto nello Pseudo-Dionigi.* Messina: Educare, 1950.

———. *Studi sul neoplatonismo, filosofia e teologia nello Pseudo-Dionigi.* Collana de Studi Filosofia 1a, 1. Messina: Educare, 1953.

Segonds, A. Ph., and C. Steel, eds. *Proclus et la Théologie Platonicienne. Actes du Colloque International de Louvain (13–16 mai 1988) En l'honneur de H. D. Safferey et L. G. Westerink.* Leuven-Paris, 2000.

Seidl, H. "L'union mystique dans l'explication philosophique de Plotin." *Revue thomiste* 85 (1985): 253–64.

Sells, Michael. "Apophasis in Plotinus: A Critical Approach." *Harvard Theological Review* 78 (1985): 47–50.

———. *Mystical Languages of Unsaying.* Chicago: University of Chicago Press, 1994.

Semmelroth, Otto. "Erlösung und Erlöser im System des Ps.-Dioysius Areopagite." *Scholastik* 24 (1949): 367–403.

————. "Gottes geeinte Vielheit. Zur Gotteslehre des Ps.-Dionysius Areopagita." *Scholastik* 25 (1950): 389–403.

————. "Gottes überwesentliche Einheit. Zur Gottellehre des Ps.-Dionysius Areopagita." *Scholastik* 25 (1950): 209–34.

————. "Die *Theologia symbolike* des Ps.-Dionysius Areopagita." *Scholastik* 27 (1952): 1–11.

————. "Gottes ausstrahlendes Licht. Zur Schöpfungs- und Offenbarungslehre des Ps.-Dionysius Areopagita." *Scholastik* 28 (1953): 481–503.

————. "Die Lehre des Ps.-Dionysius Areopagita vom Aufstieg der Kreatur zum göttlichen Licht." *Scholastik* 29 (1954): 24–52.

Sheldon-Williams, I. P. "The *Ecclesiastical Hierarchy* of Pseudo-Dionysius." *Downside Review* 82 (1964): 293–302; *Downside Review* 83 (1965): 20–31.

————. "The ps.-Dionysius and the Holy Hierotheos." *Studia Patristica* 8. Berlin, 1966.

————. "The Greek Christian Platonist Tradition from the Cappadocians to Maximus and Eriugena." In *The Cambridge History of Later Greek and Early Medieval Philosophy*. Ed. A. H. Armstrong. Cambridge: Cambridge University Press, 1967.

————. "Henads and Angels: Proclus and the ps.-Dionysius." *Studia Patristica* 11. Berlin, 1972.

Sherrard, Philip. *The Rape of Man and Nature: An Enquiry into the Origins and Consequences of Modern Science*. Ipswich: Golgonooza, 1987.

————. *Human Image: World Image. The Death and Resurrection of Sacred Cosmology*. Ipswich: Golgonooza, 1992.

Siorvanes, L. *Proclus: Neo-Platonic Philosophy and Science*. New Haven: Yale University Press, 1996.

Spearritt, Placid. "A Philosophical Enquiry into Dionysian Mysticism." Ph.D. Dissertation. University of Fribourg, Switzerland, 1968.

————. "The Soul's Participation in God according to Pseudo-Dionysius." *Downside Review* 83 (1970): 378–92.

————. "Dionysius the Pseudo-Areopagite." In *Dictionary of Christian Theology*. London: SCM, 1969.

Stein, E. "Ways to Know God: The Symbolic Theology of Dionysius the Areopagite and Its Factual Presuppositions." *The Thomist* 9 (1946): 379–420.

Suchla, Beata-Regina. "Subjektivität und Ethik bei dem christlichen Neuplatoniker Dionysius Areopagita." In *Selbst-Singularität-Subjektivität: Vom Neuplatonismus zum Deutschen Idealismus*. Ed. Mojsisch Burkhard. Amsterdam: Gruner, 2002.

Sweeney, Leo. "Infinity in Plotinus." *Gregorianum* 42 (1957): 515–35, 713–32.

————. "The Origin of Participant and of Participated Perfections in Proclus' *Elements of Theology*." In *Wisdom in Depth: Essays in Honor of H. Renard*. Milwaukee: Bruce, 1966.

————. "Participation and the Structure of Being in Proclus' *Elements of Theology*." In *The Structure of Being: A Neoplatonic Approach*. Ed. R. Baine Harris. Albany: State University of New York Press, 1982.

Terezis, C. "The Metaphysical Foundation of Gnosiology in the Neoplatonist Proclus." *Philosophical Inquiry* 16 (1994): 62–73.

Theill-Wunder, H. *Die archaische Verborgenheit, Die philosophischen Wurzeln der negativen Theologie.* Munich: Fink, 1970.

Trouillard, J. "La présence de Dieu selon Plotin." *Revue métaphysique et morale* 59 (1954): 38–45.

———. "Le cosmos du Pseudo-Denys." *Revue de théologie et de philosophie*, Série 3, 5 (1955): 51–57.

———. *La procession plotinienne.* Paris: Presses Universitaires de France, 1955.

———. "Le sens des médiations proclusiennes." *Revue philosophique de Louvain* 55 (1957): 331–42.

———. " 'Agir par son être même,' La causalité selon Proclus." *Revue des sciences religieuses* 32 (1958): 347–57.

———. "Âme et esprit selon Proclus." *Revue des études augustiniennes* 5 (1959): 1–12.

———. "Note sur *proousios* et *pronoia* chez Proclus." *Revue des études grecques* 73 (1960): 80–87.

———. "L'antithèse fondamentale de la procession selon Proclos." *Archives de philosophie* 34 (1971): 433–49.

———. "La *mone* selon Proclus." In *Le Néoplatonisme. Colloque de Royaumont 9–13 juin 1969.* Paris: Centre Nationale de la Recherche Scientifique, 1971.

———. *L'Un et l'âme selon Proclos.* Paris, 1972.

———. "Procession néoplatonicienne et création judéo-chrétienne." In *Néoplatonisme: Mélanges offerts à Jean Trouillard.* Fontenay aux Roses: Les Cahiers de Fontenay, 1981.

Van den Berg, R. M. *Proclus' Hymns.* Leiden: Brill, 2001.

Van den Daele, Albert. *Indices Pseudo-Dionysiani.* Louvain: Bibliothèque de l'Université, 1941.

Vanneste, Jean. *Le mystère de Dieu. Essai sur la structure rationnelle de la doctrine mystique du Pseudo-Denys l'Aréopagite.* Louvain: De Brouwer, 1959.

———. "Endre von Ivankas Studien über Pseudo-Dionysius." *Kairos* 2 (1960): 183–85.

———. "La théologie mystique du Pseudo-Denys l'Aréopagite." *Studia Patristica* 5 (1962): 401–15.

———. "Is the Mysticism of Pseudo-Dionysius Genuine?" *International Philosophical Quarterly* 3 (1963): 286–306.

———. "La doctrine des trois voies dans la *Théologie Mystique* du Pseudo-Denys l'Aréopagite." *Studia Patristica* 8 (1966): 462–67.

Vogel, C. J. de. "Amor quo caelum regitur." *Vivarium* 1 (1963): 2–34.

———. "Greek Cosmic Love and the Christian Love of God. Boethius, Dionysius the Areopagite and the Author of the Fourth Gospel." *Vigiliae Christianae* 35 (1981): 57–81.

Völker, Walther. *Kontemplation und Ekstase bei Pseudo-Dionysius Areopagita.* Wiesbaden: Steiner, 1958.

Volpe, G. *Della la dottrina del Areopagita e i suoi presuppositi neoplatonici.* Rome, 1941.

Wagner, M. "Plotinus' World." *Dionysius* 6 (1982): 13–42.

———. "Vertical Causation in Plotinus." In *The Structure of Being.* Ed. R. Baine Harris. Albany: State University of New York Press, 1982.

Wallis, R.T. *Neoplatonism.* London: Duckworth, 1972.

Weischede. W. "Dionysios Areopagita als philosophischer Theologe." In *Festschrift für Joseph Klein.* Ed. E. Fries. Göttingen: Vandenhoeck and Ruprecht, 1967.

Wesche, K. P. "Christological Doctrine and Liturgical Interpretation in Pseudo-Dionysius." *St. Vladimir's Theological Quarterly* 33 (1989): 53–73.

Whittemore, R. C. "Panentheism in Neo-Platonism." *Tulane Studies in Philosophy* 4 (1966): 47–70.

Yannaras, Christos. *De l'absence et de l'inconnaissance de Dieu d'après les écrits aréopagitiques et Martin Heidegger.* Tr. J. Touraille. Paris: Editions du Cerf, 1971.

INDEX

153

and immanence, 20, 23–24, 30, 44–
45, 112, 121n5, 121n10, 132n27,
137n23, 138n6
See also under God: and being:
beyond being; Good, the: beyond
being; One, the: beyond being
trinitarian doctrine, 2–3, 122n24
Trouillard, Jean, 123n30, 126n38,
127n45, 127n47, 127n49, 128n14,
129n18, 131n22, 131n24, 132n29
truth, 8–9, 35, 85, 90, 106, 108, 112,
137n14, 138n4

unfolding. *See* enfolding-unfolding
union, 1, 4, 79, 84, 89–91, 93–97,
104–5, 107–8, 119n19, 135n20,
135n23, 137n19

unity. *See* One, the
unknowing, 14, 31, 92–96, 101, 104–8,
135n20, 136n28

Van den Berg, R. M., 137n12
Vanneste, Jean, 115n6
vision, 8, 56, 84–87, 92–95, 98, 104,
108
Vogel, Cornelia J. de, 117n11, 125n28,
125n30, 126n35

Wagner, Michael, 120n3
wisdom, 3, 29, 65–67, 69–72, 83, 90,
98
word, 13–14, 16, 29, 102–3, 108

Made in the USA
Middletown, DE
03 July 2017